HIGH CAMP

Volume 2

JOAN CRAWFORD (1906–1977), looks as though she's ready to give Lizzie Borden some lessons in wielding a pretty mean axe in this scene from *Straightjacket* (Columbia, 1963).

HIGH CAMP

*A Gay Guide to Camp
and Cult Films*

Volume 2

PAUL ROEN

LEYLAND PUBLICATIONS
San Francisco

Dedication:
This one's for Walt

Front cover photo: Steve Reeves won Mr. America and Mr. Universe bodybuilding championships before he began to make his numerous muscleman epics of the 1950s–60s. Publicity photo from one of his films.

Cover layout by Rupert Kinnard

ISBN 0–943595–54–1 (paperback)

Library of Congress Catalog Card Number: 93-80253

Leyland Publications
P.O. Box 410690
San Francisco, CA 94141
Complete catalogue of available books: $1 ppd.

CONTENTS
Titles marked with an asterisk are available on video.

*Arabian Nights	11	Death in Small Doses	45
*Andy Warhol's Bad	11	*Death in Venice	45
*Athena	12	Design for Living	46
*Atlantis, the Lost Continent	13	*Destry Rides Again	48
*Auntie Mame	14	*Die! Die! My Darling!	48
*Bagdad Cafe	16	*Dino	50
*Balalaika	17	*Dr. Christian Meets the Women	52
The Beast of Hollow Mountain	18	*Dr. Jekyll and Sister Hyde	52
*Becky Sharp	18	*Dream Boys	53
*Belle of the Nineties	19	*Dreamwood	54
*Berserk	20	*Drifting	54
*Big Business	21	*Ecco	55
*The Bitter Tears of Petra Von Kant	22	*Ed Wood	55
*Blood and Sand	23	*Edward II	57
Bomba and the Jungle Girl	25	*Entertaining Mr. Sloane	57
*The Boy Friend	26	*Erotikus	58
*Boys in the Sand	26	*Fangs of the Living Dead	59
*The Boys of Cellblock Q	27	The Female Animal	60
*Caravaggio	28	Female on the Beach	63
*The Caretakers	30	*A Fool There Was	64
*Carnival Story	31	*Fortune and Men's Eyes	66
*Un Chant d'Amour	31	*The Fourth Man	67
*Class Reunion	32	*Fun Down There	67
*Cleopatra	33	The Furies	68
*The Climax	34	The Garden of Allah	69
The Cobweb	35	*The Gay Deceivers	70
*The Conquest of Mycenae	37	*The Giant of Metropolis	71
*Colossus and the Headhunters	38	*The Girl Can't Help It	71
*Copacabana	39	*Go Kill and Come Back	72
*Cover Girl	39	*Girls Town	74
*Crime of Passion	40	*Goin' to Town	75
The Damned Don't Cry	41	*Go West, Young Man	77
*Dancing Lady	43	*Goliath and the Vampires	77
*Dark Victory	43	Greenwich Village	78
*Daughters of Darkness	44	*The Grim Reaper	79
		*Gypsy	80
		Gypsy Wildcat	81
		*The Harvey Girls	82
		Hercules and the Amazon Women	83

Hercules and the
  Lost Kingdom 83
*Hercules and the
  Masked Rider 84
*Hercules in the
  Haunted World 85
*Hero of Babylon 86
*Hurricane. 86
*Hollywood Horror House . 88
If I'm Lucky 89
*Imitation of Life. 89
Island of Doomed Men . . . 91
*Isle of Forgotten Sins 92
*Ivan the Terrible, Part II . . 92
*Jerker 93
Jet Over the Atlantic 94
*The Jungle Book 95
*Jungle Hell 96
*Jupiter's Darling. 96
*Just a Gigolo 97
*Just for the Hell of It 97
*Kansas City Trucking Co. . 98
*Killer Nun 99
*The Killing of
  Sister George 101
*Kiss Today Goodbye 102
*Kitten with a Whip 103
*Klondike Annie 104
*Ladies They Talk About . . 105
*The Lair of the
  White Worm 106
*Land of the Minotaur 106
*The Last Days of
  Pompeii 108
*Laughing Sinners 108
*The Leech Woman. 109
*Les Girls. 110
*Liane, Jungle Goddess 111
*Little Men 111
*Like a Horse 113
*The Lion of St. Mark 114
*The Living Coffin 115
Look in Any Window 115
Love and Kisses 116
*Love Bites 118
Love Has Many Faces 118

*Love Letters of a
  Portuguese Nun 119
The Loved One 121
Ludwig. 122
*M. Butterfly 122
*Macho Dancer 123
*The Mad Ghoul 124
*Madame X 126
*Mademoiselle 127
*Mame. 127
The Mating Season 128
*The Merry Widow 129
*Messalina Against the
  Son of Hercules 129
*The Midnight Girl 131
*Mishima: A Life in Four
  Chapters 131
Montana Belle 132
*Morgan the Pirate 133
*My Own Private Idaho . . . 134
*Mystery of Marie Roget . . 134
*The Night Walker 135
*99 Women 136
*No Escape 136
*The Oscar 137
*On Approval 138
*The Painted Veil 140
*Paradise Plantation 140
*Passing Strangers 141
Pearl of the South Pacific . . 141
*Parrish 142
*The Phantom Empire. 142
*Pink Narcissus 145
*Poison 146
*Powertool. 147
Problem Girls. 148
*The Purchase Price. 148
Quantrill's Raiders 150
*Queen Bee 151
*Rock Hudson's Home
  Movies. 152
*Ruthless People 154
*Salo 154
*Salome's Last Dance 155
*Salon Kitty 156
Scorpio Rising 156

*Sebastiane 158
*Serial Mom 158
*The Servant 159
*Sex Garage 161
*The Shanghai Gesture 162
*She 163
Sign of the Gladiator 163
The Silver Cord 164
*Sins of Rome 165
*Skin Deep 166
*Slaves in Bondage 166
*Sodom and Gomorrah 167
*Song of India 168
Song of Scheherazade 168
*Song of the Loon 169
*So's Your Aunt Emma! . . . 171
South Sea Sinner 171
*The Spider Woman 172
The Spider Woman Strikes
   Back 173
*Stella Dallas 175
The Story of
   Esther Costello 177
*Strait-Jacket 177
Sudan 179
*Sudden Fear 179
*Tabu 180
*Tam Lin 181
*The Terror of the Steppes . 182
*That Certain Woman 182
That Night in Rio 184

*Theodora, Slave Empress . 185
*Thin Ice 187
*These Bases Are Loaded . . 188
*The Thorn 188
*Thoroughly Modern Millie 189
*Tie Me Up!
   Tie Me Down! 189
*To Please a Lady 190
*Torch Song 191
*The Tramplers 191
The Triumph of Hercules . 192
*The Undersea Kingdom . . . 193
*Urinal 195
*Valentino 196
*Valley of the Dolls 198
*Venus in Furs 200
Victim 201
*Voodoo Island 201
*Week-end in Havana 202
Walk on the Wild Side 204
*What's the Matter with
   Helen? 205
*Where Love Has Gone 205
*White Cargo 207
White Savage 208
*The White Warrior 208
*Woman's World 210
Yellowstone Kelly 211
*Youth Aflame 211
*You'll Never Get Rich 212
*Zachariah 214

INTRODUCTION

When I was about three or four years old, my mother took me to the local five and dime and let me pick out my very first comic book (the first of hundreds). I immediately selected the most lurid, gruesome cover displayed on the rack. "Put that back," said my mother. "That's a bad one. Pick out a good one."

Of course, I wasn't aware of it then, but the seeds of my esthetic destiny were contained in my reply: "I don't want a good one. I want a *bad* one!" I've been picking the bad ones ever since.

Like so many other lovers of bad art, I gravitated toward the cinema as I grew older. And, inevitably, I became a devotee of camp, particularly (since I'm gay) those strains of it which most appeal to homosexuals.

The function of this introduction is to explain and define camp. A thumbnail sketch will have to suffice. (For a fuller definition, see the introduction to Volume One.) Camp is the triumph of style over substance. It's a phoniness that glories in its phoniness. Camp is also irony, the acknowledged disparity between appearances and reality (a disparity, I might add, that gays and lesbians are all too well aware of). Camp is fun. And also funny. Oftentimes, camp is something so bad that it's good. This concept is particularly important, if only because it drives our conservative enemies right up the wall (they can't stand the thought of good and bad being turned upside down). In the realm of camp, "esthetic standards" are not only reversed, but also utterly discombobulated. Camp, as my mother would surely point out, is not in "good taste"; camp is glorious, uproarious *bad* taste.

A lesbian friend hit the nail on the head when I talked to her about the movie *Auntie Mame* (reviewed in this volume). She said, "Things like this are what we liked when we were kids, but we didn't know *why* we liked them." Camp, it may be said, offers us a theory of why we liked them. The various facets of this theory are reflected in the diverse genres of film discussed in this book. As before, I've covered an ample assortment of camp films. And, once again, I've also included an array of gay cult films—that is to say, films which, for one reason or another, have attracted a sizable gay cult following. Some of these movies also qualify as camp; some do not.

In this volume I've included, under the cult heading, a sampling of gay male erotic films. Each of the principal directors laboring in this particular vineyard is represented by a characteristic work (two works in the case of William Higgins, who has directed dozens).

*　　*　　*

Obviously, a project of this sort involves the help of many people. I regret that I haven't space to thank each one. Most of all, I wish to thank the many readers of Volume One who wrote me letters containing suggestions for this present book. I especially want to thank the people who loaned me videotapes of favorite films. Special thanks, also, to my publisher, Winston Leyland. And a final tip of the hat to the fine folks at Video Search of Miami, who were kind enough to rush me some tapes when my deadline was drawing nigh.

*　　*　　*

Titles marked with an asterisk are available on video. Five of the many sources from which videos can be obtained:

MOVIES UNLIMITED
6736 Castor Avenue
Philadelphia, Pennsylvania 19149

FACETS MULTIMEDIA
1517 West Fullerton Avenue
Chicago, Illinois 60614

BIJOU VIDEO (mainly erotica)
1363 N. Wells
Chicago, Illinois 60610

SINISTER CINEMA
P.O. Box 4369
Medford, Oregon 97501

VIDEO SEARCH OF MIAMI
P.O. Box 16-1917
Miami, Florida 33116-1917

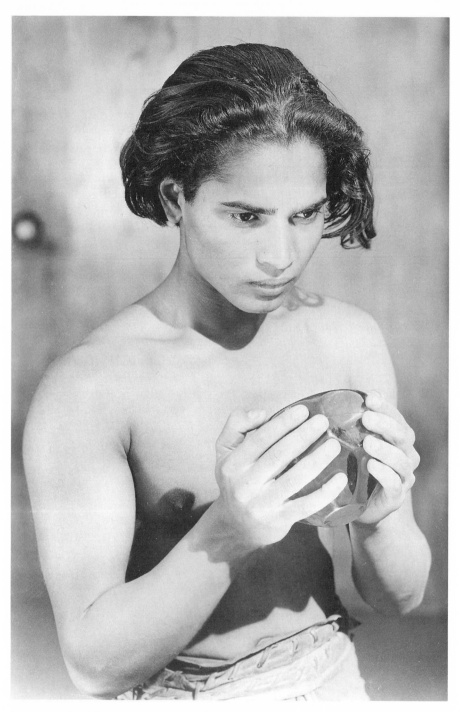

SABU (1924–1963) gazes into a crystal ball in a pensive scene from *The Thief of Baghdad* (United Artists 1940).

Arabian Nights* (U.S. 1942 C)

Arabian Nights goes down in camp history as being the film that made a star of the sublimely talentless Maria Montez. She's cast as Sherazade (which is pronounced Scheherazade), a dancing girl for love of whom Leif Erickson usurps the throne of his brother (Jon Hall), the rightful Caliph of Baghdad. Sabu, the juvenile acrobat who precedes Maria on the playbill of the local circus, climbs a human pyramid of brawny, bare-chested men and, from this enviable perch, spies Jon getting clobbered by Erickson's henchmen. The charming scamp whisks the erstwhile sovereign to safety. Maria (somewhat peevishly; the acclaim of her fickle public has left her jaded) nurses Jon back to health. Then, victimized by a palace intrigue, she is kidnapped by Turhan Bey and sold into slavery. (It grieves me to note that Turhan's role is small. Perhaps as compensation, he gets to play a truly spectacular torture-and-bondage death scene seminude on a rack in the requisite clammy dungeon.)

The best scene is the one in the slave market: horny bidders on the one hand, half-naked merchandise (male and female) on the other. This film is so rich, it's probably fattening. It's got everything: lush music, sumptuous Technicolor, gaudy costumes, absurd melodramatics, etc. (For reasons too humorous to mention, Maria must wear an ornate ring filled with deadly poison, which she then is obliged to dump into Leif Erickson's goblet right in the middle of her big Oriental dance number.) It's even got fat Billy Gilbert in drag. ("What a beautiful distribution of flesh!" someone comments.) Maria is really not as terrible a performer as she was often cracked up to be. As a matter of fact, she could be quite entertaining. Camp always is.

Andy Warhol's Bad* (U.S. 1977 C)

For an Andy Warhol epic, this is a pretty professional-looking flick. It's a surreal contemplation of working-class gracelessness (and it begins, appropriately enough, with a public toilet being vandalized). Our leading lady is Carroll Baker, cast as a housewife who lives in Queens with her sad-sack, marginally retarded daughter-in-law (Susan Tyrrell). Carroll operates an electrolysis parlor in her home. "Nobody likes hair," she tells us. "Everybody today wants to be more feminine."

"Yeah," somebody answers. "Even some women are getting into that, too."

To supplement her income, Carroll oversees a murder-for-hire operation. The victims are mainly pets and children. (Carroll is so avaricious, she even stoops to stealing from a blind street peddler.) In the film's most famous scene, a baby is tossed out of a window. Over the years, I'd read about this scene several times. I was supposing they'd merely show us the kid being dropped from the casement, and that's that. But no; I was wrong to expect even that much good taste from an Andy Warhol film. We see a very realistic-seeming baby-doll falling several stories through the air to explode in a bloody mess on the sidewalk below, splashing gore on a screaming passerby (Jane Forth).

This is the sort of film that's more interesting in retrospect than it is while you're watching it. The grunge gets depressing, after a while. One line of dialogue succinctly sums up the prevailing philosophy: "People stink. They all do. All they do is eat, fuck, and watch TV."

A Warhol film is not complete without the presence of an oversexed stud. Joe Dallesandro normally fulfills this function, but this movie gives us Perry King in his place. I was more intrigued with Baker, the former sex bombshell. I have it on good authority that she considers this performance her finest hour, and, in fact, it did mark her successful transition to character roles. I like Carroll; players in Warhol pictures tend to have extremely abrasive speaking voices, but hers is so pleasant that it's almost musical. In this movie she's got a lavish boudoir (kept carefully under lock and key, of course) that's straight out of her Joe Levine heyday, when she was making glitzy trash like *The Carpetbaggers* and *Harlow*. She may not be a superstar on a par with Holly Woodlawn, but she manages to hold her own.

Athena* (U.S. 1954 C)

This movie presents us with Edmund Purdom in the role of a conservative political candidate whose backers are distressed because he's unmarried and living alone with his charming, diminutive Japanese houseboy. So then he takes up with the title character, a New Age type portrayed by Jane Powell. (What a hit *she'll* make with the Religious Right!) She manages to win over his more stuffy supporters by warbling them a coloratura aria from Donizetti's *La fille du régiment*. But trouble looms on the horizon. Her previous suitor was Steve Reeves, and he's the jealous type.

Sparks fly when she brings the two of them together. First she offers Purdom a peanutburger (she's into health foods). He turns it down. "He probably wants roast beef," says Steve disdainfully. "He's the kind of guy that likes to eat animals." Purdom pulls another boner when he thoughtlessly lights up a cigarette. Steve rudely snatches it away from him. ("What are you trying to do? Suffocate us?!") This movie was way ahead of its time.

Then there's the part where Purdom is introduced to Jane's family. He's somewhat taken aback when Grandpa (Louis Calhern) tries to cop a feel of his thigh. You probably think I'm making this up. As a matter of fact, there were moments when I couldn't believe my eyes . . . or my ears. Like the scene where Vic Damone sings to co-star Debbie Reynolds: "I'd drench you with damp devotion. / I'd pour it before you and roar!" (What does that sound like to you?) Later, Vic brings Debbie an orchid, but Steve mistakes it for a veggie and eats it! The grand finale is a Mr. Universe pageant. The worthy contenders are many, but Steve takes top honors, of course. His clench-jawed style of acting is a continual source of hilarity, but you have to admit that this picture finds him strutting his stuff in his glorious prime. And, in a couple of numbers, he even gets to function as a chorus boy.

Atlantis, the Lost Continent* (U.S. 1960 C)

I must confess I'd never before heard of Anthony Hall, star of *Atlantis, the Lost Continent*. He's no great shakes in the muscles department, but at least he knows how to pose. Cast as a Greek fisherman named Demetrius, he rescues the Princess of Atlantis (Joyce Taylor). "Your food tempts me not," she declaims haughtily, when he offers her a bite to eat. "Do not touch me! You smell of fish!" she sneers.

She changes her tune when he consents to take her back where she came from. Along the way, they encounter an Atlantean submarine. The captain is John Dall, the movie's only bona fide star. (He's probably best known for playing a homosexual in Hitchcock's *Rope*.) Everyone appears to be pleasant enough, but there's something slightly sinister about the way Dall gives Hall the once-over and then says, "Guard! Take him aboard!"

Sure enough, our hero is soon in chains, his antediluvian charms laid bare. He sweats lustily. He reclines seminude on a leopard-skin rug. He even gets flogged (for peevishly hurling a clod of mud at that fickle princess). Slaves are conveyed on a clothesline contraption over a yawning chasm. One old fellow (Jay Novello) loses his grip, but Hall manages to save him. The old guy clings to the boy's waist for dear life, gratefully burying his head in Hall's groin. A bawdy guffaw is heard from the guards.

Atlantis is portrayed as a kind of prehistoric Nazi Germany. One old queen (Berry Kroeger) is a mad scientist transforming slaves into animals. "Why do they always take my best specimens away from me?" he grumbles, when Hall is snatched from his clutches in a nick of time. In order to escape, Hall must cozy up to Dall, who, I might add, is only too eager to be taken in. ("I may have need of your services again," he leers, handing the handsome lad a bag full of coins.) Atlantis, depraved and decadent, ultimately sinks beneath the sea. It didn't teach me a lesson, but it did remind me to soak my feet.

Auntie Mame* (U.S. 1958 C)

Auntie Mame is based on the popular 'Fifties novel about the madcap misadventures of a Manhattan playgirl trying to give her orphaned nephew a rather avant-garde upbringing during the busy and eventful second quarter of this century. The best and easiest way to approach and comprehend the character of Auntie Mame is to view her as a disguised, transsexualized version of a very hip, urban, sophisticated male homosexual. (Notes from the cover blurb of the 1956 paperback edition: "The daring adventures of an unconventional woman." "Auntie Mame is the gayest, most unconventional aunt you've ever known and you'll love her." "She could take on anyone! None of Mame's gay habits was more startling than her worldly-wise way with men!") I read this book the summer after I was in fifth grade. I was a very gay child.

The film is, of course, somewhat less provocative than the novel. Case in point: To build her ward's vocabulary, Mame instructs him to write down every word he hears that he doesn't understand. In the book, the second word on his list is "Lesbian." The movie naturally omits this term, replacing it with "heterosexual." 'Nuff said.

Much of the film is sentimental schmaltz. I suppose this is unavoidable, since the very basis of the plot is the replication of "family values" in an unexpected, bohemian setting. As far as explicitly homosexual

Coral Browne (1913–1991), left, and Rosalind Russell (1908–1976) in a publicity photo from *Auntie Mame* (Warner 1958).

characters are concerned, the one I had my eye on was Ito (Yuki Shimoda), Mame's flighty, cackling Japanese houseboy. (I should note that lesbians are plainly visible in the party scene at the beginning.) Mame herself is delineated by Rosalind Russell, who gives an insufferably strident, overbearing performance. The film seems determined to showcase her most annoying mannerisms. She struggles valiantly to convince us that she's the incarnation of flamboyance and the sworn enemy of conservatism. "Life is a banquet, and most poor suckers are starving to death," she keeps insisting. Try though I might, I somehow couldn't bring myself to forget that, in real life, Rosalind Russell was a staunch Republican.

Bagdad Cafe* (Germany 1988 C)

Bagdad Cafe is a strange little movie that provides an admirable showcase for splendidly campy performances by a pair of sublimely off-the-wall players: the Felliniesque zoftig Marianne Sägebrecht and the explosive black actress CCH Pounder. Ms. Pounder is cast as the proprietress of a run-down motel, cafe and gas station situated somewhere in the middle of the Mojave Desert. Early on, she and her husband have an energetically bombastic altercation. It's the kind of scene where he asks her if she's got the rag on and she responds by throwing empty oil cans at him. Ms. Sägebrecht is a fat, overdressed German lady with a funny feathered hat. She shows up out of nowhere and Pounder immediately assumes that she's a transvestite or a lesbian or some other kind of deviate. Contrariwise, Jack Palance is cast as a chubbychasing elderly hippie who promptly takes a shine to her. The supporting cast includes Christine Kaufmann (remarkably well-preserved) in the role of a tattoo artist who sits around all day reading *Death in Venice*. I'm not sure what, if anything, all this has to do with homosexuality, but I should at least mention that at one point there's a song-and-dance number in which Pounder and Sägebrecht get themselves up in Dietrich-style male drag. The most remarkable thing about this movie is that it's German. I can't remember the last time I saw a movie that seemed more American.

Balalaika* (U.S. 1939 B&W)

Balalaika begins with Russian peasants happily going about their business in a sleepy village somewhere near St. Petersburg. Then a horde of Cossacks come stampeding into town, hefty Nelson Eddy at their head, leading them in hearty song. Parents whisk their daughters indoors, apparently afraid that they'll be ravished. Seems unlikely. The song is about "men and leather." Indeed, those are the first words to emerge from Nelson's mouth.

Cut to the Balalaika cafe. Nelson is bellowing just as loudly as before (a piece by Glinka, I believe). When his song draws to a close, he underscores the moment by hurling a wine glass at the camera. Then he catches sight of Ilona Massey. They are a well-matched pair: with her coloratura soprano singing voice, she can break every bit as much glassware as he can. But, alas, she is one of those wacky Bolsheviks, which means that he must present himself to her in the guise of a penniless student. Behind the scenes, however, he's using his considerable influence to make of her an opera star. She is to be launched in a wild Oriental farrago based on Rimsky-Korsakov's *Scheherazade*. So then what happens? Cossacks kill her brother for being a leftist political agitator. Her Marxist dad (Lionel Atwill) seeks revenge by plotting to assassinate Nelson's father, a hated aristocrat played by C. Aubrey Smith (who is far too British for these proceedings). What's worse, he plans to commit this heinous deed at the opera house, right in the middle of Ilona's debut! Not that the performance wouldn't be interrupted, anyway: World War I is declared that night, adding to the zany confusion. After the Revolution, Nelson finds himself working at a posh restaurant in Paris, where he's obliged to serenade obnoxious American tourists whose arrogance is almost enough to make him turn Commie.

This ideological crazy quilt was Massey's Hollywood debut. Her career zenith (*Frankenstein Meets the Wolf Man*, in which she's top-billed) was still a few years down the road. I must admit that, if I made movies, *Balalaika* is what I would want them to look like: music made visual.

The Beast of Hollow Mountain   (Mexico 1956 C)

The Beast of Hollow Mountain starts out pretty much the same as any other typical Guy Madison homoerotic horse opera. Our hero comes to the rescue of a handsome caballero (Carlos Rivas) who has landed in a patch of quicksand. "You'd better go to the el rancho and dry out," says Guy, taking note of the fellow's clinging, mud-soaked pants. Further along in the film, Guy gets into a fight with the villain (Eduardo Noriega). "I'm going to find out what kind of an hombre you really are," says Guy. "Unbuckle your gun belt!" The bad guy objects to the lascivious way he helps Patricia Medina down from her mount. Patricia is a sultry señorita who wears off-the-shoulder peasant blouses and no brassiere. She's got a yen for the good-looking gringo. They rendezvous in a cemetery, nearby a majestic mountain range, and share a tender tête-à-tête while seated on the grave of her Auntie Maria. But duty calls and new adventures beckon. A dinosaur picks up a steer with its teeth, stampeding the rest of the herd. At this point occurs an amusing attempt at suspense, grotesque in its ineffectiveness: we cut back and forth between the oncoming cattle and the weirdly costumed dancers at a village festival. Once again it's Guy who averts disaster, luring the dinosaur into a bottomless bog. All in a day's work for this troubleshooting cowpoke.

No one seems very startled to see the nineteenth-century Mexican setting disrupted by a denizen of the primordial ooze. No one even gets a chance to ask, "What ees dat theeng?!"; they're all too busy running for their lives. Madison is equal to the athletic demands of his role; the histrionic demands, if any, are too slight to signify. The monster walks with a funny, effeminate, broad-in-the-hips sashay and boasts an obscenely agile tongue that unfurls like a party favor. This is an incredibly surreal motion picture.

Becky Sharp*   (U.S. 1935 C)

Becky Sharp is Miriam Hopkins as literature's most notorious little bitch. Not that she's got much use for literature: the movie begins and ends with Hopkins hurling a book at pious hypocrites. Aye, she's a saucy wench and a brazen hussy, too. The plot, derived from Thackeray's *Vanity Fair*, depicts her erotic intrigues before and after the Battle of Waterloo. The extreme, almost Wildean archness with which these low doings are depicted is the basis, the very essence of the comedy. Hopkins' acting may seem overly mannered, shrill, and superficial, but, without her waspish wit and vituperative vitriol, this movie would be approximately as interesting as a Classics Illustrated comic book version of a Regency romance. She's cunning, sly, duplicitous, and sufficiently manipulative to have men hopping through hoops at her command. It's about what they deserve.

The guys in this film are a singularly uninspiring bunch: Alan Mowbray (portly, phlegmatic), Nigel Bruce (bumblingly ineffectual, as always), and Sir Cedric Hardwicke, who appears to be trying out for the role of Dracula. When our heroine hears that Mowbray is "as worthless a scoundrel as ever wore the King's uniform," her face lights up as though she's found the love of her life. Maybe you were expecting a movie more genteel, less campy, more literary? Sorry to disappoint you, dear, but, as Becky puts it, "There's too much bad poetry in the world, anyway."

Belle of the Nineties* (U.S. 1934 B&W)

Mae West is a genre unto herself. Her vehicles are not, strictly speaking, good movies. Put another actress in the starring role and the thinness of the material would be readily apparent. In *Belle of the Nineties*, she's supposed to be a vaudeville star, yet she does virtually nothing when she's onstage. She just stands there, striking poses and giving off vibrations. She doesn't move; she pulsates. It's like she's getting paid to breathe.

That's when she's in St. Louis. When she opens at a place called "the Sensation House" in New Orleans, with Duke Ellington and his Orchestra backing her up, she deigns at least to vocalize. And, indeed, she knows how to put a song across with memorable oomph. The men in this picture are plenty dumb, but they're smart enough to do what she tells them. (Furthermore, they work out. The sweaty ambience of a Gay Nineties gym does much to enhance the film's visual appeal.) As for the women, the only other one of any consequence is sloe-eyed Katherine DeMille, who's a little more torrid than the usual ingenues who end up sharing the bill with Mae. Perhaps this explains why Miss DeMille is frequently photographed from the back. Not that our leading lady has anything to worry about.

Oddly enough, Mae epitomizes the kind of ethereal, angelic beauty which typifies the Victorian era. Perhaps that's why so many of her films take place in the 1890s. This particular one doesn't have much of a plot (somebody steals her jewels and she gets them back), but at least it provides her with plenty of chances to get in some witty ripostes. Her best moment doesn't require words, however. She tells a group of her male admirers that she needs to go home and get some rest, whereupon one of them protests, "The fun's all over, if *you* go to bed." She gives the young man a sly chuckle.

---

*Berserk** (G.B. 1967 C)

This absurd suspense melodrama was the next-to-last film of Joan Crawford's career. She's cast as Monica Rivers (a typically glamorous Joan Crawford character name), owner and ringmistress of a circus where strange murders occur. In the very first scene, a tightrope walker falls to his death. Joan takes charge immediately, shooing away the paparazzi and sending out a contingent of clowns, who flap their arms to amuse and distract the audience. "We're running a circus, not a charm school," she points out, "and, most important, people have to be entertained!"

The critical reception was surprisingly respectful when this schlocker was first unveiled. Everyone agreed that Crawford, then in her sixties, still managed to fill out her tights very admirably. Even so, the script makes her out to be a bit too improbably irresistible to menfolk. Her principal romantic interest is hunky Ty Hardin, approximately twenty-five years her junior. Her rival for his affections is the blonde sex-bomb, Diana Dors, who is roughly the same age he is. But she, poor dear, is obliged to labor under the distinct disadvantage of playing somebody named Matilda. And she ends up getting gored by a buzz saw during a magic act.

Does anybody mind if I reveal the killer's identity? I thought not. (Nobody sits through a movie like this just to find out who done it.) The murderess is Judy Geeson, who is cast as Joan's daughter. (Joan was plagued with homicidal daughters from *Mildred Pierce* onward.) Judy is supposed to be attending charm school (not a circus), but she gets expelled because she's constantly sneaking out at night and killing people. ("You've always had a knack for causing trouble," Joan complains.)

The script never explains how such a wee slip of a girl could manage to drive a tent spike through Michael Gough's head. Judy ends up getting struck dead by lightning. And Ty fatally tumbles on a bed of bayonets. All this carnage tends to make the slogan over the circus refreshment stand seem like a gruesome joke: "Come alive! With Pepsi!"

Big Business* (U.S. 1988 C)

This one's a natural. It's got a double dose of Bette Midler (at her most flamboyantly vulgar) and a double dose of Lily Tomlin (at her most high-strung and delightfully demented). These leading ladies are cast as two sets of identical twin sisters who get separated—and switched—at birth. Who among us can resist such a devastating instance of high concept?

The wildly improbable plot does not readily lend itself to succinct synopsis. A millionaire businessman and his very bitchy, very pregnant spouse happen to be passing in the vicinity of a Southern hick town when their car hits a bump and the wife suddenly goes into labor. At the local hospital, she gives birth to a pair of twin girls. In the room across the hall, meanwhile, a poor, down-home farmwife does likewise. The presiding nurse, however, is in her dotage and somewhat incompetent. (Earlier, we saw her mislay a urine sample on a tray that's laden with cups of cider.) Suffice it to say that both sets of parents get one wrong twin and one right one.

Forty years pass. In New York, Bette Midler wears power suits and looks every inch the corporate cutthroat, marching crisply down corridors and issuing commands much like her namesake, Bette Davis. Meanwhile, her meek, submissive sister is Lily Tomlin, who adopts stray dogs and longs for the simple life. They are, in a word, mismatched.

At the same time, down South, the other Lily Tomlin is a rabble-rousin' country gal whose sister, the other Bette Midler, likes to put on airs and pretend to be Joan Collins on *Dynasty*. (This cornpone Bette, in a memorable screen moment, yodels a C&W song while rhythmically milking a cow.) The local factory (Hollowmade Furniture) is about to be put out of business, all because of the wicked financial maneuvers of Big Apple Bette up North. So Hillbilly Lily puts on her best duds and heads for New York to raise some hell. And her sis tags along to see the sights.

21

Obviously, these four women are headed for a hilarious climactic confrontation. Along the way, mistaken identity humor abounds. Need I add that there's an abundance of gay camp humor also? The Down South Lily has a beau (Fred Ward) who's a muscular hunk of studflesh. He follows her to the big city, where he mistakenly sweeps the other Lily off of her feet, just like she's the heroine of a Harlequin romance. But then he falls into the clutches of the bad Bette's executive aides, an explicitly homosexual couple played by Edward Herrmann and Daniel Gerroll. The three guys wind up sharing the same hotel suite. Says the bumpkin: "Hey, I like your kimono. Ya get that in Nam?" "Uh . . . no. Fire Island."

This comedy may sound confusing when described in a brief summary, but the actresses characterize their dual roles so skillfully that we're always able to tell at a glance which one they're playing at any given moment. We've come to expect a certain gay-friendly savoir-faire from Tomlin. Which no doubt explains why this is the campiest Bette Midler project since her days at the Continental Baths.

The Bitter Tears of Petra Von Kant* (Germany 1972 C)

This excessively lachrymal lesbian soap opera is precisely the sort of four-handkerchief weeper Joan Crawford might have starred in—that is, if lesbian soap operas were being made back in those days. The all-female cast is headed by Margit Carstensen, who portrays the title character, a sapphic fashion designer who likes to suffer in high style. The film takes place entirely in her apartment, which she shares with her obsessively devoted secretary/servant (Irm Hermann), who's even more masochistic than she is. The film's most piquant image has the pair of them dancing to "Smoke Gets in Your Eyes." The director is Rainer Werner Fassbinder, who seems to have been heavily influenced by old Douglas Sirk movies. Furthermore, Petra's in debt to a money-lender who's got the same name as the director of All About Eve. The costumes and coiffures are so outlandish, we momentarily think the film takes place in the Third Reich (which it doesn't). Ms. Hermann looks exactly like Margaret Thatcher (this can't have been intentional). When bitchy Petra finally offers her some kindness and compassion, she abruptly moves out as if she'd been insulted. But the film is mainly about Petra's heartbreaking love affair with a spoiled, selfish model, who is played by Hanna Schygulla, a full-fledged cult actress and probably this movie's campiest component.

Blood and Sand* (U.S. 1941 C)

Blood and Sand, a bullfighting epic, is the color remake of a Rudolph Valentino silent picture. The cast includes a fascinating assortment of homosexual stars: Tyrone Power as the matador, Alla Nazimova as his mother, and Laird Cregar as a sports columnist (if you can call bullfighting a sport). Furthermore, the film has left its mark in the realm of literature: it inspired Manuel Puig's book, *Betrayed by Rita Hayworth*. Puig (best known for his novel, *Kiss of the Spider Woman*) no doubt found plenty to capture his interest here: this is precisely the sort of corny, campy melodrama his characters so frequently favor. The images, painterly in their Technicolor richness, are so luridly over-the-top as to be almost surreal.

The setting is a feverishly vivid Spain that could only exist in romantic stories. When first we encounter the Tyrone Power character, he's a delinquent youth who smashes a bottle on Laird Cregar's head, thereby touching off a tavern brawl (the gypsy vocalist, her back to the wall, never misses a beat as the place is reduced to a shambles). At any rate, this kid is a born bullfighter: to get to the corrida in Madrid, he stops a train just by waving his cape at it.

When the lad grows up to be Tyrone Power, the film turns into an esthetic hodgepodge. He kneels before a mammoth crucifix all too obviously in the style of El Greco; then Rita Hayworth comes striding into the chapel, clad in purple and so clearly a vamp, she might have stepped out of an etching by Aubrey Beardsley. She tarries with him for a while, then moves on to Anthony Quinn, perhaps because he blows such pretty smoke rings. Speaking of things oral, one image is emblematic of the entire film: during the big corrida sequence, a woman in the stands gets carried away and goes into a violent ecstasy, smearing her lip rouge all over her face. The prevailing delirium carries over into Alfred Newman's music score: the death motif, set to a muffled roll of drums, sounds inexplicably like a Muslim call to worship, echoing dimly from some Moorish minaret of repressed national memory.

Power's pert little bottom, encased in an assortment of tight pants, practically functions as a supporting character in the drama. At times

Muscular JOHNNY SHEFFIELD (1931–   ), playing Bomba the Jungle Boy in *The Golden Idol* (Allied Artists 1954), appears headed for trouble if we can believe the leering/admiring glances from the accompanying Bedouin.

I almost expected him to grow a fluffy little tail. One scene finds him wearing just his underpants, while Cregar, like a squatting toad, sits appreciatively absorbing the view. The Cregar character, who is definitely depicted as being gay, is unsympathetic, which means that the film is subtly homophobic. And anti-critic (since he wields his pen to make or break bullfighters). Speaking as a homosexual critic, this naturally disturbs me. But every frame of this crazy movie is beautiful, and I love it.

Bomba and the Jungle Girl   (U.S. 1952 B&W)

The "Bomba the Jungle Boy" films were a godsend to chicken fanciers of the late 'Forties. Johnny Sheffield, the star of the series, was somewhat past his prime by the time he appeared in *Bomba and the Jungle Girl*. In fact, he was well above the legal age of consent. He looks rather like a college sophomore: husky, stolid, petulant, rather dim. Though he'd probably be more comfortable on a football field, he's obliged instead to roam the back lot jungles in the company of a chimp (the utterly shameless "Nakimba"). Bomba's a bargain basement Siegfried stranded on Poverty Row, his only garment a skimpy leopard-skin loincloth. We see plenty of haunch and ripely rounded buttock. There's no chance of seeing more, however, since the two sides of the loincloth are discreetly joined at the crotch. This becomes apparent fairly early in the proceedings, in a scene which has Bomba straddling the railing of a porch. It's still more glaringly apparent in a fight scene later on, when Bomba lands sprawling on his back and his front flap immediately falls backward upon his belly. The embarrassed gesture with which he smooths it back down again is obscenely amusing; he looks like a flustered maiden lady pulling the hem of her skirt down over her knees. At one point a group of native warriors lay hands upon him. The carnal potentials are unfortunately overshadowed by the political incorrectness implicit in the Bomba genre. We know perfectly well that most of these "natives" probably reside in some L.A. slum and are likely being paid next to nothing for their degrading efforts herein. The film is watchable in its mediocre fashion, but, like all these cut-rate jungle epics, ultimately descends into dull gray tedium. Still, we scholars of the cinema—and of cinematic boyflesh—must needs persevere with our studies. There is, after all, great plenty to study: the "Bomba" series runs to a dozen titles, including such promising-sounding ones as *Killer*

Leopard (with the ineffable Beverly Garland), *The Golden Idol*, *The Lost Volcano*, and *Bomba and the Elephant Stampede*.

The Boy Friend* (G.B. 1971 C)

If you weren't around in the 'Sixties, you've probably never heard of Twiggy, a sort of unisex supermodel. Her abortive bid for movie stardom was this seemingly interminable compendium of backstage musical clichés. She's the understudy who goes on in place of the leading lady (Glenda Jackson) on the very day when a famous Hollywood director is in the audience. "You're going out there as a youngster," she's told. "You've got to come back—a *star*!" The period is sometime in the Art Deco 'Twenties or 'Thirties. The girls seem to be all eyes and teeth, as if they were auditioning for a vampire picture. (My favorite is the scene-stealer played by Antonia Ellis, who's got one of those Martha Raye smiles that seems to go all the way around her head.)

This is a Ken Russell movie, which means we'd better keep an eye on the chorus boys. The leading man is Christopher Gable, Tchaikovsky's male amour in Russell's *The Music Lovers*. Here he's ostensibly straight, but we can't help but notice ambiguous moments—for instance, when he's dressed just like the Philip Morris bellboy and when he sings the word "fallacies" in a way that sounds like "phalluses." Best of all is the bacchanal sequence, in which he's awakened from a sleeping beauty trance by none other than Tommy Tune.

Boys in the Sand* (U.S. 1971 C)

Boys in the Sand, directed by Wakefield Poole, was a ground-breaking gay erotica film and therefore one of the first unequivocally gay cult movies. It is, in many respects, a rather crude and primitive effort. Today it is principally remembered as a showcase for Mr. Casey Donovan, a true superstar of homoerotica. He is first seen arising from the ocean surf (rather like the Botticelli Venus) and running in slow motion toward the camera (rather like the girl in a Clairol commercial), his huge cock merrily bobbing up and down. To the musical accompaniment of Debussy, he and his partner repair to a sylvan glade for the usual sucking and fucking. Afterward, the other guy disappears (while yet un-

26

dressed) and Casey makes off with his bell bottoms.

In the second segment, Casey answers a personal ad in a gay newspaper. Instead of a written reply, he receives a package containing what looks like a large tablet of Alka-Seltzer. He tosses the Alka-Seltzer into his swimming pool, whereupon a handsome brunette materializes. Predictable lovemaking ensues.

In the third and final segment, the tony Fire Island ambience is penetrated by a prole: a telephone repairman who is not only working-class, but also black. He is a lineman for the county and, as he goes about his business, he can't help but take notice of Casey, who is practically hanging out of a window, jacking off.

In 1986 Wakefield Poole made a direct-to-video sequel entitled *Boys in the Sand, II.* In this opus we notice that Casey's hairline is receding and his ass is definitely starting to droop. The music sounds sad.

The Boys of Cellblock Q* (U.S. 1993 C)

A women's prison picture with an all-male cast?! Well, why not? Direct-to-video producers cater to even the most specialized tastes, and few palates are as overbred as mine. What we've got here is a homoerotic parody of those old AIP programmers that starred the likes of Gloria Castillo and Adele Jergens. With a little bit of *Fortune and Men's Eyes* thrown in for good measure, of course.

The setting is Sunnyvale Juvenile Correctional Farm and, as the pre-credit crawl would have it, "When so many young sweaty boys were placed in close proximity, male liasons (sic) were formed." The chaplain, who seems to be doing a very bad impression of Barry Fitzgerald, spells it all out for us with grave sincerity: "You'd be shocked if I told you what I've seen some boys do for a *Superman* comic book or a frozen banana bar." But where did these straying kids learn to be so campy? Even the supposedly butch number gives himself away, becoming a bit flustered at one point and blurting the name Florence Henderson when he means to say Florence Nightingale. How do tough young criminal types happen to know so much about the great ladies of American popular culture? And why are they so obsessed with male sex organs? The sadistic guard mutters disgustedly, "Is that all you guys do? Stand around and look at each other's dicks?" He needs somebody to explain it all to him, and somebody does: "That's why it's called a *penal* colony." Hardy-har-har.

There's plenty of nudity (including full frontal), but not much in the way of sexual activity. The performances, though far from polished, are at least competent, and some of the "boys" have real charm, particularly Lewis Alante as "Beef," the "top cock" of the cell block. The entire production exudes gay camp so comprehensively, it could practically function as a dictionary definition of the term. A single exchange of dialogue says it better than I ever could. Timmy, the "new fish," declaims dramatically, "I don't have any answers . . . just questions." And then "Lana," the resident flaming queen, responds to this outburst as follows: "I've seen this place do a lot of things to a lot of people, but I've never seen anybody turn into Susan Hayward right in front of my eyes!"

---

*Caravaggio** (G.B. 1986 C)

Derek Jarman, the British art film director who died of AIDS in 1994, was quoted in '91 as follows regarding his artistic mission: "I'm simply trying to demystify areas of life which are very ordinary, such as HIV infection or my sexuality." He is similarly matter-of-fact regarding Caravaggio's homosexuality. The late Renaissance Italian artist is portrayed by Nigel Terry as a former street tough attracted to other street toughs. Gayness is clearly no big deal. In this movie, even the Pope is a screaming queen.

In many respects, *Caravaggio* is typical of Jarman's films. The images are appropriately painterly and the props, costumes, and background details deliberately anachronistic. The pace is languorous, even somewhat lethargic. Most untypically, toward the end, the action veers into melodrama: the plot commences to hinge on who killed leading lady Tilda Swinton.

Terry has a sexy, sonorous voice, but I prefer the rolling, sepulchral tones of co-star Michael Gough, who is cast as a cardinal. This role must have been a refreshing change of pace for Gough, who is more accustomed to the realm of horror pictures such as *Trog* and *Berserk*. Incredibly enough, at one point he bares his chest. I suppose it's rather perverse of me to confess that, in a film that's teeming with attractive young fellows in various states of undress, I was most profoundly moved by the seminudity of a sixty-nine-year-old man.

NIGEL TERRY (1945–   ) plays the Renaissance artist Caravaggio in the film of the same name (1986), directed by Derek Jarman—a core representative of the "Queer Film Movement." Many of Jarman's films are becoming gay cult (see also *Edward II* and *Sebastiane* elsewhere in this volume). Photo: Mike Laye.

The Caretakers* (U.S. 1963 B&W)

The Caretakers, one of several morbid 'Sixties films about mental hospitals, starts out with Polly Bergen stumbling along a busy downtown sidewalk. Anguished by the noise and chaos of modern metropolitan life, she seeks sanctuary in, of all places, a movie theatre. A poor choice, obviously: she has a nervous breakdown during the newsreel and misses the main feature (*West Side Story*). Polly is consigned to the state hospital, where she declares that her fellow patients are "a dirty bunch of women." When her husband (Robert Vaughn) pays her a call, she becomes hysterical and starts ripping her dress off. She attempts escape, but gets no further than the men's ward, where serious unpleasantness nearly befalls her. It's only too clear that poor Polly needs looking after.

Joan Crawford is cast as Lucretia, the reactionary head nurse, who opposes newfangled notions like group therapy. "You know the kind of discipline I believe in," she purrs malevolently (these words must've sent cold chills running down the spines of her real-life adopted kids). In the film's most memorable scene, she dons black leotards and conducts a gym class, teaching the other nurses how to protect themselves with judo. Joan knows how to deal with refractory patients ("They can only be handled by the intelligent use of *force*!"). She appears repelled, yet fascinated by both the liberal concepts and the sheer physical presence of the progressive physician played by Robert Stack. A wooden, mostly inexpressive actor, Stack is the ideal choice for his role as one of those psychiatric wizards, known only to Hollywood, who can calm even the most rabid maniac with a few gentle words, spoken in a soft, carefully measured tone.

Mental illness isn't funny, but this is still a pretty campy flick. I don't know why I'm so fascinated by the spectacle of a bunch of actresses in a psycho ward, but I do know I'm not the only gay man who finds this film enthralling. Bergen provides a frantic, eyeball-rolling performance which is more entertaining than convincing. She is outshone at every turn by co-star Janis Paige, cast as a man-hungry ex-hooker whose incarcerated condition is never adequately explained (she shows no sign of psychosis). Also on hand are Sharon Hugueny, Constance Ford, Ellen Corby, Susan Oliver, and Diane McBain. Joan's the only one who leaves an indelible impression. At any rate, she sure must've impressed me; when I later read Ken Kesey's *One Flew Over the Cuckoo's Nest*, I found myself picturing her as Nurse Ratched.

Carnival Story* (U.S. 1954 C)

We each of us have our favorite cinematic heartthrobs. Mine is Steve Cochran, a swarthy male sexpot who enjoyed a brief (*very* brief) popularity in the early 'Fifties. *Carnival Story* casts Steve as a barker in a sleazy freak show touring the hinterlands of postwar Germany. His loud, sporty apparel and smooth, oily manner serve to make him immediately noticeable, even in such a phantasmagorical chaos of midgets, hermaphrodites, and sword swallowers. When a starving waif (Anne Baxter) picks his pocket, he mistakes her for a kindred spirit and offers her a job washing dishes in the cook tent. Anne is more than grateful. Then she captures the fancy of the daredevil high-diving artist (Lyle Bettger). He trains her to participate in his dangerous line of work. As they stand together, poised on the topmost pinnacle of his diving platform, he asks if she'll be his bride, while the stylized lights of a cardboard city twinkle expressionistically in the soundstage distance beyond. Although she responds affirmatively, her heart still belongs to Steve. He's a real heel who'd have her steal the savings of her husband. The furtive pair share clandestine meetings beside the carousel. "Till I met you, I never knew how rotten I was!" intones Anne fiercely. "Don't fight it, baby!" Steve urges delightedly, while the background music goes woozy with rapture. Steve's even got his own theme in this picture: a seductive siren song befitting a homoerotic Lorelei. But the clinches in this opus are strictly heterosexual. We cut from Cochran and Baxter locked in an embrace to a shot of Anne awakening in bed and looking as contented as is humanly possible. Then she discovers that her room has been ransacked. By this time, Steve has murdered Lyle, and now he's made off with the nest egg she inherited. Some louse, huh? Of course, he must come to a bad end, but at least it's a spectacular one. From the ferris wheel he is flung to his death by a crazed pinhead (Ady Berber). What a way to go!

Un Chant d'Amour* (France 1950 B&W)

Un Chant d'Amour, Jean Genet's film about boys in prison, is what most people would consider an old movie (it's even silent). Therefore we're somewhat startled to see hard cocks being masturbated. Not all of the jailhouse antics are this blunt, however. Indeed, the film is quite subtle and oblique in its use of homoeroticism. Flowers are employed as symbols of sexual desire; arms reaching blindly through barred windows attempt to pass them from one cell to the next. Two guys attempt to share a cigarette by blowing "secondhand smoke" through a hole in the wall. A stud massages a picture of a vampy-looking girl tattooed on his left bicep. Everybody's in solitary confinement. We become so accustomed to this that, when at last a pair of guys are seen to be sharing the same frame, we're so startled, we scarcely notice that they're locked in a passionate embrace. A guard, jealous and frustrated, takes off his belt and whips someone with it. Then he takes out his gun and forces the guy to go down on the barrel. Even the most hapless innocent can plainly see what's being portrayed. Not everyone would call it a song of love, but at least there's a sense of narrative impulse (however tentative, as befits a brief, impressionistic art film). *Un Chant d'Amour* is a genuine artifact of gay culture. And "culture," I might add, begins with the world "cult."

Class Reunion* (U.S. 1983 C)

Twenty-one gay male porn stars gather 'round a swimming pool (presumably that of director William Higgins) for a photographic study of bronze flesh tones and cerulean water. The usual orgy, in other words. After a while, it all starts to look like something out of Hieronymus Bosch. About a half hour into the film, a dachshund wanders through the festivities. He looks like he's wondering what the hell is going on. Toward the end, there's a perfectly spectacular aerial shot of all twenty-one guys ranged around the pool in a mind-boggling synchronized daisy chain of cocksucking. Whereupon my viewing companion exclaimed, "My God! It's . . . it's like an Esther Williams movie!" How true. Essentially, this film is an explicit gay sex version of a Busby Berkeley production number, somehow dragged out to feature length.

Cleopatra* (U.S. 1934 B&W)

Not long ago, I dreamt that I was watching television, and, as so often happens in dreams, I was somehow unable to grasp the substance of what I was seeing. The program was either the old Claudette Colbert movie of *Cleopatra* or a performance of the Zandonai opera, *Francesca da Rimini*. In the muzziness of my mind, I couldn't quite distinguish between the two. Upon my waking, I immediately attempted to analyze the dream. I knew at once I could divine its relevance to myself if I could determine what the title characters of these two stories have in common. Of course, the answer was readily, stunningly apparent: both were queens who died for love.

A discussion of dreams provides an appropriate introduction to *Cleopatra*, a Depression era extravaganza that begins with a virtual delirium of ancient Egyptian imagery. This opening montage includes idols, pyramids, sphinxes, palm trees, and a great stone gate sliding open to reveal a naked woman brandishing a pair of Oriental lamps. A discussion of queens is also pertinent, since the role of Marc Antony is portrayed by Henry Wilcoxon, an actor who, according to Boyd McDonald's *Cruising the Movies*, was not above dicking a queen now and then.

But, let's face it, this is Claudette Colbert's show. She's brought to Julius Caesar (Warren William) disguised as a rug, which, once unrolled, reveals her in a sexy halter top and a shimmy-shimmy skirt with slits up the side. Her belly button is covered, but practically everything else is visible. "Egypt! Sit down!" Caesar commands her. She offers to help him conquer India. (Claudette never really abandoned her dreams of empire. There are those who say that Ronald Reagan invaded Grenada in order to protect her mansion in Barbados.)

Wilcoxon makes his entrance wearing a breastplate molded to match his pectorals. Moments later, Caesar enters Rome, preceded by a bevy of maidens scattering rose petals. Behind him is Cleopatra on a golden throne, borne by a battalion of Nubians. Pomp, glitz, and sizzle: they dazzle the mob, both in ancient days and in times more recent. We laugh at Claudette, with her bee-stung lips and crescent moon eyebrows. Her act may look corny, but it worked; epics like these are cunningly crafted to make the masses love their chains. Princess Diana has a somewhat different shtick, and so, no doubt, did the actual Cleo. But it always amounts to the same thing.

Colbert seduces Wilcoxon with great quantities of wine and vast, elaborate production numbers. It isn't easy. Maybe she's heard that he prefers guys; the ballet she stages includes a muscular lion-tamer prancing about in a remarkably explicit costume that not only shows haunch, but also buttock. When at last the curtain is drawn on Cleo and Marc Antony, a slave commences to beat upon a drum, thereby setting the pace for their lovemaking. Slow and languorous. She likes a man who takes his time.

But let's return to earth for a moment, shall we? The director, Cecil B. DeMille, somehow manages to endow this very old-fashioned movie with a surprisingly modern sensibility, at the same time explicating a plot that's rife with political complexities. I like this film, though I really shouldn't. It's hokey and phony and sexist and racist. Besides which, it shamelessly romanticizes the ruling classes. But film, like poetry, must bypass the intellect and make its appeal directly to the heart. *Cleopatra* may be a bad movie, but it's a good dream. Why fight it? After all, doesn't my own subconscious assure me that I am a queen, as well?

A note on the 1963 remake: it's got everything from eunuchs to witches, as well it should, since it's more than four hours long. We get to see Elizabeth Taylor and Richard Burton, the supreme 'Sixties couple, doing their thing together. More interesting is the spectacle of a major studio (20th Century Fox) losing touch with reality and almost bankrupting itself.

The Climax* (U.S. 1944 C)

No, *The Climax* is not a film about orgasms. Would that it were, since the hero is played by sucky Turhan Bey. Top billing, however, goes to Boris Karloff, who scowls his way through the role of the resident physician at the Paris Opera. (I'm not certain why such an establishment would require the full-time services of a physician; I've heard that Europeans take the arts more seriously than we do, but this seems a trifle much.) When leading lady Susanna Foster makes her triumphant debut, he accosts her like any stage door Johnny. "It's a rule of the theatre to have your throat examined after each performance," he asserts, patiently leading the credulous child up the stairs to his private office. I trust he finds the depth of her throat satisfactory. Turhan likes her, too: earlier, when she was singing her big aria, he got so carried away, he ate his program.

Karloff sits her down in front of a hypnotically spinning wheel and orders her to sing no more. Later, he keeps her a prisoner in his house. But she escapes. The King of France has decreed that she must participate in a command performance. Karloff retaliates by mailing her an atomizer loaded with a rather dubious-looking throat spray.

As the preceding plot summary abundantly indicates, *The Climax* is rich, febrile camp. The crowning touch (functioning almost as an insignia, if you will) is the presence of Gale Sondergaard in the role of (what else?) the sinister housekeeper. The film, intended as a follow-up to *The Phantom of the Opera*, flopped resoundingly at the box office and cast a pall on the career of everyone connected with it. Appropriately enough, shades of green and orange dominate the production design. This rather nauseous color scheme reaches its apotheosis in Susanna's big number—a dizzy piece of folderol which has tutu-clad lady's maids (sporting powder-puff chapeaux) prancing madly to and fro in the opulent confines of Madame's dressing chamber. Climax, indeed: it's a transvestite's wet dream.

The Cobweb (U.S. 1955 C)

The Cobweb is a great movie for queens, since it's all about drapes. Lauren Bacall wants them to be muslin. Lillian Gish, meanwhile, has decided on a whole other kind of cotton. And Gloria Grahame has made up her mind that they absolutely have to be brocaded satin. As you can see, we've already got the makings of a first-class catfight. The fact that the drapes in question will hang in the library of a lunatic asylum doesn't do very much to decrease the tension. John Kerr (of *Tea and Sympathy* fame) wants to design the pattern himself. This is a very star-studded boobyhatch. The head administrator of the hospital is Charles Boyer, who's married to Fay Wray, but he's also porking his secretary, who's played by Adele Jergens.

Richard Widmark gets top billing. He's supposed to be a heroic, daring, innovative psychoanalyst, but I notice that he treats women (especially nurses) like shit. His secretary is Virginia Christine ("Mrs. Olson" from the Folger's coffee commercials) and his maid is Marjorie Bennett (Victor Buono's mother in *What Ever Happened to Baby Jane?*). His little boy is Tommy Rettig and his wife is Miss Grahame, who ultimately takes matters into her own hands and puts up the curtains herself, at which point John Kerr throws a snit fit (he even calls

GORDON SCOTT (1927–   ) in a publicity photo showing off his muscular bod—probably for one of his 1950s Tarzan films.

her a "nymphomaniac") and attempts to drown himself. Obviously, this is a film I can recommend to all or most of my friends. It's not for me, however. I've never made a personal commitment to interior decoration.

The Conquest of Mycenae*
(Italy 1963 Released in color. Shown on TV generally only in B&W)

The Conquest of Mycenae presents us with a mythical kingdom in ancient Greece, where the good guys worship "the great earth goddess, the mother of us all" and the bad guys worship a cat-headed god named Moloch. The queen is a Moloch-worshipping bitch who demands human sacrifices from neighboring principalities. This movie looks and sounds like some gloriously bad opera. Unfortunately, the entrance of Gordon Scott, ever the bellicose, truculent muscleman, marks a disappointing descent into ordinariness. "Avenge us, I beg you," someone says to him, early on. There's never any need to ask him twice. But, after the sensual stylishness and the grandiose luridness of the opening scenes, I was in no mood for his brand of sadistic bloodshed. Things go downhill fast, from that point on.

The most outrageously campy ingredient in this depraved concoction is borrowed from the horror genre: the queen has a crazed son who dwells in a hellish grotto beneath the palace. He's got the gorgeously sexy physique of a bodybuilder. Unfortunately, he's obliged to go about in a Halloween mask. His "real" face is awfully unsightly: another Halloween mask, courtesy of the folks in the makeup department. He thinks like a retarded Marquis de Sade. An accomplished archer, he uses attractive women for target practice. Surrounding him is a retinue of beauteous slave girls, much of whose time is devoted to pounding on bongo drums and striking provocative poses for the camera. Such are the fruits of a corrupt monarchy.

Real fruits, meanwhile, are provided with precious little to munch on. Gordon is given a token girlfriend. She's a ludicrous little prig with a dubbed-in British accent that's insufferably la-di-da. Unsurprisingly, he shows a definite inclination toward bisexuality. He tells the queen, "I've always wanted to see your son and admire him." "The earth would swallow the man who dared," she haughtily replies. Yes, but what would *he* get to swallow?

37

Colossus and the Headhunters* (Italy 1963 C)

Colossus and the Headhunters starts out with a tropical island being sundered by a volcanic eruption. White-hot lava is spewing and spurting all over the place. (Have I got your attention? Good.) The inhabitants are shrieking and rushing to and fro. Here and there, the earth opens crevices to swallow them. Pandemonium reigns. And then, seemingly out of nowhere, a well-proportioned young bodybuilder (Kirk Morris) with an Elvis pompadour comes idly moseying into their midst.

"Who are you?" someone asks.

"This is no time for questions," Morris rather unhelpfully replies. "Just follow me if you want to escape. Come on! To the sea!"

Unfortunately, there is only room aboard his raft for an assortment of musclebound studs clad in briefs (and a scant scattering of girls, for variety's sake). "Where are we going?" somebody asks.

"I don't know myself yet," Morris explains. "I'd been at sea for a month when I saw your island." We're all at sea by now. Seldom have I encountered a less forthcoming Greek demigod. They end up in what seems to be a Peruvian jungle, where the locals consider severed human heads to be an essential element of municipal decoration.

The muscles of Mr. Morris are so copiously oiled, they seem to gleam through a sheen of perpetual sweat. The elderly king, who is blind, gets to cop a free feel in order to reassure himself that Kirk is not, in fact, someone else. Like, for instance, the bad guy who's intent on wedding the queen, which seems rather odd, since he and his male henchman, Arros (pronounced "Arse"), are all too clearly lovers.

The villain, much like the rest of us, would like to learn more about Kirk: "Who was that man? Where did he come from?"

"I have no idea," the queen replies haughtily, "and, even if I had, I wouldn't tell you!" (At times it seems they actually want this movie to not make sense.) The queen's handmaiden gets the marriage ceremony underway by performing a ritual dance (which would've been far more impressive if she'd at least *attempted* to move in time with the music). Midway through the picture, there's a fight scene in the royal tent. One of the guys falls backward on the throne of the queen, his legs spread, his knees flailing wildly in the air. The other guy eagerly falls upon him and, for several seconds, seems to be furiously fucking him in the butt. It qualifies as one of those privileged peplum moments so blatantly homoerotic, you can't help but wonder if maybe it wasn't intentional.

Copacabana* (U.S. 1947 B&W)

In the opening scene of *Copacabana*, Groucho Marx and Carmen Miranda arrive at the title nite spot in hopes of auditioning their act for the manager, Steve Cochran. "Throw 'em out," he growls, without even laying an eye on them. Later on, Carmen gets to try out on her own. "She'll do," Cochran brusquely remarks, after the poor kid has all but busted her hump in yet another of her hyperkinetic Banana Belt specialty numbers. Carmen's sparkle and glitter, her turbans and other exotic headgear, not to mention her exaggerated gestures and constant gesticulations—all serve to suggest that her desperation in this film verges on hysteria. Not that Groucho is any greater model of composure: at one point, festooned with flowers, he threateningly brandishes a dead turkey at a fellow. "Guess you boys want to be alone," says Steve enigmatically.

Steve—who, incidentally, is cast as someone with the same first name as himself—is contrastingly cool and smooth, his suave, silky, tranquilized voice purring like a well-oiled engine. He's got sublime (even somewhat effete) sophistication written all over him: his pencil-thin sliver of a moustache, the dainty way he sips his coffee and puffs his cigarette, even the way he writes his name (the S in Steve is a treble clef sign). He's the lone outpost of sanity in this otherwise hopelessly pixilated enterprise. In this entire musical he's the only performer who seems frankly startled when, apropos of nothing, people start singing right in his face. As for Groucho, he does drag (two times) and, at one point, claims he used to be Steve's college roommate.

Cover Girl* (U.S. 1944 C)

Cover Girl, a lavish, near-psychedelic Technicolor musical, concerns itself with the world of glossy magazine publishing. Eve Arden is cast as a hard-boiled executive assistant. Her name is Miss Jackson, but everybody calls her "Stonewall." In one scene, she and Anita Colby give the once-over to prospective models. "That redhead isn't bad," Anita coolly observes, catching sight of leading lady Rita Hayworth. "Carry on, Colby!" says Eve encouragingly, patting Anita warmly on the shoulder. The lesbian overtones are low-key, but undeniably present. The publishing realm is made to seem intriguingly inverted: the male fashion photographer is noticeably swishy; female business types, meanwhile, wear power suits that make the working attire of today look downright wimpy in comparison.

The plot is pretty much a cliché: Otto Kruger wants to make a cover girl of Rita Hayworth, all because she happens to resemble his old flame. Her true love, however, is Gene Kelly. Through the magic of trick photography, he dances with himself. Later he and Phil Silvers entertain the troops with a dismally unfunny "sissy" routine. The grand finale is a production number featuring every wartime cover girl from Martha Outlaw of *Redbook* to Dusty Anderson of *Farm Journal*. What makes the movie camp, however, is Arden and her endless supply of bittersweet wisecracks.

Crime of Passion* (U.S. 1957 B&W)

Crime of Passion casts Barbara Stanwyck in the role of a lovelorn columnist. I can think of more compassionate people to confide one's troubles to. She perceives the weepy and woebegone as being her bread and butter. In the opening scene, a colleague points out that there must be *some* happy people left in town. "Not if I can help it," Stanwyck snarls. Faced with a letter from a seventeen-year-old girl who wants to run off with a married man, she jokingly advises, "Forget the man. Run away with his wife." These are her first two lines of dialogue in the film.

Her editor sends her off to get an angle on a story about a female fugitive wanted for murdering her husband. She finds the cops somewhat less than cooperative.

"You have your work to do; we have ours!" Barbara protests.

Royal Dano eyes her coolly. "Your work should be raising a family . . . having dinner ready for your husband when he gets home."

Barbara goes ahead and writes her story, anyhow. It's an open letter to the alleged murderess. We see a pair of lesbian cab drivers reading it aloud ("Let me stand by your side in your fight for justice and compassion in a world made by men and for men!"). The fugitive, who trusts Barbara (hah!), is moved to get in touch with her. You can guess the rest. This is a 'Fifties movie, which means all that feminist rhetoric isn't worth a plugged nickel.

At this point the story shifts gears. Barbara gets married to Dano's partner, a police detective played by Sterling Hayden. Sterling installs her in a quiet suburban neighborhood and expects her to submissively assume the role of a placid 'Fifties homemaker. Of course, we know right away this will never work. And, sure enough, she almost immediately turns into an ambitious, conniving shrew. To the movie's credit, we see with stunning clarity the reasons for her discontentment. The suburban milieu is portrayed as a wasteland: shallow, sterile, mindless. This is a revisionist film noir, which means that cozy traditional family values are turned on their ear. Barbara's so bored and frustrated, she tries to advance her husband's career by having a love affair with his boss (Raymond Burr). It ends very badly, as the title of the movie indicates. The scene where she shoots Burr dead is handled audaciously: we don't see the gun . . . just her eyes as she pulls the trigger.

A housewife who will literally kill to keep up with the Joneses is, I think, a supremely appropriate heroine for a subversively campy 'Fifties melodrama like this one. As for Hayden, since he's the one who cracks the case and then marches his better half to the hoosegow, I'd say he deserves the promotion she's won for him.

The Damned Don't Cry   (U.S. 1950 B&W)

A correspondent in London writes, "Has there ever been any man as alluring and yet uncaring about his allure as Steve Cochran?" I'm inclined to doubt it. And I'm sure I couldn't have put it better myself. In *The Damned Don't Cry*, his romantic interest is none other than Joan Crawford. As a couple, they haven't much chemistry; in fact, he seems slightly frightened of her. I guess I can't say that I blame him. She's a ball-breaker in this one, and Steve's got a lot to protect.

This melodramatic film noir, made in 1949, but released in '50, qualifies as a kind of transitional vehicle for Crawford. The opening scenes are pure *Mildred Pierce*: she's wanted for questioning in connection with a murder, but a flashback hastens to inform us that she used to be just another downtrodden postwar housewife, wearily exchanging snarls with her redneck husband (Richard Egan) in the hick town tract house they share with her whining parents. Joan loses no time in freeing herself from this domestic hornet's nest. She lands a job as a mannequin at Fit-Rite Frocks, where she quickly discovers that some of the out-of-town buyers are veritable octopi. "It's still modeling, only it pays better at night," someone points out.

Then she catches the eye of David Brian, a gangland kingpin who takes a shine to her. This nouveau riche scoundrel is unsettled by her coarse accoutrements and tells her so. "I don't like being made to look like two cents," she fumes, which makes us wonder why she's wearing that hat she's got on. When she saunters into his private office, he ostentatiously opens a window, then asks her, "What kind of perfume are you using?"

" 'Temptation,' " she replies.

"Yes. I suppose it *is*, in some quarters."

Under his careful tutelage, the tart is transformed into a well-bred and cultured society beauty, hostess of soirees attended by the cream of the upper crust. Significantly, at this stage she bobs her shoulder-length 'Forties hair and wears it in a short pageboy, a style Crawford stuck with throughout the 'Fifties.

At Brian's behest, Joan embarks on a mission of intrigue. He packs her off to Nevada, where she's ordered to seduce and betray a rival mobster: a slick, oily, oversexed punk who, of course, is portrayed by Steve. At this point, Joan settles naturally into the role of the "older" woman struggling to repress the desire she feels for an obviously younger man. This sort of thing was to become her stock-in-trade throughout the decade ahead, which placed her opposite leading men like Jeff Chandler and Cliff Robertson. Cochran comes on to her at a diving exhibition. It grieves me to report that he's fully clothed (worse yet, he's wearing a plaid sportcoat), but then he turns up in bathing trunks later on. "The best-looking scenery in the West," he says, taking the words right out of my mouth. (Unfortunately, and rather unbelievably, he's referring to Crawford at the time.)

After dark, Joan interrupts a gangster confab at Cochran's home. Claiming she was worried he was with another woman, she's relieved to perceive that the party is all-male. No need for her to fret, after all! Right?

At one point Joan has a line which practiced ears will recognize as a textbook example, summing up the kind of roles that she and Davis and Stanwyck made their own: "You gotta kick and punch and belt your way up, 'cause nobody's gonna give you a lift!" All three of the principals in this movie—Crawford, Cochran, and Brian—wind up dodging bullets. It comes as no surprise that Joan is the sole survivor.

Dancing Lady* (U.S. 1933 B&W)

In *Dancing Lady*, Joan Crawford's first scene finds her clad in little more than a scattering of sequins. She's a chorus girl in a burlesque house, and her performance is interrupted by a vice raid. A Park Avenue swell (Franchot Tone) bails her out of jail. He inspires her to make a try for Broadway. First, though, she has to charm a certain Broadway director, and she's so determined to do so, she almost follows him into a Turkish bath. Before you assume that he's gay, I'd better mention that he's played by Clark Gable.

The piano player at her audition is one of the Three Stooges (I mean that literally), but she gets the job anyhow. And Gable's so impressed, he decides to make her the star of the show. Which means a complete rewrite is in order. It's fun watching Gable tell the playwright this, since he's played by Sterling Holloway doing a temperamental fag routine.

Some of the geopolitical trimmings are more than a little ironic, in light of later events. Tone, for example, takes Crawford to Cuba on holiday. Later, clad in dirndl and lederhosen, Crawford and her dancing partner (none other than Fred Astaire) perform a number entitled "Let's Go Bavarian," a rather controversial suggestion in 1933, the year that Hitler came to power. But perhaps I'm taking this frothy concoction too seriously. What matters is that Crawford and Gable were two of the most gorgeous creatures to ever grace the screen. They seldom looked better than they do herein.

Dark Victory* (U.S. 1939 B&W)

Brendan Behan once said he would rather be dead than think about death; this movie thinks about virtually nothing else. It's a Bette Davis cult film of the highest magnitude, beloved by her fans and non-fans alike. I, however, have always found it morbid and depressing. She's cast as Judith Traherne, a darling of the horsy set, who's plagued by ghastly headaches and double vision and the odd habit of falling down stairs. George Brent, that constant plodder, is the surgeon who diagnoses her brain tumor. He's determined to shield her from the fact of her impending doom, but then he leaves her file out in plain sight where she can get at it. When she learns the truth, she's so upset, she goes flying into the arms of co-star *Ronald Reagan*! She's a sick girl.

The cast also includes Humphrey Bogart as a stablehand. He seems hard-boiled, but he's a softy at heart. The setting is American, but Davis has seldom seemed more British. (The 1963 remake, *Stolen Hours*, takes place in Britain, but stars Susan Hayward, who is clearly American.) The film is justly famed for the spirit of nobility and self-sacrifice which Bette brings to her lugubrious death scene. It could wring tears from a statue. Unfortunately, in this case, I guess I'm harder than a statue.

Daughters of Darkness* (Belgium 1971 C)

Daughters of Darkness qualifies as an art film, despite its lurid subject matter and overtones of camp. Delphine Seyrig (from *Last Year at Marienbad*) stars as a glamorous lesbian vampire who shows up at a ritzy Belgian resort during the off-season. The concierge recalls that she stayed there forty years previous, when he was just a lowly bellboy. She tries, unsuccessfully, to convince him that he must be thinking of her mother. He knows better. She looks precisely the same as she did back in 1931: marcelled hair and shiny, high-gloss costumes, lipstick, and nail polish. She is Art Deco incarnate and the very image of Depression era Dietrich.

Delphine is drawn to a honeymooning couple lodged in the Royal Suite. The husband is John Karlen (from *Dark Shadows*). He's a kinky bisexual nervously endeavoring to put off the day when his bride (Daniele Ouimet) will inevitably encounter his aristocratic "mother" (actually, the wealthy, middle-aged male lover who's been keeping him). The newspapers are full of grisly stories about a series of throatslittings in nearby Bruges. With typical horror movie logic, the newlyweds repair to Bruges on a sightseeing jaunt, arriving just in time to witness the discovery of the latest victim's corpse. Back at the hotel, Seyrig regales the young couple with stories of her notorious ancestress, Countess Elizabeth Bathory, who bathed in the blood of virgins. In the movie's campiest scene, Seyrig and Karlen turn each other on with a verbal inventory of the Countess's crimes.

In point of fact, however, Delphine only has eyes for Daniele. John is odd man out and we know it's only a matter of time before the bloodsucker fixes his wagon. Waiting for her to do so is the basis of the film's suspense. That's why, although he's unsympathetically portrayed, the movie's gay male anti-hero practically functions as its endangered heroine.

Death in Small Doses   (U.S. 1957 B&W)

Based on a *Saturday Evening Post* exposé, this quintessentially 'Fifties drug film could well be the gay camp *Reefer Madness*. We know right off the bat that Peter Graves is with the Feds: first they show us the Capitol dome and then we see him sitting in an office with a picture of George Washington on the wall. Ere long, he's making an undercover trip to L.A., where he moves into a rooming house that caters to truckers. Sounds like an interesting place to live. Just down the hall is Chuck Connors, who's cast as someone named "Mink" (as in "fucking like minks"). Seems like he never gets any sleep. Instead, he spends all his time jitterbugging, listening to bebop records, and poppin' pills. And he sure makes a lot of unannounced visits to Peter's bedroom. "Hey, I've got just the thing for that tired-all-over feeling," babbles Chuck. Is he hopped up or is he just plain horny?

Good ol' Pete is investigating amphetamine abuse among truck-drivers. He and Chuck are employed by "Boomer Freight Lines," where everyone seems to either be freaking out, dropping dead, or gulping bennies. Chuck eats 'em like candy. Pete has a tendency to poop out at parties, so Chuck shows him how to get that extra burst of vim and vigor. This is a deliriously funny movie (with an especially ludicrous surprise ending). I think it must have been financed by a consortium of stimulant companies. There's a blatant plug for Coke and, in practically every scene, someone's either smoking a cigarette or drinking coffee. It's like a feature-length commercial for caffeine and nicotine.

Death in Venice* (Italy 1971 C)

There is nothing remotely amusing about *Death in Venice*, Luchino Visconti's gloomy film of Thomas Mann's equally grim novelette. The movie nonetheless qualifies for inclusion as a cult film on the basis of its cinematic depiction of boy-love (said depiction, while hardly flattering, is rendered with the utmost romanticism). The film is a lethargically languorous evocation of fin-de-siècle decadence. Dirk Bogarde is cast as a celebrated German composer who becomes hopelessly infatuated with a bored-looking adolescent boy whom he encounters at a fashionable seaside resort. Bogarde plays the musician as a fussy, rather pathetic-seeming martinet. His mad passion is intended to signify a sort of final surrender to overripe sensuality, symptomatic of a life-denying obsession with youth and beauty for their own sakes. It proves to be the death of poor Dirk. His all-consuming yearning leads him to linger overlong in Venice, though he's well aware that the city is gripped by pestilence.

The camerawork seems random, rambling, and diffuse. Visconti makes surprisingly little of the architectural panoply that is Venice. Though the subject matter is superficially similar to that of *Lolita*, this art film is actually more akin to the realm of vintage bloodcurdlers. Both the turn-of-the-century period and the Art Nouveau decor were once, two or three decades ago, the common province of British and Italian Gothic horror movies. The philosophical concerns displayed are also like those of the blood-and-thunder school: life and death, good and evil, love and lust, purity and corruption, and, most importantly, the destructive effects of the sexual impulse. These topics turn up, not only in thrillers, but also in far more respected forms of dramaturgy. Of course, I do not mean to classify *Death in Venice* as a thriller. Far from it. Indeed, the film contains only a single moment of genuine horror: our initial intimation of the plague's presence, when a decrepit old vagrant twitchingly succumbs in a crowded railway depot.

Design for Living   (U.S. 1933 B&W)

This campy depiction of a ménage à trois involving Miriam Hopkins, Gary Cooper, and Fredric March tries terribly hard to be heterosexual. But how straight can it be when the source material is by Noel Coward and the supporting cast includes both Edward Everett Horton and Franklin Pangborn? For that matter, when Miriam first encounters March and Cooper, they are sleeping together, albeit with their clothes on (the setting for this opening scene is a train compartment). "A thing happened to me that usually happens to men," she tells the boys, early on. This remark gets her their undivided attention. As for Horton, he is cast as a rival for Miriam's affections. No such fantastic premise disfigures Pangborn's performance. He is his usual self. I particularly appreciated the way he says "Heavens, no!" just like I do.

FRANKLIN PANGBORN (1893–1958), shown here in *Design for Living* (Paramount 1933), was often cast by Hollywood in stereotyped "nervous nellie" roles.

Destry Rides Again* (U.S. 1939 B&W)

Destry Rides Again is a western, a genre which some consider inhospitable to camp. However, there can't be much doubt about this opus, particularly when Marlene Dietrich, cast in the role of a saloon singer named Frenchy, launches herself wholeheartedly into a remarkably energetic and protracted cat fight with Una Merkel, in the process of which she wantonly rips off most of Merkel's ginghams. Then Jimmy Stewart intervenes by dousing them both with a bucket of water, absolutely ruining Dietrich's elaborate coiffure.

Una Merkel is married to the ever-effeminate Mischa Auer. He loses his pants to Dietrich in a poker game. Una won't buy him new ones, so he steals a pair from Billy Gilbert. Una returns them, cautioning Gilbert to take better care of them in the future. "You watch your husband. I'll watch my pants," Billy grumbles. (It's a wise wife who won't let her spouse exchange trousers with the guy nextdoor.)

Stewart strives to disprove charges that he's a frontier pantywaist, a reputation brought about by the fact that he drinks milk and won't wear a gun. Dietrich sings one of her most celebrated numbers: "See What the Boys in the Back Room Will Have." In the gay bar culture of the late 'Seventies, this song took on a whole new layer of meaning.

Die! Die! My Darling!* (G.B. 1965 C)

It is, of course, a sublime irony that Tallulah Bankhead's final film performance was in the role of a right-wing religious zealot. In her very first scene she announces how glad she is that her son died a virgin. This is a woman who eschews, abhors, and abjures tobacco, make-up, strong drink, theatrical entertainments, and all shades of the color red. She's also opposed to mirrors, telephones, and salt ("God's food should be eaten unadorned."). It's a challenging role. I mean, this is a woman who doesn't believe in lipstick. And it must have required sandpaper to remove all traces of lipstick from Tallulah's lips.

Tallulah's staff of servants in the film is suitably peculiar. The housekeeper (Yootha Joyce) is practically a case study of repressed hostility and aggression. Her husband, the groundskeeper (Peter Vaughan), is a sadistic lech. There's also a severely retarded handyman (played by

The inimitable TALLULAH BANKHEAD (1903–1968) packs a gun while reading the Bible in *Die! Die! My Darling!* (Columbia 1965).

Donald Sutherland, at a very early stage in his career).

A crisis strikes Tallulah's homestead when Stefanie Powers shows up. She's cast as the fiancée of the aforementioned deceased son. But she says they wouldn't have married, even if he'd lived. Details are lacking, but it's a cinch that no one could grow up straight in this ménage. At any rate, Bankhead is heartily pissed to learn that Stefanie's not a virgin. "You must die . . . DIE, my dahling!" Tallulah declaims dramatically. Since this is a horror film, we're subjected to a Grand Guignol finale, with everyone stabbing and shooting each other. I realize that Bankhead was one of the all-time great actresses, but in this film she's so hammy (and campy), she reminds us of an evil queen (the female kind) in a Disney animated cartoon.

Dino* (U.S. 1957 B&W)

Dino is babyfaced prettyboy Sal Mineo butching it up as a hardened delinquent. Just out of reform school, where he served a three-and-a-half-year sentence for offing a night watchman, Sal is now getting therapy from a settlement house caseworker. This shrink is played by Brian Keith, who, in 1957, looks like a hunky football quarterback. Much of what Sal has to say is surly. In light of his later career, however, his words take on a whole new layer of meaning. Like, for instance, when he talks about life in the reformatory: "Did you ever sleep forty guys in a room? Yeah! What goes on in there? Everything you can think of!"

"I just want to help you feel better, that's all," Brian offers, consolingly.

"So why don't you give me a rubdown?" Sal suggests. "I don't remember no one ever kissing me. . . . How come nobody ever kissed me?" To conceal his tears, he flips over on his stomach, thrusting his denim-clad butt at the camera.

Ironic double entendres, however unintentional, surely qualify as camp. I should also mention the pensive scene in which Sal contemplates killing his mom and dad in their sleep. I must admit I was shocked: we see the parents sharing a double bed, a 'Fifties movie taboo.

Publicity photo of 18-year-old SAL MINEO (1939–1976) in the same year he made *Dino*.
But were juvenile delinquents ever this adorably cute in reality?

Dr. Christian Meets the Women* (U.S. 1940 B&W)

Dr. Christian Meets the Women is a film that takes pains to establish its heterosexual credentials early on. The opening scene presents us with a pair of newlyweds setting out on their honeymoon; virtually the entire town has gone to the station to see them off. What a heartwarming celebration of family values! The only dissonant note is struck by a couple of giggly fat girls (twins, identically dressed) who look like they stepped right out of a Diane Arbus photo.

Since this is a film about proper diet and exercise, these full-figured gals make recurring appearances and are used as a sort of leitmotif. They are the ghosts of meals not eaten, the specter of pounds which were lost and are soon to be regained. A quack doctor comes to town and plays on the vanity of the local females, persuading them to embark upon his supposedly beautifying regimen. This hard-muscled gent is played by Rod La Rocque (a name of commendable firmness). One young woman is so swayed by his pitch, she becomes an anorectic. Her mother, meanwhile, is so hot for La Rocque, she invites him to stay at her home, and even turns her decor topsy-turvy to accommodate his exercise equipment. He gives the girls bennies; no wonder they get so high-strung and temperamental. And it's no wonder that business slacks off at the local grocery. Nobody's eating food anymore; it just isn't done.

Seldom have I seen womanhood more unflatteringly pictured. All the more ironic, then, that the ludicrous malaise which afflicts these ladies is fueled by a desire to make themselves attractive to men. In scene after scene, they're misled by a man. It remains for the saintly, condescending Dr. Christian (Jean Hersholt) to set them on the path to good nutrition. (La Rocque is portrayed as being a kind of vampire. And the anorectic is saved by a blood transfusion from the man she loves.) If I were a woman, I'd beware of any movie that had the word "women" in the title. It's almost always a sign of rampant sexism.

Dr. Jekyll and Sister Hyde* (G.B. 1971 C)

Just as a mere title, Dr. Jekyll and Sister Hyde immediately expresses its sexual transgressiveness. Similarly, the elegantly languorous waltz which accompanies the opening title design (white candle in a silver stick, set against red velvet draperies) just as firmly establishes a mood of high-tone camp. Ralph Bates is Dr. Jekyll, who swallows a potion mostly made up of female sex hormones. He staggers around awhile, makes a bit of a ruckus, then looks into a mirror and . . . Why, it's Martine Beswick!

The randy chap who lives upstairs comes down to see what the noise is all about. He peeks in the door and sees the erstwhile doctor still stationed before the mirror, massaging her naked and newly developed tits. But the sex change is short-lived. Ralph wants more hormones. (Maybe he just wants to hear the violins welling up on the soundtrack one more time.) The morgue is fresh out of nubile cadavers, so he kills a prostitute ("I'm very popular with *real* gentlemen—on account of the fact that I speak fluent French."). The murder is attributed to Jack the Ripper. Earlier, the doctor bargained for bodies with Burke and Hare. (Never mind that these two practiced their grisly trade in the 1820s, whereas the Ripper was only active in 1888.)

When Beswick becomes the more dominant side of Ralph's personality, he finds himself slipping into feminine mannerisms while still appearing outwardly male. For instance, he starts coming on to the upstairs neighbor when the latter fellow happens to espy him emerging from the corsetmaker's shop. Whoops!

Beswick's blatantly perverse presence is basically all the film has going for it. The two sides of her face seem oddly mismatched; her eyes look like they're not on the same level with one another. The overpowering sexuality of her performance tends to ruin the provocative gay camp aspects. When she makes love to the guy upstairs, we totally forget that we're witnessing a technically homosexual act.

Dream Boys* (France 1986 C)

The French approach to gay male erotica is different from ours. The first of the films on this tape (all of them directed by Jean-Daniel Cadinot) presents us with a pair of guys garbed in white, frolicking on a farm to the tasteful accompaniment of classical music. An erect member seems almost a rude intrusion under such high-flown circumstances. Considerably more erotic is the episode which concludes the tape: a hitchhiker and a dazzlingly handsome motorcyclist get it on in an abandoned bus. Traffic signs are intercut to provide a witty commentary on the action.

The longest segment takes place in a hospital where the simple act of taking a patient's temperature with a rectal thermometer inevitably leads to an interracial threeway. This orgy is presented as a flashback as one of the participants tells his priest about it during confession. Maybe that's why the cum shot is accompanied by a fanfare from the Berlioz Requiem.

Cadinot has directed many other superb gay male erotic films. Worth checking out (on their way to cult status) are *Sex Bazaar*, *Tough and Tender*, *All of Me*, and *Becoming Men*.

---

*Dreamwood** (U.S. 1972 C)

James Broughton is a maker of short experimental films of great gay cultural value. *Dreamwood*, one of his more ambitious works, presents us with a good-looking naked man frolicking in the forest. (He bears a passing resemblance to Melanie Griffith, only he's got a moustache.) He's haunted by strange visions of an Egyptian princess straight out of some old Hammer horror film about mummies. He axe-murders a drag queen who attempts to ply him with costume jewelry. A middle-aged nun does a strip. Our leading man takes a piss. (He also takes a crap, in full view of the camera. This may be a screen "first.") This kinky Siegfried eventually awakens a leather-clad Brunhilde of indeterminate gender. He gives him/her a good whipping. Despite its more lurid qualities, the film is actually quite a pretty pastoral piece. The colors have a tactile quality one can almost taste.

Broughton's best-known and liveliest work is *The Bed*, a witty and charmingly playful film which illustrates the many and various ways a bed can be put to use. Perhaps his most "Warholian" film is *Hermes Bird*, which consists of an extended close-up of a cock getting hard.

---

*Drifting** (Israel 1983 C)

I was, I must admit, a tad surprised to encounter a gay film from Israel, hardly a country known for its excessive tolerance toward homosexuality. And, in fact, the topic of this movie is how hard it is to make a gay film in Israel. Thus, by its very existence, the movie undercuts its own argument. I could relate to the filmmaker hero (Amos Guttman), who is clearly fascinated by camp icons such as Greta Garbo, Ramon Novarro, Rudolph Valentino, and Jayne Mansfield. The title is apt: he's bored, he's aimless, he's discontented, he works at his grandmother's grocery store, and he's constantly kvetching about how he wants to make movies. I was more interested in the decor: rooms and furnishings in Israel tend to be white, a circumstance which, I must say, makes English subtitles devilishly difficult to read.

Ecco* (Italy 1965 C)

George Sanders killed himself in 1972. His suicide note read as follows:

> Dear World,
> I am leaving because I am bored.

Ecco, a documentary narrated by Sanders, takes us on a round-the-world tour. As always, he does sound rather jaded. We may, however, safely assume that the doings onscreen kept his audience enthralled. Sure held my interest, at any rate. We get to see Brazilian drag queens, American bodybuilders, Swedish teddy boys, plus a huge, seething mass of seminude Japanese youths, all tangled together and writhing in a quaint religious ceremony which appears far more sensual than sacred. ("The steam rising from the bodies actually fogs our camera lens," George informs us.)

The most charmingly picturesque sequence involves a reindeer roundup in Lapland. A Nordic maiden, her blonde head topped with a pert and festive bonnet, castrates one of the animals with her teeth.

George's screen persona could easily be "read" as homosexual. It appears, however, that, in reality, he was not. After all, he was at one time married to Zsa Zsa Gabor.

Ed Wood* (U.S. 1994 B&W)

Ed Wood is that true rarity—a camp classic which also legitimately qualifies as a great motion picture. Why is this film able to have it both ways? Probably because it's the true-life story of a gentleman who actually *was* a camp classic: Edward D. Wood, Jr. (arguably the worst director of all time).

Wood's oeuvre includes such acknowledged "masterworks" as *Jail Bait*, *The Sinister Urge*, and other oddities which I fully described in *High Camp*, Volume One. This new film takes place in the middle to later 'Fifties, Wood's most fecund period, during which he gave the world *Glen or Glenda?*, *Bride of the Monster*, and the immortal *Plan 9 from Outer Space*. *Glen or Glenda?* holds a special meaning for gays because . . . well, because it's a romantic melodrama about transvestites. Since Wood himself was a transvestite, we may safely assume that the film was especially significant to him, as well. According to *Ed Wood*, the project saw its genesis when he happened to spot a *Variety* item about a Poverty Row studio planning a screen bio of Christine Jorgensen. ("Boy-to-Chick Flick to Click," leers the headline.) As played (with clammy zeal) by Johnny Depp, Wood experiences a moment of bona fide creative inspiration. Can this be the story he was born to tell? Can this be the film he was born to direct? Can this be the ideal way to let his girlfriend (Sarah Jessica Parker) know about his sexual quirk? ("Where's my pink sweater? I can never seem to find my clothes anymore!" she's been heard to loudly complain of late.) Perhaps she's just not ready to accept the truth. ("Ed, it's over. I need a normal life," she sighs defeatedly, after watching him perform an exotic dance in full drag.)

Wood's most fruitful relationships are with his professional colleagues: washed-up horror actor Bela Lugosi (an Oscar-caliber performance by Martin Landau), camp diva Bunny Breckinridge (a swishy performance by Bill Murray), and preening "psychic" Criswell (Jeffrey Jones, who's a dead ringer for the genuine article). All three appear in his magnum opus, *Plan 9 from Outer Space*, an incoherent miasma of mismatched footage, cardboard props, and laughably slipshod special effects. The financial backers of this mess are a group of Baptists, who, predictably enough, object when Wood shows up for work in feminine attire. But he perseveres. At *Plan 9*'s premiere, he has a prophetic vision, the veracity of which has been confirmed by history: "This is the one! This is the one I'll be remembered for!" (Two years after his death, *Plan 9* was declared the worst film ever made. Which only goes to prove that a genius is never properly appreciated during his lifetime.)

Despite all the grungy weirdness, this is actually quite an inspiring tale. Sort of like an upbeat *Day of the Locust*, if you can imagine such a thing. The film has a high-gloss polish that Wood himself couldn't have achieved in a million years (although, with a million *bucks*, he might have come close). The clanky, skanky music score is performed by the London Philharmonic Orchestra. That should give you some idea of what I mean.

Edward II* (G.B. 1992 C)

Edward II, Derek Jarman's film of Christopher Marlowe's classic play, has a relatively simple and uncomplicated plot. The King of England (Steven Waddington) is madly in love with a man (Andrew Tiernan) who, worse luck, is clearly lower-class. The church, the military, the upper crust (in short, the usual suspects) consider this a scandalous state of affairs. Encouraged by the jealous and neglected Queen (Tilda Swinton), they take decisive action: the commoner is merely choked to death; the King, on the other hand, is sodomized with a white-hot poker.

The opening scene is favored with a felicitous device: if we tire of the elegant Elizabethan speeches, we may direct our attention to the background, where a couple of sailors are having sex. Jarman indulges his usual penchant for conscious anachronism: the King's adherents in the ongoing political struggle are a suitably unruly gang of ACT UP demonstrators. (It should perhaps be mentioned that this movie was made midway through the director's battle with AIDS.) The Queen complains that the King and his favorite "jest at Our attire. T'is *this* that makes *me* impatient." Homosexuals have long been known for their keenly discerning taste in clothes, and it must be said that Swinton makes of herself an eminently suitable target for sartorial japery. She is gowned in the style of a *Vogue* fashion model from the late 'Fifties (one of the more bizarre and grotesque periods in the history of haute couture). On the other hand, I must also admit that the reactionary bad guys are much more coherent, articulate, and interesting than the overly histrionic and obnoxious renegade heroes. Is it mere perversity on my part that it seems so, or is this simply the way things are? It can't have been what Jarman intended.

Entertaining Mr. Sloane* (G.B. 1970 C)

Entertaining Mr. Sloane, based on a fairly notorious play by Joe Orton (a gay cultural icon if ever there was one), was Beryl Reid's follow-up film to *The Killing of Sister George*. It is, if possible, an even less heterosexual vehicle. On the other hand, it offers her a far more heterosexual role. She's cast as your typical middle-aged butterball who fancies herself a sweet, alluring young thing. And let it never be said that she prizes her dignity too highly: she spends the opening third of the movie clad in a sheer, diaphanous see-through miniskirt with absolutely nothing underneath it. Her roly-poly torso thus attired, she entices the titular Mr. Sloane to follow her home, mainly by promising him free board and lodgings. He is a handsome, hard-bodied ne'er-do-well (Peter McEnery), his demeanor youthful, his morals negligible. She has little difficulty coaxing him into the sack.

Soon, however, he encounters Beryl's brother (I almost wrote "sister"). Portrayed by Harry Andrews, he is a closeted, cashmere-coated homosexual who drives a huge, pink convertible with tailfins. The camera presents Mr. Sloane from his viewpoint in a sequence as blatantly homoerotic as you'll ever see outside of a porn flick. Later he takes the lad swimming, and thoughtfully helps him apply sun tan lotion to his smooth, yet muscular back and shoulders. He also outfits the boy as his chauffeur; the uniform, of course, is leather. Contrary to the title, Mr. Sloane is the one who ends up doing most of the "entertaining." He oversteps his bounds, however, when he plays too rough with the siblings' dad: an addled, semi-senile old gent (Alan Webb) whose battered corpse gives Beryl and Harry a chance to blackmail Mr. Sloane into going further with them than he's ever gone before. Indeed, he "weds" them both in a highly informal ceremony which concludes with the two of them kissing him, simultaneously, one to a cheek. That this is, in fact, an unmitigatedly happy ending is signaled by the why-the-hell-not?, things-could-be-worse expression which flickers across McEnery's handsome face.

Erotikus* (U.S. 1983 C)

Erotikus, a history of gay porno flicks, compiled by director Tom De Simone and narrated by the heavily macho Fred Halsted, is most informative in its discussion of the genre's early days, when studios such as the Athletic Model Guild were cranking out crude, rude nudies with guys like Ed Fury (soon to be a star of Italian pepla) and Glenn Corbett (soon to be replacing George Maharis on *Route 66*).

All too soon, however, we're plunged into the hardcore stuff: sordid couplings and spurting pricks in rooms with tacky wallpaper. The movies excerpted, however, are fascinatingly primitive and obscure. There's apparently a little bit of Jane lurking in the title character of *Tarzan the Fearless*: for his rendezvous with a succulent youth, he wears a flower in his hair. *Duffy's Tavern* features a poolroom scene which is notable for its intensely erotic mood of pent-up sexual need and frustration: a guy fondling his pool cue or rubbing his denim-clad crotch turns out to be far more compelling than the inserted "fantasy" shots of explicit sex. Best of all, however, are the clips from an outdoorsy opus called *Dust Unto Dust*: an ersatz spaghetti western about a blonde-haired frontiersman befriended by a pair of *really* wild Indians.

An interesting historical footnote: I recognized the background music used in the early sections of *Erotikus*. It's appropriated from Neal Hefti's score for the Carroll Baker vehicle, *Harlow*. Nice to know that we all buy the same movie soundtrack albums.

---

*Fangs of the Living Dead** (Spain 1968 C)

In the early 'Sixties, Anita Ekberg was being directed by Fellini. In the later 'Sixties, she ended up making this vampire sexploitation picture. I've no idea how or why this came to pass. As a camp fancier, all I can do is bow my head in silent gratitude.

Anita is the only certified star on hand. Cast as "the most beautiful model in Italy," she jets from Rome to Central Europe for a look at the ancestral mansion she's inherited. She makes quite a sight, sweeping into the local village tavern. She's wearing an orange pantsuit with matching cape. In a scene that's practically a parody, all the rustics freeze in their tracks when she chances to mention her destination and the fact that she is the new Contessa. The castle is indeed a handsome edifice, and the final leg of her journey there is accomplished via coach, which serves to firmly establish the proper genre tone. Upon being shown to her room, she changes clothes. The burly coachman peers through the keyhole to watch Anita disrobe. Surprised by a parlormaid, he retreats to his own quarters, presumably to jack off.

Appropriately enough, the most impressive chamber of the castle is its crypt, all blue with dank, sweating stonework and golden with the glow of a profusion of candles and torches. From there arises "Glinka," a pale brunette lesbian vampire who nocturnally prowls the premises, candelabra in hand. Encounters with such castle denizens as this gradually convince Anita that she herself is a victim of the vampiric curse which has plagued the family for generations. Anita's uncle—who is, in fact, the chieftain of the vampires—is the one who tells her this sorry ancestral saga. At first she's inclined to disbelieve him, and even questions his sanity, telling him he needs "a long rest" in "some peaceful place." (If only she knew!) He, however, is persistent enough to gain the upper hand, and she's just dumb enough to let him.

The men in this film are a fine-looking bunch. The "uncle" is a gaunt, ascetic type with a charmingly devilish Vandyke beard and moustache. The hero's sidekick is cuter still, though someone should have warned him never to wear a brown leather jacket over a red turtleneck sweater. The hero himself did not impress me favorably until the very end, when we discover him bound to an inverted cross, with chains encircling his naked, hairy chest. Anita releases him so he can stake down the bad guy, who is temporarily distracted because he's gawking at a vampire catfight on the staircase. Lecherous voyeurism is punished again! An odd conclusion for a peep show like this.

The Female Animal   (U.S. 1958 B&W)

Hooray for Hollywood! Especially the lurid, decadent 'Fifties Hollywood that all the gay boys of the Eisenhower era wished they could run away to. *The Female Animal* (love that sordid title!) purports to give us a behind-the-scenes glimpse of Tinseltown reality. Hedy Lamarr plays a fading star of overstuffed historical epics. The opening scene finds her staggering out of her dressing room one step behind a discarded liquor bottle. The hell with rehearsals, she tells her director. "Just shoot it." Famous last words. She falls off a bridge during the fight scene they're filming. We get a glimpse of her undies as she plummets down, down to the water below.

Hedy goes from crisis to crisis in this pic. Next a well-muscled extra (George Nader) saves her from being crushed beneath a falling spotlight. Grateful, she asks that he escort her to a premiere. "You look very handsome in your dinner jacket," she says after the show, implying that he'd look even better out of it. "Do you have to go home or something? Is someone waiting for you?" She invites him to her "little place" down by the beach. After their midnight swim, they passionately kiss while reclining in the sand. The water droplets on George's back and shoulders glitter like falling stars.

Just when things are getting hot and heavy, the telephone rings. Hedy

GEORGE NADER (1921–   ), hunky star of many 50s films, is shown here in a publicity photo (U-I). In the 1970s he wrote a gay-themed sci-fi novel, *Chrome*, and came out openly as a gay man.

is summoned home to her Bel Air mansion, where her delinquent daughter (Jane Powell) is throwing a drunken tantrum. A grown-up child can be a major inconvenience (in more ways than one) to a celluloid siren. No matter: Hedy installs George in her Malibu hideaway as a "caretaker," though it's unclear who's taking care of whom. But then he's offered the lead in a horror flick about a giant, man-eating orchid. The producer (Jerry Paris) enthuses, "There won't be a florist in this country that won't carry a big blow-up picture of you . . . with your clothes half torn off, in orchids up to your navel!" Hedy knows that George can't be a star unless he looks like one, so she buys him a different suit for every day of the week. "If I took them, I'd be a tramp!" George protests. Shades of *Sunset Boulevard*!

Jan Sterling has a memorable cameo in the role of a has-been cinemoppet. "I was the first child star ever to be chased around a desk," she boasts. She and her latest gigolo share an excruciating scene with Hedy and George in the foyer of an expensive night club. "I adore the clean-limbed American type, too," says Jan approvingly, after giving George the eye.

"Leaping to conclusions again?" Hedy purrs.

"What else is there to leap at? Except men." When Hedy confides that George has acting aspirations, Jan is quick to caution her: "My dear, that's a mistake. Never let them have a career. . . . Keep 'em sharecropping, dear. It's the only way."

Before very long, the soap operatic complications have become ludicrous. Hedy's in danger of losing George to her dear, demented daughter, so she plays her trump card and proposes marriage. ("This story, I think, should go to Hedda.") Nothing like keeping it all in the family. Sweet little Jane Powell is not very good at playing drunk scenes. George, however, is simply superb at showing off the beef. He plays most of his scenes in swimming trunks and (as I've indicated) the lighting is fabulously imaginative. My favorite line, however, has nothing to do with sex. A little boy exclaims to Hedy, "Hey! I know you! You're on TV!" Her quick retort: "Hasn't your mother taught you not to say that naughty word?"

Female on the Beach   (U.S. 1955 B&W)

Movies about male prostitutes were considered rather avant-garde in 1955, but that didn't stop Joan Crawford and Jeff Chandler from making one. Even the opening titles (their names, written in the sand, are erased by the rushing tide) identify the film as being camp. Jeff is a former sailor and a part-time gigolo. His pimps are Cecil Kellaway (Lana Turner's husband in *The Postman Always Rings Twice*) and Natalie (*Gilligan's Island*) Schafer. In the opening scene, he's breaking things off with a client (Judith Evelyn) who's been taking too much of his time. Blinded by tears and booze (she's been swilling brandy out of a huge snifter), she takes a fatal tumble off her balcony. Was it accidental? A suicide? Murder? Before the body is even cold, Joan Crawford moves into the house. She's a wealthy widow from Las Vegas. The real estate agent (Jan Sterling) tells her nothing at all regarding the previous evening's awkward contretemps. Therefore Joan is in for a nasty shock when the cops start buzzing around. She's further discomfited when Jeff comes blithely strolling into the house one morning. He and his friends reside just up the beach. He thought he'd drop by and fix her some breakfast. She asks him how he got in. He says he has a key.

"I'm glad I didn't know that last night," she remarks, drily.

"I never come in at night . . . unless asked," he replies, with a leer.

Jeff spends a good deal of the film in various stages of undress. (His studio forced him to shave his chest. Must've itched him like crazy.) His mentors, Schafer and Kellaway, watch him like a hawk. They even give him hints on how to sunbathe. "Not over your face, dear," Natalie chides, when he pulls his captain's hat down to keep the light out of his eyes. "It spoils that gorgeous tan. And we have quite an investment in your tan." Natalie, fearing that Joan may be lonesome, urges him to pursue a relationship: "It'd be an act of goodness for you to offer her your friendship . . . *all* of it." Yeah, right. All seven inches of it. Joan is outdoors on her dock, reclining with a book of poetry. Jeff comes splashing over and starts applying sun tan lotion to her leg. "You're cold," he says, referring more to her frosty demeanor than to her actual body temperature. "Let me warm you." So she pays him a nocturnal visit aboard his boat. He takes her in his arms, after first removing the batcape she's got draped over her shoulders.

"I wish I could afford you," she coos huskily.

"Why don't you save your pennies?" he says.

In one of their love scenes he starts getting rough with her. "A woman's no good to a man unless she's a little afraid of him," he philosophizes. So she bites him to show she isn't. Then she goes running across the beach, but she stumbles on a rock and goes sprawling in a mad swirl of legs and petticoats. She gets up. He tears her dress off. She slaps him. They embrace. But then weeks and weeks go by and he doesn't even call her. Joan starts hitting the sauce, just like Judith did. She makes up her mind she's gonna marry him, but first she's gotta get his present caretakers out of the picture.

KELLAWAY: Would you like us to go?

CRAWFORD: As far as you like. Another continent, preferably.

Shortly before the nuptials, the real estate lady comes barging in all sloppy drunk and starts dropping ugly hints that maybe Jeff was somehow implicated in Judith's fatal plunge. (It occurs to me that he has a real knack for driving women to drink.) After the ceremony, Joan commences to fear for her own life. She tries to call the police, but Jeff intervenes, so she beans him with the telephone receiver. Threats! Accusations! Suspicions! Recriminations! Violence! A typical night of wedded bliss (the first of many) at the Crawford residence.

A Fool There Was* (U.S. 1915 B&W)

A Fool There Was, suggested by Kipling's famous poem, "The Vampire," is the movie that made a star of Theda Bara and furthermore added the word "vamp" to the English language. Ms. Bara, her name a rather obvious anagram for "Arab death," was the first great lady of camp (though I'm sure she was blissfully unaware of it at the time). She specialized in the portrayal of exotic, predatory, and generally ill-humored temptresses. Pity the men who fall into her clutches! Merely by uttering the words "Kiss me, my fool," she is able to persuade a discarded lover to stop threatening her with a pistol and promptly turn it against himself. Another suitor is reduced by her to a state of utter penury. Now a pathetic vagrant, he approaches her on the street, whereupon she summons a cop to make him stop bothering her.

The "fool" of the title is a wealthy big shot who's been sent by President Wilson on a diplomatic mission to England. Apparently, she seduces him to avenge herself on his wife, who once snubbed her, probably because of the godawful dress she had on. Or maybe she's merely curious about his endowments; after all, he's sailing aboard the S.S.

THEDA BARA (1890–1955), "the first great lady of camp," in a publicity photo from one of her early exotic films, perhaps *Cleopatra* (1916).

"Gigantic." She persuades the steward to give him the deck chair next to hers. Before you know it, she's lured the poor sap to sunny Italy. What will President Wilson think?

But, no matter whom she fucks, she can't get into high society. We can tell that her victim and his erstwhile happy family are respectable: their servants are white people. Theda, meanwhile, is waited on by a Chinaman and a Negress. We can almost hear the audience clucking.

The men in this movie tend to look alike, mainly because they all wear too much eye shadow. When I see a movie this ancient, however, I am less interested in looking at the people and more interested in looking at the cars and the dresses and the furnishings and general decor. Print quality may be variable, but, when you're dealing with a film made in 1915, you should count yourself lucky you can see it at all.

Fortune and Men's Eyes* (Canada 1971 C)

Homosexual rape in a prison setting may be a rather grim topic for a movie, but any film that second-bills Michael Greer (the Franklin Pangborn of the late 'Sixties/early 'Seventies) can't be very far from the realm of camp. This one at least tries to be, however. It's a gritty, anti-erotic tale of a middle-class straight boy (Wendell Burton) who is slowly but surely corrupted by life in the big house. (The level of discourse is, I fear, none too sophisticated. We know he's straight because they underline it for us: his girlfriend saying goodbye to him is virtually the first thing we see in the movie.)

Greer is cast as "Queenie," the bitch of the cell block. She knows all the ropes and won't let nobody mess with her. The highlight of Greer's performance is, of course, his drag routine at the Christmas party talent show. He starts out as Marlene Dietrich, turns into Gypsy Rose Lee, and ends up showing cock. This scene-stealing display lands him in solitary (the warden, the administrative staff, and all their wives were in the audience). Not much to write home about, perhaps, but it does dramatically demonstrate the transgressive power of camp, of drag, of homosexuality, and, need I add, of the male sexual organ itself. That said, I should mention that I can't stand characters such as the one Greer plays herein. For one thing, he precipitates the tragic finale, mainly because he's so damn hard-boiled, he can't stand the sight of two men showing genuine love for one another.

66

The Fourth Man* (Netherlands 1984 C)

The Fourth Man, a stylish suspense/horror opus, has for its main character an excruciatingly handsome, but severely maladjusted homosexual author (Jeroen Krabbe) who embroils himself in a passionate love affair with a woman solely because he's got the hots for her other boyfriend. She's a beautician (played by Renee Soutendijk) and at one point she gives him a desperately needed style perm (he's having a bad hair day in the first couple reels). She's also a fiendish black widow type, which comes as a surprise to him, but not to us, since the film is utterly steeped in ominous dream imagery, much of it only subtly sinister, but most of it gruesomely macabre. (Like, for instance, when he has a nightmare in which she snips off his sausage with her clippers. Did Mrs. Bobbitt ever see this film?)

A morbid Catholicism pervades the entire movie. Our hero imagines he sees the title character (the male object of his desire, played by Thom Hoffman) nailed to a huge cross in a cathedral. Which doesn't stop him from feeling up the crotch of this Christ figure. Later they make love in an open tomb. ("I read about those cemetery whores," clucks Thom disapprovingly, before indicating that he is one.) Coincidentally enough, it proves to be the crypt of Renee's three husbands, each of whom met with a strange and violent demise. This realization, not at all surprisingly, causes Jeroen to lose his hard-on, though he's certainly been more than sufficiently horny up until this point. He makes love to Renee by pretending she's a boy and, in the film's most pathetic scene, masturbates while peering through a keyhole at her and Thom getting it on. This may not be a gay film, but it's certainly bisexual. Maybe even polymorphously perverse.

Fun Down There* (U.S. 1990 C)

Fun Down There, a gay slice-of-life movie, depicts a rather dull-witted farm laborer (Michael Waite) who resides with his parents in upstate New York. Privacy proves rather elusive in this rural setting; he has to row out into the lake just to beat off. The film is subtitled "A Week in the Life." A day-by-day breakdown of the week would look something like this:

Monday—Beat off. Get ears pierced. Fight with sis over the latest issue of *Playgirl*.

Tuesday—Move to New York City. Find a boyfriend. Have sex on a rooftop.

Wednesday—Get a hotel room.

Thursday—Get a job washing dishes at a cafe.

Friday—Have sex again. Also smooch with busboy at the restaurant.

Saturday—Go sightseeing. Have sex with busboy.

Sunday—Move in with first boyfriend. Call home.

Though I think this is a somewhat idealized portrait of life in the big city, I must admit that colorful supporting characters enrich the film. Just when we're starting to wonder if a guy is gay or straight, he suddenly launches into a word-for-word recitation of scenes from *All About Eve* and *Valley of the Dolls*.

The Furies   (U.S. 1950 B&W)

The Furies are Barbara Stanwyck, Blanche Yurka, Beulah Bondi, and Dame Judith Anderson. And you better believe they're tough! Toughest of the lot, of course, is Stanwyck. At first we think there's something kinky about her relationship with her father (a hard-driving cattle baron played by Walter Huston), but then she develops a passion for Wendell Corey. I guess there's no accounting for taste. She even bakes him a cake. I personally find it difficult to imagine Barbara Stanwyck baking *anyone* a cake.

Blanche Yurka spits on the floor when Barbara enters the room. Barbara's the prize bitch of the Wild West in this picture. She gives Wendell a good slap (he gives her one back). She hurls a pair of scissors in Dame Judith's face (it doesn't kill her, but it sure doesn't do her any good). What touches off that particular squabble is Judith's announcement that she and Walter have plighted their troth. Barbara's jealous, and that makes her mean. Walter gets his revenge by stringing up Gilbert Roland, her dearest pal. But Gilbert's the eldest son of Blanche Yurka, who shotguns Walter in the back. A lot of gay men don't cotton to westerns, but I can't resist the ones where women take the reins. Virtually every female character in this film behaves like a man. What's really remarkable, however, is that *all* the characters are varmints (most of them murderous), yet none of them is unlikable.

The Garden of Allah (U.S. 1936 C)

As I persevere in my exploration of exotic decadence, I find that good, pulpy camp provides precisely the trite, superficial trivialities I need to maintain my fragile, ever-more-precarious innocence. Did you know, for example, that the Sahara Desert is sometimes called *The Garden of Allah*? In the opening scene, Marlene Dietrich is discovered in a convent, piously praying to the Blessed Virgin. Despite her vast wealth and exquisite wardrobe, she has found that, for her, life has become empty and meaningless. The Mother Superior (Lucile Watson) advises her to go out in the wilderness, there to contemplate things eternal and infinite.

Marlene is next discovered aboard a railway carriage, sharing a compartment with Charles Boyer, a Trappist monk who has renounced and forsaken his vows. A dancing girl (Tilly Losch), wearing a see-through blouse and just enough necklaces to satisfy the Production Code, comes at him with the studied sinuousness of a snake-woman in a horror picture. She prostrates herself, bent over backward before him, and fixes him with her deep, hypnotic gaze. He drops a coin on her forehead to get rid of her. Later, at the oasis, Marlene encounters a count (Basil Rathbone) disguised in the robes of an Arabian. He brings her to a soothsayer, whose palm she crosses with silver. The soothsayer warns her to beware, beware . . .

C. Aubrey Smith plays a stern old priest who tells Marlene to keep her distance from Charles. There's an astonishingly gorgeous shot of her standing in a doorway, bathed in the orangish glow of the setting (or is it the rising?) sun as she announces that she's obliged to follow the dictates of her heart. She and Charles are wed in a tiny chapel rocked by a sandstorm. Their honeymoon is a religious pilgrimage into the desert vastness. Marlene utters yet another orison: "Put my love to the proof! The uttermost proof! So he may know that nothing can destroy our love! Nothing!" Talk about tempting fate! And, of course, her prayer is answered. You see, Marlene is *still* unaware that Charles is a spouse of Holy Mother Church. So, naturally, in the middle of the Sahara, their caravan runs into a lost patrol containing the one and only soldier in the French Foreign Legion who is able to identify Charles as a former monk. Yes, this is indeed the Garden of Allah!

Nothing but heartache from this point on. And it's not all heterosexual, either. The supporting cast includes Joseph Schildkraut wearing a fez and sporting a carnation behind one ear. He attaches himself to

Marlene at the railway station and remains with her for the duration of her stay in North Africa. His function is to stand around reciting bad poetry. Guys like him only turn up in overripe romances like this one.

The Gay Deceivers* (U.S. 1969 C)

The Gay Deceivers is a real historical artifact. This time capsule from 1969 presents us with a pair of straight guys (Kevin Coughlin and Larry Casey) who evade the draft by pretending to be lovers. The film is a smarmy sex comedy and very politically incorrect, but you have to put it in its proper context: Nixon is President, the Vietnam war is raging, and these two guys are firmly convinced that the only way to save their asses is to move into a gay neighborhood and stop dating girls. But guess what? Turns out that they don't have the balls to cut it in the gay world. One loses his job; the other loses his fiancée. They end up begging Uncle Sam to induct them. The message is clear: posing as a homosexual will ruin your life.

This was the film that introduced Michael Greer (see the review of *Fortune and Men's Eyes*). Cast as the swishy landlord whose decorating taste is straight out of a Lana Turner movie, he brings a measure of integrity to a role that could have been nothing more than a caricature. And, of course, he's got all the best lines. Fussing over a favorite recipe, he notes, "Maria Montez served it to her lover in *The Son of the Cobra Queen*." Arguing with a woman who unwittingly trampled his garden, he shrills, "I may not know my flowers, but I know a bitch when I see one!" At the climax, he stages a costume ball, inviting everybody to come dressed as their favorite campy character. One shows up as "Judy Streisand." ("She went over the rainbow, and somebody broke her nose!") Yes, Greer may be a mere cartoon, but at least he comes out of it looking better than the straights. Coughlin claims to want nothing more than to become a lawyer, get married, and have children. Worse yet, the woman he wants to marry is Brooke Bundy, who at one point gawks at a denizen of a gay bar and screeches, "He's wearing an earring!!"

The Giant of Metropolis* (Italy 1962 C)

The Giant of Metropolis is a highly unusual muscleman epic, in the sense that it's set in a past so distant, it might as well be the future. The tale transpires in the capital of Atlantis, which is depicted as being a superscientific civilization that sinks beneath the sea as punishment for having defied the gods. The king of this realm is so consumed with over-weening hubris, he not only raises the dead, but also seeks the secret of eternal life. The bodybuilder hero, played by Gordon Mitchell, is an emissary from far-off climes, come to warn this Promethean monarch of the perils implicit in such avant-garde research.

The ambience is surprisingly contemporary. This is especially true of the principal choreographic interlude—a bisexual, interracial mating ritual featuring a black man, an Oriental youth, and a girl. This very modern dance concludes with one of the men caressing the other. Mitchell is also sexually memorable. (And a competent actor; his agony is convincing in the torture scenes.) I have never been a connoisseur of muscles, but even I couldn't help but be impressed with his physique. His body resembles some classical sculpture. Which brings us to the film's most hilarious moment: when he sweeps the heroine into his arms and says, "I love you, Mercede. You're made like I am." Not so's you'd notice.

The Girl Can't Help It* (U.S. 1956 C)

The Girl Can't Help It is a kinky, almost surreal depiction of the 'Fifties pop music scene. On the one hand, we're presented with night clubs full of weird, well-dressed, middle-class middlebrows (parental types, in other words) responding respectfully and favorably to rock 'n' roll at its most raw and primitive. And then, at the climax, we're confronted with a mob of teenage rockers who promptly cease their cavorting and listen attentively as leading lady Jayne Mansfield serenades them with cocktail music.

Like most of Jayne's movies, this one uses women in a kind of psychedelic capacity. Tom Ewell is cast as an alcoholic theatrical agent who's nursing an unrequited passion for a torch singer (Julie London, literally playing herself in the guise of a hallucinatory vision). Edmond

O'Brien portrays a former gambling czar who entertains musical ambitions. O'Brien aims to make a star of his girlfriend (Mansfield), so he engages Ewell to "handle" her. After a couple days on the job, Tom protests that his "hands are full" (even though she's got "a good pair of lungs"). Jayne, meanwhile, would like to abandon show business, settle down, and raise a family. She complains that no one believes she's "equipped for motherhood."

As I have just indicated, Mansfield's physical presence encourages a proliferation of double entendres. Her body, so opulently proportioned, appears to be locked in desperate contention with every dress she puts on. She says goodbye with her mouth; then, when she turns around and walks away, she seems to be waving goodbye with her buttocks. Perhaps to explain her gluteus maximus, the script specifies that she comes from a well-muscled family. She proudly displays a photograph of her brothers, all of them bodybuilder types so freakish, they look like they belong on a carnival midway. (Appropriately enough, the living room of her home in this movie is dominated by a grand staircase which resembles a circus runway.) There is also a motif of milk bottles. In what is perhaps the film's most notorious shot, she cradles a pair of them against her ample bosoms. Another one explodes as she walks past. Maybe I should say that it ejaculates.

So much for the purely carnal level. On a more ethereal esthetic plane, the picture constitutes some sort of cosmic comment on color contrasts: mostly masculine blues and seductive shades of scarlet, with plenty of turquoise and lavender to complicate the decor. The mise en scène is sparkling with sequins and red glitz. Edmond O'Brien (who's got a laugh that sounds like a tommy-gun) makes his entrance wearing an orange plaid sportcoat. Gaudiness throbs and pulsates wherever we look. Mention must also be made of the ubiquitous jukeboxes, which, aflush with neon colors and attended by gyrating acolytes, would seem to personify Moloch in a "Let's party!" mood.

Go Kill and Come Back* (Italy 1969 C)

Go Kill and Come Back is a spaghetti western which combines the talents of Guy Madison and Edd "Kookie" Byrnes, a pair of cinema studs who, while generally forgotten by the mainstream, will always be fondly remembered by the cognoscenti. Their screen chemistry is potently powerful in this ultraviolent oater. Whether allied or opposed to one

GUY MADISON (1922–1996), handsome hunk star of the 40s–50s in *Massacre River* (RKO 1949).

another, they always manage to evidence plenty of passion. And why not? They've got a lot in common: both appear to be homicidal maniacs. Indeed, the recurrent line in Madison's dialogue is "Kill them!" Kookie, meanwhile, hides beneath a straw sombrero and hopes someone will mistake him for Clint Eastwood.

Guy is cast as one of those obsessed Confederate colonels who refuse to admit that the Civil War is over. He'll bind and gag anyone who dares to utter a discouraging word. And he'll shoot a man for even less than that. "You make friends too quickly," he complains, just prior to plugging a fellow. "I don't like shooting at still targets," he grouses while practicing his marksmanship. "I need something moving! Something *alive!*" His stronghold is a tall and impregnable tower, high on a hill (a phallic image that's as resonant for Fascists as it is for homosexuals).

His comrades are as crazy as he is. This movie includes one of the most sissified torture scenes I've ever witnessed: the baddies take someone's shoe off and tickle the sole of his foot with a feather. Kookie (despite the countless murders he's already participated in) is grossed out by this and attempts to intervene. Which gets him into a brawl with the ringleader, who whips out his knife and asserts, to Guy, "It's just a little family quarrel. Sometimes even brothers gotta fight to get it out of their system. I'm just gonna mark his pretty face up a little so he won't forget me." (Never fear; Kookie's dazzling face escapes unharmed and unscathed.)

The final gunfight takes place in an underground tomb that's lined with mummified Indians. It's not the bloodshed and grue that make Italian westerns so wonderfully bizarre; it's the stylish perversity with which all this carnage is orchestrated.

Girls Town* (U.S. 1959 B&W)

Girls Town asks us to believe that Elinor Donahue ("Betty" from *Father Knows Best*) is Mamie Van Doren's sister. Elinor wears a blonde wig and heavy make-up, but we're still not convinced. We're also presented with Mel Torme as a rather elderly teenager, complete with a prominent double chin. "You're in Queersville, man!" Mamie tells him, just before creaming him with a custard pie.

Mamie ends up in Girls Town, a Catholic institution presided over by Mother Veronica (Maggie Hayes). "Many girls need love. / Many girls need care. / And, if they're not attended to, there's trouble everywhere!" screeches the title song. Mamie doesn't mesh very well with such a cloistered environment. Her room has a picture of Jesus at one end and a photo of Paul Anka at the other. "Any studs around here?" she inquires.

"Any *what*?" her roommate replies, authentically perplexed.

Gloria Talbott is cast as the resident bull dyke. "You don't look so tough to me!" Mamie tells her. "You do everything the sisters tell you to do."

"I give them a fair shake; they give me a fair shake," says Gloria.

"I'll *bet* you do!" Mamie sneers.

Mel kidnaps Elinor and threatens to sell her into white slavery down Mexico way (Tijuana, specifically). But Mamie prays to St. Jude and Gloria defeats the bad guys with judo. Anka sings "Ave Maria" while Mamie breaks down in tears. Yes, his performance really *is* that bad.

Goin' to Town* (U.S. 1935 B&W)

I love opera and I love Mae West. Thus I find *Goin' to Town*, in which she sings the female lead in *Samson and Delilah*, to be quite irresistible. The odd thing is that this foray into high culture starts out as a horse opera. Mae is betrothed to a rancher who gets himself shot dead while rustling some steers. She's his sole beneficiary. His fancy male secretary offers to be of assistance: "I suppose I'll have to stay and look after the cattle and the men for you."

"Just the cattle!" she specifies, with good-humored alarm. "I'll take care of the men."

Actually, the film is more concerned with social class than sex. (Mae was forced to resort to such ploys by the advent of the Production Code.) Despite her background as a dance hall dame, she sets her cap for an English earl (Paul Cavanagh). She manages to land him and, in the process of doing so, she scores her biggest laughs at the expense of the haut monde. This was all very satisfying to me, since I have often been attracted to the aristocratic type (a pursuit, I might add, in which I'm invariably frustrated). But, really, I found myself laughing even when she wasn't doing or saying anything particularly humorous. For the truly attuned, she's able to be funny simply by the fact of her existence.

MAE WEST (1892–1980) in a publicity photo of the 30s. She wrote and directed the play, *Drag* (1927) about homosexuals and is one of the catalytic gay icons.

Go West, Young Man* (U.S. 1936 B&W)

As the title would seem to suggest, Mae West is essentially portraying herself in *Go West, Young Man*. She is cast as "Mavis Arden," glittering goddess of the silver screen, on a personal appearance tour for her studio ("Stupefyin' Pitchuhs"). The opening scene presents her in a film-within-the-film: a drama of hot-blooded passion and queenly stances. This stupefying picture is what she's promoting on her tour. The next stop is Harrisburg and a rendezvous with Lyle Talbot, but her limousine conks out at a hick town en route. She is, of course, somewhat vexed, but then she catches sight of a local boy—none other than Randolph Scott—lifting the front end of a car with little more than a flex of his pelvis (which, by the way, is facing the camera; he's holding the car behind him, almost as if it were balanced on his buttocks). "Mmm. What large and sinewy muscles," remarks Mae-vis.

Randolph plays an inventor. She persuades him to take her on a tour of his workshop. She also halfway coaxes him into reclining with her in a haystack. This roll in the hay is rudely interrupted by Warren William, her p.r.-minded press agent. His job, you see, is to protect her reputation by keeping her away from men. Needless to say, he's got his work cut out for him. He finally convinces her that Randy's got a girlfriend who's knitting little booties in preparation for a blessed event.

"They're just babes," says Warren of the erring pair. "Babes in the woods!"

"Yeah? Well, they should have kept out of the woods," Mae observes drily.

Her dialogue is a babbling brook—or should I say a garbling stream? —of delicious malapropisms. Equally flavorsome are the supporting turns by Elizabeth Patterson and Isabel Jewell. The latter, as a servant both starstruck and butterfingered, is almost as funny as our leading lady.

Goliath and the Vampires* (Italy 1964 C)

Goliath and the Vampires starts out with our title hero (Gordon Scott) plowing a field. Like any typical farmer, he wears nothing but a loincloth as he uproots stumps and boulders with his bare hands. His labors are interrupted when he hears a drowning child calling for help. He dives into the ocean (adjacent to his farm), carrying along an axe in case he has to battle any sea monsters. (Don't *you* bring along an axe when you go swimming?)

Meanwhile the female population of his village is being carried off by pirates. "Throw the old women to the sharks!" the captain orders, once they're out in the open sea. I must say, he's somewhat lacking in chivalry. And what does he want with the younger women? To feed them to the vampires, of course! The girls are brought to an island under the thumb of a bloodsucking overlord who stages ghastly impalements in the marketplace. The local sultan is rather depressed over such goings-on, as well he should be. His consort (Gianna Maria Canale) offers him words of comfort: "Don't feel so badly. Life can be quite gay." Then the whole harem comes in and does a dance. The girls wear diamonds (or are they zircons?) in their navels.

Gordon shows up before too long. I love the way he grits his teeth all the time and runs around with next to nothing on. Even on ceremonial occasions, he appears in the equivalent of swimming trunks. Gianna attempts to seduce him, but he maintains his purity. ("These few moments are made for love." "No! Not while the monster still lives!") At the climax, the vampire disguises himself by taking Gordon's form and shape. A fight ensues: the real Goliath vs. the fake one. (I have it on good authority that Gordon's double in this scene is none other than his archrival, Steve Reeves—which would seem to indicate that their rivalry was strictly tongue-in-cheek.) This ludicrous situation is a treat because it affords Gordon the opportunity to act the role of a villain. His grimaces are hilarious.

Greenwich Village   (U.S. 1944 C)

A Carmen Miranda movie called *Greenwich Village* sounds like something that should clearly be of interest to readers of this book. Carmen gets top billing, but, as usual, her role is rather peripheral to the action. The 'Forties were a fairly puritanical period in movie history, but the film is sufficiently plain-spoken to call Greenwich Village a domain of "long-haired men and short-haired women, . . . free-living, free-thinking!" And, in fact, many of the women we see are mannish, while the men are plainly "artistic" types. (True, Don Ameche has a scene where he's in bed with Vivian Blaine. But he stays on *top* of the covers.)

Aside from Carmen, camp interest resides with co-star William Bendix, cast as an entrepreneur who's producing a show called *Greenwich Village Gaieties*. One scene finds him dancing with a man in drag. Bendix even gives the guy's cheek a playful pinch. ("Not here, dearie, in front of all these people. I know a better place.") As so often happens in cases like this, the affair concludes with an ugly altercation in an alley. Oddly enough, the movie transpires in the Roaring 'Twenties. (You were hoping for the Gay 'Nineties?)

---

*The Grim Reaper** (U.S. 1976 C)

I remember when this film, ostensibly a "Christian" horror show, was presented at a fundamentalist church in my vicinity. I suggested to my closest friend that it might be a hoot to drop by and have a look at it. He strenuously disagreed, and I suspect that he was right to do so. Mocking one's enemies on their home turf is seldom a wise idea. Furthermore, the delights of camp are meant to be savored in friendlier surroundings.

Which makes this epic a natural for home video. The film begins at the funeral of a young man named Frankie, whose soul is burning in hell because he never accepted Christ as his personal savior. Flashbacks reveal that, while his pious mother and his insufferably priggish brother were attending Sunday worship services at their church, Frankie was home watching sporting events on television and (gasp!) drinking beer. Now his parents—whose names, by the way, are Verne and Ruby— are tortured by troubling dreams and nightmares, especially Verne, who has always maintained that conservative Protestant doctrine is "like something from a paperback novel." Rival theologies, such as Catholicism and New Age spiritualism, are subjected to a ritual tongue-lashing. Bible stories are acted out with Sunday school pageant verisimilitude. We learn, for example, that the Witch of Endor wore a black, pointed hat and that, furthermore, all the prophets and patriarchs spoke with down home Southern accents. In one such Scripture-based interlude, those ungrateful Israelites complain to Moses about traveling conditions in the Sinai Desert, whereupon they are all bitten to death by poisonous serpents. This demonstrates, as clearly as anything might, the masturbatory sadism which resides at the heart of "that good old-time religion." The infernal scenes, by the way, have much more cinematic conviction than the preachy ones, but this, I suppose, should not surprise us, since the director—Ron Ormond—helmed such earlier gems as *Mesa of Lost Women* and *The Monster and the Stripper*.

Various Christian celebrities such as Jack Van Impe put in their two cents here and there. I'm sure you'll be inspired to hear that the Rev. Jerry Falwell is among those present. Thanks to bad lighting, we can actually see the sweat dripping from his jowls. (Now *that's* horror.) In this movie, demons are invariably portrayed as screaming queens. Same could be said for some of the evangelists. And why do they all have to comb their hair in that ungodly fashion?

Speaking of hair, I should mention the dynamic participation of "actress" Viola Walden, who, in the role of Ruby, wears flamboyant 'Seventies wigs all through the film. (She even sleeps in them.) Approximately twenty years too old for her middle-aged role, she exhibits an amateurish enthusiasm which reminded me of the late, great Edith Massey. Ah, what histrionic wonders Walden might have wrought, if only John Waters had discovered her before Ron Ormond did!

Gypsy* (U.S. 1962 C)

"The movie that changed my life, if ever there was one! Now—I know that it isn't really strictly 'gay' or camp, and that there are no gorgeous half naked men in it, or even great acknowledged gay cult stars. But I insist that *Gypsy* has a homoerotic feel to it, and, if it has helped me and countless others to be proud about our gayness, then it definitely deserves an entry in Volume 2!"

So writes a reader in Malmö, Sweden, who is clearly a huge fan of this brassy musical about the youthful Gypsy Rose Lee. He contends that watching Natalie Wood (in the title role) grow increasingly confident as a stripper gave him the courage to come out as a gay man.

The film has a deeply personal meaning for me, as well. It played the Norshor theatre in Duluth, Minnesota, just prior to *What Ever Happened to Baby Jane?* and, in its evocation of seedy, early-twentieth-century vaudeville houses, it could almost serve as a Technicolor prologue to the Davis/Crawford opus. Or so it seemed to me and my best friend when we saw it together (his mother took us) in January of 1963. For one thing, much of the film is devoted to the career of Gypsy's sister, a frustrated child star named "Baby June" (who grew up to be June Havoc). The show even has a horrific quality, incarnated in Rosalind Russell's performance as a fiendishly aggressive stage mother. Strident, domineering indefatigability was always Russell's strongest characteristic (I hesitate to call it an asset), and it's refreshing to see it played for subtle chills. She has, in my opinion, the best number: a song entitled "Some People," which today sounds like it could almost serve as an anthem for gay men of my generation who left the Midwest for more hospitable climes. Sample lyrics: "Some people can thrive and bloom / livin' life in a livin' room. / That's perfect / for some people / of one-hundred-and-five." "Goodbye / to blueberry pie! / Good riddance to / all the socials I had to go to, / all the lodges I had to play, / all the Shriners I said hello to. / Hey, New York, I'm comin' your way!"

Gypsy Wildcat (U.S. 1944 C)

The "wildcat" of the title is Maria Montez, clad in a scarlet dirndl and rattling a tambourine. The plot is like a child's fever dream of Verdi's *Il Trovatore*; the music, meanwhile, sounds more like Enesco. The setting is a Middle European medieval never-never land so impossibly romantic, I wish that I could go there right now. Jon Hall disguises himself as a clown (kind of redundant, under the circumstances). He and the villain (Douglass Dumbrille) get to roll around on the floor together while dressed in tights. Peter Coe wears so much make-up, I began to suspect that Edward D. Wood, his real-life drinking buddy, must've been giving him beauty tips. Coe's mom in the film is Gale Sondergaard, who, at one point, improbably entices the guard who's posted at the door of her dungeon. (What do you call a movie that combines the talents of Maria Montez and Gale Sondergaard? If you've been paying attention, I shouldn't need to tell you.) Douglass wants to marry Montez, because he's discovered she's really a long-lost countess who supposedly was drowned in a shipwreck during infancy, but actually was brought up by gypsy vagabonds. Co-star Nigel Bruce must've felt like he was right back in Hitchcock's *Rebecca*, since so much of the narrative hinges on the heroine's resemblance to a portrait. It is, of course, a ghoulishly obscene coincidence that Hollywood was cranking out flossy entertainments like this at precisely the historical moment when Europe's real gypsies were being exterminated.

The Harvey Girls* (U.S. 1946 C)

The Harvey Girls are a bevy of winsome waitresses who conquer the Wild West. Thanks to them, the prevailing outlaw culture is ultimately supplanted by traditional family values. Furthermore, all of the bad waitresses (dance hall girls, saloon hostesses) are sent packing at the film's conclusion, while the good waitresses get married and live happily ever after.

Sounds dreadful, doesn't it? And that's not even the half of it. The Harvey Girls have a housemother (Selena Royle) who tells them that they represent "the symbol and the promise of the order that is to come." So, you see, these young ladies have been entrusted with a sacred mission. The cause of civilization is supposedly advanced by the proliferation of wholesome amusements, perhaps best typified by the scene in which the good guys square-dance to "Skip to My Lou." One wonders what Sam Peckinpah would have made of all this. I mean, where are the Wild Bunch when we really need them? As one disgruntled fellow tartly observes, "Nice women can ruin a town."

There's something deeply reactionary about a movie which can't imagine any woman (good or "bad") in any capacity other than subservient (and what, after all, could be more subservient than a waitress?). In the final analysis, this is an inadvertently noirish musical western with overtones of Gothic melodrama (the restaurant burns down at the climax). The songs have no period charm whatsoever. They are pure 'Forties cornpone, complete with inane, asinine lyrics. Cowpoke chorus boys feign heterosexuality, casting calf-eyed glances at leading lady Judy Garland and rhythmically rocking to and fro while she sings. Miss Garland is presented to us in the role of a mail-order bride who is placed in diametric opposition to a Fatal Woman (Angela Lansbury; she and her cohorts look like prostitutes in a Jack the Ripper movie). There's nothing quite so ferocious-looking as a man-hungry gal, especially if it's Judy Garland. However, she just about faints when hunky John Hodiak takes her into his brawny arms and kisses her. Which, I guess, goes to show that outlaws (sexual ones, at any rate) do have a place in the scheme of things.

Hercules and the Amazon Women (U.S. 1994 C)

I was inclined to feel that made-for-TV movies were outside the province of this book, but then someone alerted me to the fact that these very 'Nineties Hercules flicks are just too dreadful to miss. He was right. See, the idea is to make old Herc "politically correct." We can sense the prevailing mindset right from the start. "Go play with a doll or something!" a little Athenian boy snorts to a little girl who wants to join in his ball game. "He's right, Lilia," her mother points out. "Now come and help me wash your father's feet." Get the point? Women of the ancient world were (gasp) downtrodden!

Shortly thereafter, the goddess Hera manifests herself in the guise of an obscenely phallic serpent—rendered even more obscene when Hercules (Kevin Sorbo) decapitates it. (Or should I say he circumcises it?) Hercules makes an appeal to his father, Zeus (Anthony Quinn). "Get her off my back!" Hercules whines. "After all, she *is* your wife."

The Amazons show up wearing animal masks that are so cute, I was reminded of Playboy bunnies. They take Hercules' clothes off and tie him up, so I guess they can't be all bad. But then they perform the unforgivable: they raise his consciousness.

"Women need respect and loyalty just as much as you do," the Queen of the Amazons tells him. "But you'll never understand that."

"What if I tried to change?" Hercules whimpers.

TV is pretty raunchy nowadays. I must admit I was surprised to see the Amazons ride into a village and rape all the men. I was even more surprised to see Anthony Quinn having sex with an Amazon young enough to be his granddaughter. But a Hercules movie can't hope to succeed without a dark, muscular dreamboat in the title role. Sorbo is not only scrawny; he's blonde.

Hercules and the Lost Kingdom (U.S. 1994 C)

This one starts out with a giant troll whose lackluster sex life has left him feeling fierce. "I want Hercules!" he announces. (It's his opening line of dialogue.) The giant, unsurprisingly, carries a big stick, but Sorbo takes it away from him and beans him with it. Which goes to show that what we want and what we get are two very different things.

The heroine is a lost princess (she's from Troy) who thinks she can get her way by calling people eunuchs. (Not always, however. At one point she impatiently says to a bodybuilder, "Will you get out of my way, you mountain of meat?") A bartender asks if she's a slave. "Do I look like a slave?" she angrily replies. "She's a Master?!" the bartender mutters disbelievingly, thereby showing a keen awareness of S&M terminology.

Of course, that old phallic serpent has to put in another appearance. It eats Hercules. (I think somebody's got things a little backward, don't you?) But never fear: he gets vomited up. I couldn't digest this shit, either.

Hercules and the Masked Rider* (Italy 1964 C)

Title to the contrary, this is a swashbuckler, not a peplum. The story takes place in Renaissance times. The setting is literally a castle in Spain. And the film is as gay as a fiesta. Take, for example, the oddly gratuitous little scene in which a group of seminude men are ordered to whip one another to death. Since there's not a drop of blood to be seen, nor even so much as a lashmark, the point of it all is obviously not violence, but blatant homoeroticism. I might add that, in this movie, whenever a pair of men collapse (whether in death, fatigue, unconsciousness, or whatever), they always manage to land right on top of each other, as if they'd just finished having sex.

Hercules is played by Italian muscleman Alan Steel, his hair and beard dyed a decidedly unnatural shade of orange. Throughout the film, he is always dressed exactly the same way: stripped to the waist and wearing a pair of very, very tight black trousers, with a wide black leather belt. This attire is flattering; he photographs well. (The shots from behind are especially revealing.) According to the plot, he's a bodybuilder who's joined up with a roving band of gypsies. What's really remarkable, however, is the fact that he's clearly portrayed as being homosexual. He's constantly in the company of an effeminate gypsy musician who wears golden earrings. They reside together in a cozy little tree house. (Hanging just beside the front door of this domicile is a drinking flask that resembles a heart-shaped pillow.) These two are engaged in Robin Hood antics: at one point they strip the clothes off an elegant male aristocrat who's chanced to wander through their neck of the woods. They tackle this task (and this victim) with an almost unseemly enthusiasm.

The next-to-last scene is a double wedding in which four of the heterosexual protagonists are joined together in holy matrimony. After the ceremony, Hercules puts his arm around his swishy little pal and affectionately says, "Let's go!" The concluding scene—the movie's final image—has four heterosexual couples riding past the camera, each couple sharing a single horse. Bringing up the rear is—you guessed it!—a noble steed bearing Hercules and his boyfriend. The release date on the movie is 1964. And yet the film itself is like a subliminal advertisement promoting the very 'Nineties concept of gay marriage. They should've called it *Hercules Meets La Cage aux Folles*.

---

*Hercules in the Haunted World** (Italy 1961 C)

Hercules in the Haunted World has Reg Park providing a surprisingly witty performance as the muscleman of the title. I was, however, even more taken with Giorgio Ardisson, a lithe, nimble, fair-haired pretty boy cast as Theseus, the hero's cohort, sidekick, and constant companion. The opening scene finds Theseus making love to a woman named Jocasta in a hayloft. Meanwhile, over by the waterfall, Hercules is plaintively calling for him.

"Hercules wants something," Jocasta points out.

"He always wants something," her lover grumbles.

These two guys literally go to hell in this movie, since it's the only place they can locate the magic stone with which to rescue the heroine (Leonora Ruffo), who is being pursued by a vampire (Christopher Lee, Britain's answer to Bela Lugosi). All tuckered out, Hercules and Theseus sleep together in the magic garden of the Hesperides. Theseus also reclines on the bed of Procrustes. But Hercules does not share it with him. In this movie, Procrustes is a creaking stone robot whom Hercules picks up and hurls bodily, thereby knocking a hole in the underworld, thus providing a means of entrance for living mortals.

At this point, the boys encounter the beauteous Persephone. Theseus, of course, is promptly smitten. Later, having brought the girl topside from the infernal regions, he discovers her gazing pensively at a fire in a brazier. "What's the matter?" he inquires, with tender solicitude. "Do you want to go . . . back home?"

The film is rather like a Marvel comic, but considerably more gaudy. The color scheme is dominated by warm, sun-bronzed flesh tones, often contrasting with a backdrop of deep, cool midnight-blue. You wouldn't think so from the title, but, in order to be properly appreciated, this movie requires the sensibility of an aesthete. There is much to be said for fakery, when it's pretty.

*Hero of Babylon** (Italy 1963 C)

"Bad omens for Babylon?" asks King Belshazzar rhetorically, as fire and brimstone rain down upon his city. The high priestess of Ishtar suggests that perhaps he's angered the gods by being soft on law and order. "No more leniency! I'll annihilate all these abject traitors!" promises the chastened monarch.

"God, take pity on us!" howls the heroine (named Tamira) as a slave driver whips her seven times on her pert, white-clad bottom. As for the pert, white-clad bottom of leading man Gordon Scott, we get a beautiful, coyly teasing shot of it as he bends over to pick up a log, which he then hurls at four soldiers, knocking them flat. ("Let's go. You're hopeless," clucks their leader.) "I just hate cruelty," says Gordon. Belshazzar is of a different disposition, executing his prisoners as background entertainment at a palace banquet and then grumbling because their screams make dinner table conversation difficult. ("Damn! Can't they die without all that fuss?") So he orders the harpists to play louder.

All of the usual homoerotic notations are firmly in place. Gordon has a fawningly attentive manservant who helps him get dressed (and, I take it, get undressed) and who gawks at his muscles with huge, Anna Magnani-like eyes. And, of course, there's a scene where Gordon is seminude and gets all tied up. He's photographed from a low angle, with the camera at about the level of his waist, and his nipples are so obscenely prominent that we scarcely notice such minor details as, for instance, if and when he bursts his bonds.

*Hurricane** (U.S. 1979 C)

Hurricane is a creakingly antiquated (but nonetheless diverting) South Seas melodrama. The director is Jan Troell, the cinematographer is Sven Nykvist, the music is by Nino Rota, and it would be hard to imagine three people more entirely at sea. The story eventually gets swamped by the title catastrophe, but is fairly absorbing up until that point. While

Dayton Ka'ne (1956–   ) gives one of the most homoerotic presentations in cinema in his mating dance in *Hurricane* (Paramount 1979); here accompanied by Mia Farrow (1945–   ).

the ukuleles go plunka-plunka, teenage tribal chieftain Dayton Ka'ne makes big trouble by wooing and winning wealthy white lady Mia Farrow. The sarong-clad maiden who's been promised to him in marriage is so perturbed, she gives herself to the first horny native boy who comes along. Which makes for major mortification on the night of her big defloration ceremony. This is one of the camp highlights of the picture: the high priest plunges his hand up her crotch and it comes out embarrassingly stainless. (You'd think she might have at least attempted a ruse. Like maybe cramming a piece of raw liver where it would do the most good.) Another camp episode is when hunky Dayton Ka'ne, wearing only a male sarong, does a very sexy South Seas dance—flaunting his muscles and thrusting his well-endowed crotch provocatively at the camera. A final camp highlight comes when Ka'ne is arrested and packed off to prison. Whereupon the soldier (James Keach) who's escorting him thither sees fit to preach him a sermon on the evils of self-abuse.

Hollywood Horror House* (U.S. 1975 C)

As its lurid title suggests, this rather little-known film represents the last gasp of a decadent genre that virtually defines gay camp: the *Baby Jane/Sweet Charlotte/Sunset Boulevard* ripoff. It's 1975, the cycle has pretty much run its course, and, this time around, the resident has-beens are Miriam Hopkins and Gale Sondergaard. Hopkins is cast as—what else?—a retired Hollywood glamour queen. Her initial scene more or less establishes the requisite mood: elegantly gowned and bewigged, she drunkenly topples down the staircase of her empty mansion (she thought she was making a grand entrance at a party, but it was all in her sodden mind). So now she's laid up with a cast on her leg and a male nurse is hired to look after her. He's a hippie junkie homicidal maniac (John David Garfield) who likes to chop up defenseless old ladies with a cleaver, all because his mom was a hooker and a lush. It's a longish movie, and we spend most of our time waiting for the inevitable. Sondergaard is the standout, working a variant on her customary role as the snoopy, scheming housekeeper. She's cast as Miriam's live-in secretary (named Leslie, which conveniently shortens to "Lez") and she does a lot of peering through windows. For a while, it looks like, for once, she might actually get to be the heroine. Unfortunately, she eventually gets offed, like everyone else. The plot continuity's a mess, but I like this kind of picture, even when it isn't particularly well done.

If I'm Lucky   (U.S. 1946 B&W)

If I'm Lucky presents us with Perry Como as a crooner seeking public office. "I'm a hip candidate!" he asserts. "I'll give away a haircut with every vote."

("And a manicure, too?" enthuse the chorus girls.)

Carmen Miranda helps Perry campaign. She's a harpist. Her name, improbably enough, is Michelle O'Toole. At one point she dances a samba with a straw basket balanced atop her head. (Wait a minute. I guess it's supposed to be a hat.) Her way with the English language is as idiosyncratically charming as ever. "Keep a stiff upper cut," she advises one of the other characters.

Perry wins the election. The notion of show business personalities going into politics must have seemed desperately outré in 1946. Today, of course, we know that they can even be elected President. But that won't happen again. If we're lucky.

Imitation of Life*   (U.S. 1959 C)

"I'm an actress and a good one," Lana Turner boldly asserts, attempting, more or less, to imitate life. This was her smash hit comeback film after the scandal that nearly wrecked her career. Millions flocked to see it, in hopes that they'd be witnessing an actual imitation of her life. With such a star, such a title, and such a director (Douglas Sirk, famous for his use of subtextual irony), such a blatantly false imitation can't help but be camp.

Lana's agent (Robert Alda) suggests that she sleep her way to the top, but she furiously protests, "You're trying to cheapen me. But you won't. Not me! Oh, I'll make it, Mr. Loomis, but it'll be MY WAY!" And she does, which brings us to the scene where Dan O'Herlihy takes her up to his penthouse apartment, with its panoramic view of Broadway, and he tells her, "There's your new empire! Not big . . . but it's the heart of the world!"

Lana's selfishly single-minded pursuit of stardom is compared with the behavior of Susan Kohner, cast as the light-skinned daughter of Lana's Negro maid (Juanita Moore). Susan's attempt to "pass for white" is portrayed as being inherently dishonest and misguided. Today we're

Lana Turner (1920–1995) in a publicity photo of the 50s. The film *Imitation of Life* (Universal 1959) followed by one year the stabbing of underworld macho Johnny Stompanato (Lana's lover) by Cheryl Crane (Lana's daughter).

more likely to be impatient with Juanita Moore's determined efforts to make her daughter play with chocolate-colored dolls instead of white ones and to have her matriculate at a Negro teachers' college. Susan, like Lana, wants a career in show business, but she aims for the lower end of the scale and becomes a chorus girl. We can see why she's eager to escape from the lily-white confines of Lana's house, where Juanita, lest anyone miss the point, occasionally appears in a cotton print dress with a jungle leopard skin pattern.

The cast includes Sandra Dee and Troy Donahue, future stars of *A Summer Place*. Troy is Susan's bigoted boyfriend, who beats her up when he trips to The Truth. Sandra is Lana's daughter, who's in love with John Gavin, Mom's fella. This is shameless catering to then-current suspicions regarding Lana's real-life woes. In this case, *Imitation* is the sincerest form of distortion.

Island of Doomed Men   (U.S. 1940 B&W)

The *Island of Doomed Men* belongs to Peter Lorre, who populates it with ex-cons who've been paroled into his greedy clutches. He likes to watch men getting flogged. Wielding the whip is Charles Middleton ("Ming the Merciless" from the Flash Gordon serials).

Lorre is married to Rochelle Hudson in this movie. By no stretch of the imagination does their relationship include sex. She's merely someone who hangs around his house, playing the piano and dressing up. Lorre himself looks chic and trim, not to mention natty, in an assortment of white tropical suits. He smokes cigarettes very elegantly and is one of the few men I've ever seen who looks good in a bow tie. His portrait of homosexual sadism is tastefully subdued, and seasoned with just enough of his trademark smarm. "Eddie, I hope I'll hear good reports on your conduct hereafter," he oozes to a young man who's stripped to the waist and waiting to taste the lash. I know it's politically incorrect to appreciate such exercises in gay villainy, but I don't feel obliged to apologize for being amused.

Isle of Forgotten Sins* (U.S. 1943 B&W)

Gale Sondergaard is the madame of a South Seas whorehouse in *Isle of Forgotten Sins*. The opening scene finds her slinking about in a satin dressing gown, tapping on doors and wakening her girls to let them know that a shipload of horny sailors just dropped anchor in the lagoon. Of course, this is puritanical 1943, which means her joint is officially designated a "gambling casino." Indeed, the goings-on are so chaste, we commence to wonder just what sins the title refers to. Littering? Picking your nose? Dropping buttons in the collection plate at church?

Since the girls (among them Tala Birell, Rita Quigley, and Veda Ann Borg) are so non-compliant, it's no surprise that the guys should turn to each other. You know sailors. John Carradine has a crewmate (Frank Fenton) who literally ties him to the bunk and then picks his pocket, copping a watch, a wad of bills, and a free feel, all at once. But this is no time for hanky-panky. The wind is rising, which means "much bad magic now in sky and sea," as the local native chieftain puts it. Before the monsoon hits, there's a salvage job to be done. If this underwater sequence grows tedious (and it does), it may amuse us to note the film's promiscuous borrowings from the works of Richard Wagner. We know in advance when the deep sea diver locates the sunken treasure; the "Rhinegold" motif thunders on the soundtrack. This is the only film I know that concludes with the entire cast getting inundated by a tidal wave. It's also the only film for all you pervs out there who've been waiting to see Sidney Toler in a swimsuit. (Yuck!)

Ivan the Terrible, Part II*
(Russia 1945 B&W, with some color sequences)

Eisenstein? In a book on camp?! Well, as a matter of fact, I can't really take credit for the idea. A reader in Canada was the one who alerted me to this Stalin-era propaganda spectacle, wickedly subverted by director Sergei Eisenstein's undeniably homoerotic sensibility. The Canadian correspondent singled out the opening scene and, indeed, it's a pip. A blonde and somewhat swishy Russian nobleman formally transfers his allegiance to the King of Poland. Said monarch (henceforward known as the King of the Poles) sprawls indolently upon his throne. His ladies-in-waiting resemble the brides of Dracula; his male courtiers, meanwhile, are adorned with what look like velvet bat-wings. A ludicrously large Elizabethan ruff encircles his collar; he also wears a pair of teardrop earrings. The background music (by Prokofiev) is full of epicene pomp. The Russian whips out his (very long) sword. The King fondles, caresses, strokes (should I say masturbates?) the blade. The Russian draws it back and tenderly kisses it.

Not that the rest of the film isn't just as campy. The acting is straight out of a silent movie. The stylistic notations are mainly from the realms of opera and expressionistic horror. The plot delineates the title character's political struggle with the landed gentry. He is played by Nikolai Cherkasov. It would be difficult to imagine a more unprepossessing tsar. His eyes dart like trapped insects and his long, pointed beard is so dirty, it defies gravity. The protagonists mostly drag flamboyant trains along behind them; an all-male drinking orgy, meanwhile, is staged more or less like an M-G-M production number. But how am I to respect a national hero who doesn't wash his hair?

A note on *Ivan the Terrible, Part I*: Not much homoeroticism here, but the film does have its campy element. As in *Part II*, the role of the villainous dowager is played by Serafina Birman as a bumptious frump who is seemingly modeled on the Wicked Witch in *Snow White and the Seven Dwarfs*.

---

*Jerker** (U.S. 1991 C)

This is a direct-to-video adaptation of Robert Chesley's acclaimed—not to mention notorious—homoerotic stage play. The subject is phone sex. J. R. (Joseph Stachura), a Vietnam veteran with a game leg, telephones Bert (Tom Wagner) for some hot masturbation sessions. Of course, since this is a movie, he always catches Bert at precisely the right moment—in bed, just out of the shower, etc. Such serendipity is a rare thing in the real world, where a call for phone sex is just as likely to occur when you're having the boss and his wife over for dinner. Anyway, the drama demonstrates how virtually anonymous sex can blossom into love, even though J. R. never once reveals his name (or, for that matter, his disabled status) and the relationship is suddenly cut short when Bert (it's implied) develops AIDS and dies.

Despite these downbeat aspects, the play is intended as a celebration of gay male sexuality and therefore deserves our respect. The performance preserved on video, unfortunately, has a smarmy quality which often rubbed me the wrong way (pun intended). The background music (courtesy of "Rock Hard Productions") is particularly sleazy.

Jerker's notoriety stems from the brouhaha which ensued when excerpts from the play were broadcast on public radio. The FCC unsuccessfully attempted to bring obscenity charges against the station in question. The source of the uproar was simply this: the virgin ears of the Religious Right were offended by the drama's explicit descriptions of masturbation. Do these people actually expect us to believe that they've never jacked off? (No, they just don't approve of talking about it.)

Jet Over the Atlantic   (U.S. 1960 B&W)

Letters such as this are a special source of satisfaction:

> Dear Paul Roen—
>   The first film I saw after reading *High Camp* was Byron Haskin's *Jet Over the Atlantic* and I believe it qualifies for Volume 2. . . . The star is Guy Madison—as bad as ever, but such a joy to look at. Unfortunately, he never disrobes, although there is one loving shot of his crotch as he's seated in the airplane.

This correspondent is astute in his observation and adept in his description. (Said gifts were no doubt fine-tuned by his having so recently finished reading my book.) Suffice it to say that, when I saw the film, I knew right away which crotch shot he was referring to.

The opening scenes transpire in Madrid. Virginia Mayo is cast as a night club dancer, prancing to and fro in a toreador outfit, waving a cape in time to the music. We're to assume that this is the sort of entertainment that Spaniards would fancy. Guy is her fiancé, but a G-man (George Raft) arrests him and spirits him out of the country. Virginia, at this point attired in a Folies-Bergère costume, barely manages to snag a seat on the flight that Guy is on. Whenever I see a movie character racing to catch a plane, I automatically hope they'll make it, even when, as in this case, I know perfectly well that a maniac has planted a bomb on board. Furthermore, when the jet is indeed over the Atlantic, I find myself fretting less about the human passengers and more about the pets stored in the baggage compartment. This is particularly perverse when you take into consideration that this movie features such stalwart players as Anna Lee, Margaret Lindsay, and Ilona Massey, who, as in *Balalaika*, is cast as an opera star. (Planes in movies are invariably loaded with showfolk.) At one point she bemoans the fact that she's likely to perish in a plane crash before achieving her ambition of singing at Carnegie Hall. Meanwhile the Liebestod from *Tristan und Isolde* is welling up on the soundtrack. It's that kind of film. And all around her, people are succumbing to poison gas. It's that kind of bomb.

The Jungle Book * (U.S. 1942 C)

This brilliant, kaleidoscopic, phantasmagorical film succeeds, not so much as a narrative, but as a procession of moods and colors, a blending and matching of moods and images. The gaudy 'Forties Technicolor possesses a lambent glow and a contrastingly dark, iridescent sheen. The protagonists are merely moving silhouettes in a green-shadowed wilderness of prowling beasts, exotic blooms, and lily ponds like mirrors. Birds flutter in the vaulted, vine-festooned stillness. Sunlight filters hazily through the extravagant foliage and lavish vegetation of black, towering trees. We willingly surrender ourselves to the eerie, awesome atmosphere, basking in the campy joys and pleasures of total escapism.

The central conflict is one between man and nature. Village and jungle are quite unable to coexist in harmony. Spanning the gap is Mowgli, the man-cub reared by wolves. He is played by Sabu, who, in his early scenes, while still untouched by civilization, is really, truly, honest-to-gosh naked (but you have to look quick). Torn between the world of humans and life in the savage wild, he ultimately settles for the latter. The deck is stacked: nature has its own innate nobility, and eventually swallows up all of mankind's prideful, presumptuous accomplishments. Man, it would seem, has nothing going for him but the inexplicable gift of fire. Thus the battle culminates in a visual eruption: orange flames penetrate and ignite the green darkness.

Sabu is (unsurprisingly) convincing as a native of India. Along with his glossy mane of hair and his irrepressibly feral beauty, he has the supple, natural grace of a bathing-suited pin-up girl. He tosses his long, dark tresses with elegant aplomb. His androgynous presence clearly contributes to the movie's ambiguously gorgeous decor. Enhancing all the prettiness is a Miklos Rozsa music score that's a sumptuous, sinuous, sensuous tone poem.

Jungle Hell* (U.S. 1956 B&W)

There's high camp and there's low camp. There's also bottom-of-the-barrel camp like *Jungle Hell*, with Sabu cavorting in a loincloth, as is his wont, while greatly vexed by flying saucers and radioactive rocks from outer space. His major source of annoyance, however, is a rival jungle lad (Robert Cabal) who picks a couple fights with him, thus providing a sensual thrill for those of us who enjoy watching seminude "native boys" locked in close physical contention. At least a third (perhaps as much as half) of this cheapie consists of stock footage. But otherwise we wouldn't get to see any elephants . . . and pachyderms, I might add, are by far the film's most appealing players. In 1956 Sabu was thirty-two years old, and rather long in the tooth for jungle boy antics.

Jupiter's Darling* (U.S. 1955 C)

Jupiter's Darling is an absurdly overproduced historical epic about Hannibal's attempted conquest of Rome. It looks a lot like a Hercules picture, except that the people in it sing and dance. Furthermore, the stars—Howard Keel and Esther Williams—bear a more than passing resemblance to Steve Reeves and Sylvia Lopez. The cast includes other typical denizens of the ancient world, such as William Demarest, Richard Haydn, and Marge and Gower Champion. George Sanders portrays the Dictator of Rome, who has decreed that Esther must either marry him or become a Vestal Virgin. She is taken prisoner by Hannibal (Howard Keel), who sings that "A man who is a he-male / should never trust a female." In the movie's campiest scene, some nearly nude male statues come magically to life for the purpose of joining Esther in one of her patented underwater ballets. The funniest line, meanwhile, is meant to demonstrate the general unchivalrousness of Hannibal and his barbarians. "I'll kill her myself!" snarls Keel, with reference to poor Miss Williams, whereupon his trusted lieutenant (Demarest) hopefully inquires, "Can I stay and watch?"

Just a Gigolo* (Germany 1979 C)

This decadent depiction of Berlin between wars was made by people who didn't do their history homework. Is it camp or is it just plain silly? The film gets underway with David Bowie arriving on the Western Front sometime toward the end of World War I. He's a German officer and he says all the proper, proto-Fascist things ("Heroism is my destiny," etc.). The war lost, he returns to Berlin, where he finds his mother (Maria Schell) working in a Turkish bath. His father suffered a paralytic stroke upon hearing the news of the Fatherland's defeat. Bowie comes home to them carrying a pig; a mob of hungry people attempt to relieve him of it along the way. David Hemmings is a local bigwig in the fledgling Nazi party. He comes on very macho, but he seems to have trouble letting go of Bowie's hand. (Later he waylays the unfortunate lad in a public toilet.) Bowie has an awkward encounter with Curt Jurgens while bathing. (He gets so flustered, he drops the soap. Jurgens gives it back to him by sticking it with his cane.) Marlene Dietrich (in her final film role) is housemother to a stable of gigolos. They are a collection of pretty and decorative creatures; she recruits Bowie to join them. Kim Novak hires him to sire her an heir. Meanwhile, Hemmings and his Nazis are holding their clandestine meetings inside of street kiosks.

Marlene, seventy-eight years old, looks okay, but her voice is strangely slurred as if she were on drugs. Novak looks a little *too* good —at any rate, too young-looking to require the services of a gigolo. Bowie just looks cadaverous. This is one of those rare films that really is as bad as people say it is.

Just for the Hell of It* (U.S. 1968 C)

This is a movie about hopped-up teenagers on the prowl. In the very first scene, they totally demolish a nice, respectable middle-class living room. These kids are so mean, they throw *paint* at people! They take away a blind man's cane and knock him down! They see a crippled guy coming out of a hospital, so they take away his crutches and beat him up with them! They go into a cafeteria and plaster the big fat lady cashier with a cream pie! These kids'll tear your wash right down from your clothesline and *stomp* on it! They set fire to a newspaper while somebody's *reading* it! They squirt innocent housewives with *garden hoses*! They wreck a baby carriage, but at least they have the decency to take the baby out first—and put him in a *garbage can*! They trash a greasy spoon cafe and fry the palms of the proprietor's hands on the stove! They lure a bunch of naive high school girls to a party, dope their drinks, and tear their dresses off! They even go to a doctor's office and rip up all the magazines in his waiting room! They go to the library and throw rocks through the windows! ("Librarian injured," screams the headline.) They even beat up on a bunch of little kids playing baseball!

This minimalistic exercise in anarchy and nihilism was scripted by someone named Louise Downe. I've no idea who she is, but I'll bet she lives in the suburbs and drives a paneled station wagon.

Kansas City Trucking Co.* (U.S. 1976 C)

Kansas City Trucking Co. gets underway with Richard Locke barreling down the freeway at the wheel of a big rig. His mood, however, is one of jaded boredom. We can tell because he's got the radio on and he's listening to a book review of *Born Again*, the autobiography of Charles Colson, noted anti-porn crusader. "Shit," he mutters, and changes the station.

Back at the garage, he gets it on with the dispatcher (Jack Wrangler, himself the author of an autobiography). An element of suspense is introduced: a new driver is expected momentarily. Will he show up before the guys have gotten their rocks off?

Later in the film, Locke is driving down the turnpike next to a convertible with its top down. The two guys in the front seat are smoking dope and giving each other hand jobs. In the interest of promoting highway safety, Locke honks his horn and waves at them.

Kansas City Trucking Co. is the first in a trilogy of films directed by Joe Gage (the other two are *El Paso Wrecking Corp.* and *L.A. Tool and Die*). Gage's approach to erotica is distinctive and idiosyncratic. Dramatically innovative, too. For instance, *L.A. Tool and Die* features a scene in which a divorced dad checks with the high school football coach on his son's athletic progress. This parent-teacher conference gets seriously out of hand and winds up with both men sprawled naked on the coach's desk.

Locke, who stars in all three films, has a macho, Mephistophelean handsomeness that would not be out of place in a Sergio Leone western. As for Jack Wrangler, I like the casual way he smokes a cigarette while beating off. In the world of porn, that's about as close as you can get to cool.

Killer Nun* (Italy 1977 C)

Killer Nun stars Anita Ekberg, clad in sacred vestments. This rather irreligious camp classic gets underway with a procession of holy sisters solemnly filing into a cathedral to the accompaniment of the Dies Irae. Sister Anita is meanwhile making confession. "I can't forgive him, Father," she snarls. (With neurotic compulsiveness—and phallic suggestiveness—she jabs at her hand with a crucifix.) "I have tried, but I will never forgive him. . . . May his soul burn in hell! Just the thought of what he did to me makes me want to take revenge on *all men*! To snuff them out like he snuffed out my happiness!"

Her Father Confessor, meanwhile, is all but shitting in his pants. "To forgive is the prime duty of the righteous," he admonishes. "You are no longer in a state of grace!"

Anita is Sister Gertrude, a nurse in a Catholic hospital. She pretends to be all sweetness and light, merrily traipsing down the corridors, clapping her hands and making pious exhortations. ("Let us praise Jesus Christ, our Lord! Come on, up you get! The Lord does not like lazy people!") But secretly she's a murder-obsessed morphine addict. She catches sight of a scalpel and suddenly the humming of a theremin is heard on the soundtrack. A doctor catches her disconnecting a patient's oxygen tent. But does he report her? Hah! That would spoil the plot!

Anita rings up the Mother Superior and begs to be hospitalized. The Mother Superior is Alida Valli, who munches chocolates while trying to placate her with platitudes. "It is a nun's vocation to suffer," she offers helpfully, and then hangs up the phone.

"Bitch!" Anita mutters, nervously playing with a pencil. Her anxiety manifests itself in odd and sadistic behavior. She throws a poor old lady's dentures on the floor and stomps on them. The woman promptly dies of a coronary, whereupon Anita steals her jewelry and trades it for morphine. She changes into civilian clothes and goes smoking and drinking and whoring all over town. Then she goes back to the hospital and, next thing you know, an old man is found bludgeoned to death. One of the nuns gets wise, but decides not to tell; she hopes to seduce our

JOE DALLESANDRO (1948–   ), hunky star of numerous Andy Warhol films.

leading lady into the sack. But Anita isn't impressed: "You've been rolling your eyes at me ever since you were transferred here, flaunting your big floppy breasts at me at every opportunity, hoping I'd jump into bed with you! Foolish little bitch! You're the worst kind of prostitute! I've seen how you behave with the new doctor. Perhaps you aren't as much of a lesbian as you pretend!"

The new doctor is Joe Dallesandro, of Andy Warhol fame. He maintains a certain coolness toward Anita, perhaps because of the needle tracks on her arms, perhaps because the patients are staging a hunger strike until the murders are solved. But even his professional detachment can't withstand the wiles of a horny nun. ("You *will* help me, won't you, doctor? I promise I'll make you very happy.")

There's a fairly decent trick ending. Fooled me, anyway. The actresses are somewhat less than convincing as nuns. For one thing, they wear too much eye shadow.

The Killing of Sister George* (U.S. 1968 C)

Gee, this is a good movie! Whenever I see it, it takes me pleasantly by surprise. It deserves to be regarded as a gay cult film, even though it contains no male homosexual characters (the plot is about lesbians). As a portrayal of what it's like to be gay, *The Killing of Sister George* is without equal.

The best thing about the film is Beryl Reid's performance in the central role. She is June Buckridge, a loud, vulgar, deliberately abrasive middle-aged lesbian who happens to be an actress in a popular BBC television soap opera. June is cast as "Sister George," the indefatigable village nurse, forever dispensing cheery smiles and uplifting comments. For ironic effect, the film cuts hilariously back and forth between her saintly screen persona and her rather more crude off-screen personality. (I wish I had the guts to speak to my co-workers the way she does to hers.) Crisis enters her life when she learns that she's soon to be written out of the series; Sister George is destined to have a fatal collision with a lorry. Furthermore, June is also in trouble regarding an incident off the set: a rude, lewd, drunken encounter with a pair of novitiate nuns from Ireland. ("How do you *ladies* pass your time?") Adding insult to injury is the news that her next professional assignment will be the role of Clarabelle Cow on a program called "Toddler Time." ("A flawed, credible cow . . . full of little foibles and prejudices.") As for June's love life, it is worse than problematic. Much like her acting career, it is fraught with misfortune.

The film is based on a successful play by Frank Marcus. Reid originated her role on the stage. It's sad that she didn't have a more satisfying screen career. Her type is difficult to cast; she ended up in horror movies (*The Beast in the Cellar, Dr. Phibes Rises Again!*). The cast of this film provides her with solid acting support: Susannah York as her live-in lover, Coral Browne as the hypocritical closet case who steals York away from her, and Patricia Medina as the good-hearted whore who resides just across the street. The director is Robert Aldrich. There've been some quibbles with regard to his handling of the material. York and Browne have a sex scene that's scored with ominous music and photographed with the queasy prurience so characteristic of the male heterosexual eye. There's also some rather leering footage of women dancing together at Gateways, a lesbian night club in London. Still, when it comes to show biz topics, I've always considered Aldrich a director without peer. Bear in mind that he also made *What Ever Happened to Baby Jane?*. And it shows in his direction of the pathetic scene which finds June nursing a Scotch while writing phony fan letters to herself. At this point a friend of mine was heard to remark, "That's not June Buckridge. That's Baby Jane Hudson!"

Kiss Today Goodbye* (U.S. 1980 C)

Francis Ellie's *Kiss Today Goodbye* is a gay hardcore version of the four-handkerchief soapers Lana Turner used to make. George Payne, cast as a construction worker saddled with a bitchy roommate, shares a bittersweet love affair with Lew Seager, whose heterosexual marriage is just as bad as George's gay one. Unfortunately, Payne's truculent mate gets wise to the situation. In a plot twist apparently inspired by *The Boys in the Band*, he humiliates George by inviting Lew to a birthday get-together which inevitably turns into the usual orgy. ("Fasten your seat belts! It's going to be a humpy night!") The guests amuse themselves with the newcomer (and he with them), while George does a slow burn in the corner, ultimately hurling his glass into the fireplace. The shards land on the same carpet where (sigh!), only the night before, he and Lew were making passionate love to one another. The two get back together again for a final ecstatic fling. Then Lew nobly returns to his wife and son. All this, and traditional family values too!

The background details are suitably campy. A Raggedy Ann doll sports a Joan Crawford button. There's also a plug for Crisco (something else gets plugged at the same time). It pleases me to note that the music score mainly consists of classical selections; the climaxes of the actors are timed to coincide with the rich orchestral climaxes of Ravel and Rachmaninoff. A split-screen effect is imaginatively used to enhance the erotic impact; a many-faceted lens reproduces provocative images six times over. As for George Payne, he is breathtakingly handsome in all of his particulars, and he gives a strenuously athletic performance. He's not much of an actor, but, of course, there *are* compensations.

Ellie's work (*Christopher Street Blues*, *Killing Me Softly*, *Navy Blue*, etc.) is considerably more romantic than what's popular nowadays. The cleverest title in his résumé is *Michael, Angelo and David*; you just about have to have a classically-attuned sensibility to come up with something like that.

Kitten with a Whip * (U.S. 1964 B&W)

This chef-d'oeuvre of the bad girl genre is a certified trash classic. The show begins with Ann-Margret busting out of Juvenile Hall, hopping a freight, picking her way across a construction site, getting barked at by guard dogs, etc., all while clad in a peekaboo baby-doll nightgown (probably robin's-egg blue to complement her hair, though I can't say for sure, since the film is in black-and-white). Somehow she ends up at the palatial suburban residence of John Forsythe, an aspiring senatorial candidate. (His party designation is carefully left unspecified, but he's gotta be a Republican. For one thing, we overhear him making a date to meet somebody for lunch at the country club.) She hands him a sob story about how she's running away from home 'cause her stepdad started coming on to her. Forsythe not only swallows it; he buys her a dress, shoes, undies, and a bus ticket to visit her aunt in L.A. What she needs, however, is a place to hole up till the heat is off, and Forsythe's pad suits her just fine. She won't budge. Furthermore, when he threatens to call the cops, she gets downright nasty: "You poke your finger at that dial, mister, and that's when I start screaming rape!"

At first she amuses herself with harmless mischief, like drawing a clown mouth on a portrait photo of his wife (who's conveniently out of town, visiting relatives). Then she gets on the phone and invites some of her sleazebag friends over for an evening of fun and games. These cohorts of hers include Peter Brown and James "Skip" Ward, who share a relationship that's unconventional, even by my standards. Ward's got an awful temper, and Brown actively yearns to be made the butt of it. "Hit me, Buck! Go on! Release those tensions!" he insists, offering his arm and shoulder to be punched. "Do it, buddy! Get rid of those hostilities! Go on! . . . I feel no pain!" Brown's misogynistic attitude toward our heroine is just as morbidly obsessive: "She's the female! The foulup! . . . She's the succuba . . . some kind of a demon. Comes to a man while he's sleepin' and *drains* him!"

By manipulating his fear of scandal, the kids coerce Forsythe into smuggling them across the border to Tijuana. Now, as they say, he's in a heap of trouble. His south-of-the-border misadventures are an unmitigated nightmare of violent mayhem, lurid strip joints, and tightassed embarrassment, with no relief in sight till the kids get killed in an auto mishap. This 1964 release presents us with a Goldwateresque universe in which everyone is either a psychopath or an anal retentive. There is no middle ground.

Klondike Annie* (U.S. 1936 B&W)

Klondike Annie is the most unusual film in the Mae West canon: she plays a shady lady who gets religion. Not what I would call an inspiring prospect. And yet, what could be campier than a "born-again" Mae West?

In the opening reels, she's her usual racy self. As a matter of fact, her first few scenes find her wearing what looks like a Swedish Modern Christmas tree on her head. She's the "kept woman" of a Chinese vicelord in old San Francisco. But then she escapes aboard a northbound clipper which is captained by Victor McLaglen (definitely not one of her sexiest leading men). "When you sing like that, you make me tremble all over!" he swoons. She changes her tune when she's obliged to share her cabin with a saccharine missionary lady (Helen Jerome Eddy). As soon as Mae forsakes the primrose path, we know in our hearts that this movie is headed straight for perdition. Her formerly raucous voice is now hushed; she takes to affecting pious expressions more becoming to one of the Gish sisters. Upon arrival in Nome, Alaska, she takes charge of a settlement house and goes about the business of saving souls. Victor doesn't know what to do with her. Much like the audience, he preferred her the way she was before.

Mae intended this flick as a sop to th. rious moral purity leagues that were constantly bitching about her bawdiness. The fact that she would dare presume to make a film about religion, however, only served to outrage these watchdogs of decency all the more. The essence of camp is irony, and you can't hardly get more ironic than that.

---

*Ladies They Talk About** (U.S. 1933 B&W)

Ladies They Talk About is an excellent title for a women's prison picture starring Barbara Stanwyck and Lillian Roth. "Talking" is a concept central to the plot, since everything depends on who's a snitch and who isn't. The film begins with Barbara talking on the telephone to the cops. She tells them there's a homicidal maniac running around the West Side with a butcher knife. Then she and her gang hightail it over to the East Side and stick up a bank.

Her leading man is Preston Foster, cast as an evangelist whose "old-fashioned revival" hour is broadcast nightly over the radio. Like his telegenic descendants, he has massive political clout. And, of course, he's got the hots for Barbara. She hails from his hometown and he cherishes fond memories of her (she was the deacon's daughter). She foolishly confides in him as to her role in the robbery. Next thing she knows, he's up there on the witness stand, testifying against her.

The rest of the movie mainly takes place at San Quentin, where Barbara subsists on a diet consisting primarily of beans and juteballs. One of the inmates is a mannish type who's partial to Cuban cigars. Lillian Roth gives Barbara the lowdown: "Watch out for her! She likes to wrestle."

Preston pays Barbara regular visits, in hopes of providing her with spiritual uplift. She slips him a letter to be mailed outside the wall. It contains the dope on an upcoming breakout. Next thing you know, the warden's quashed it. Has Preston squealed again? Somethin' sure stinks, and it ain't Limburger.

Of all the movie's clear and abundant camp components, co-star Maude Eburne is the standout. She's cast as a procuress who's doing time for running a "beauty parlor." Pointing out one of the other prisoners, Eburne says, "See that dame? She used to be one of my girls. She quit me. The stairs were too much for her."

The Lair of the White Worm* (G.B. 1988 C)

When I'm confronted with a film called *The Lair of the White Worm*, can you blame me for supposing that the title refers to leading man Hugh Grant's trousers? But in fact this dotty Ken Russell opus is a camp horror item about a seductive snake woman who favors blue eye shadow and masquerades as a patrician English gentlelady (Amanda Donohoe). She snacks on the occasional boy scout and can quote from Oscar Wilde and Orson Welles with equal alacrity. At the climax, she straps on a huge, pointed dildo and attempts to rape poor, sweet, virginal Catherine Oxenberg. In short, she's a menace to the patriarchal status quo which horror films hold so dear. Obviously, this woman who occasionally turns into a big, long, white snake which kills and eats men not only *has* a symbolic, castrating penis, but indeed *is* a symbolic, castrating penis. And she's far from being the only one on display. This is a film obsessed with garden hoses and vacuum cleaners. There's also a ballpoint pen which Grant holds very suggestively in his lap. When Ken Russell permits his imagination free rein, one shouldn't be surprised that the end result is an avalanche of phallic imagery.

Land of the Minotaur* (G.B. 1976 C)

This movie deserves mention both for its hilarious badness and for its sexy mise en scène of Greek paganism. A cult of devil worshipers (led by Peter Cushing, whose billing is large, though his role is small) kidnap a handsome brunette, strip him to the waist, and bind him to an altar for human sacrifice in a temple filled with statues of bulls, all of them amply endowed and standing up on their hind legs. The effect is, to put it mildly, homoerotic.

Donald Pleasence (with an awful Barry Fitzgerald accent) portrays a priest whose primary aim is to protect a group of hippie archaeologists from the depredations of the devil cult. Incidentally, he won't let the hippies share a bedroom, even if they're guys. We can tell they're hippies because they have long hair and drive around in a van covered with peace symbols. The devil cult dresses in Ku Klux Klan robes. The hippie girls emit shrieks whenever they catch sight of anyone thus attired. The guys, meanwhile, are petrified with terror when they spot

Pure camp as the hero is subjected to the third degree before a kinky statue of a naked beastie in *Land of the Minotaur* (Crown International 1976).

one of the aforementioned Minotaur statues. I realize that hippies are expected to be sort of wimpy, but getting scared of a statue, however well-hung, is kind of dumb.

*The Last Days of Pompeii** (Italy 1960 C)

The Last Days of Pompeii is surely the only Steve Reeves picture that's based on a Victorian novel. Sir Edward Bulwer Lytton's grand historical potboiler was a smash bestseller of 1834. His already melodramatic plot has been seriously distorted in order to fit the conventions of the Italian sword-and-sandal genre. This serves to trivialize, defuse, and deflate the book's substantial theatrical potential. Reeves portrays Glaucus, the hero of the piece, who is now necessarily a musclebound gladiator type. Perhaps for purposes of contrast, he's been given a nimble, frivolous pretty-boy cohort.

Reeves provides an amusingly awkward performance. He even gets to stagger his way through a drunk scene. His togas are shorter than most miniskirts: he shows great legs and plenty of haunch. Unfortunately, careful observation reveals that he's always wearing underpants. If he wanted to star in a movie based on a classic of English literature, what a pity he didn't select *The Scottish Chiefs* by Jane Porter! It has always been my understanding that Scotsmen never wear anything under their kilts.

*Laughing Sinners** (U.S. 1931 B&W)

Early on in this fire-and-brimstone soap opera, Joan Crawford performs a *Hee Haw*-flavored dance number that's as campy as anything in her entire career. All dolled up in Old McDonald drag, complete with bib overalls, a fake beard, a long and pointy putty nose, and a wide-brimmed straw hat, she cavorts in a decidedly cornball fashion to the accompaniment of a hayseed quartet.

This movie expects us to believe that Joan Crawford could be head over heels in love with stuffy, double-chinned Neil Hamilton (perhaps best known for his TV role as *Batman*'s police commissioner). About all that he's got going for him is a slick-looking moustache. She's a cafe entertainer and he's a perpetually horny traveling salesman named

Howdy. (His fellow drummers include Guy Kibbee, Roscoe Karns, and Cliff Edwards.) When he throws her over to marry the boss's daughter, she attempts to throw herself off a bridge. Clark Gable intervenes. He's a very persuasive soldier in the Salvation Army and, before you know it, he's got Joan standing on a street corner, beating a tambourine. (If this improbable spectacle isn't camp, what is?) Then Neil comes back and seduces her into one night of sin. But she quickly sees him for the jerk he is and goes right back to her hymn-singing. These melodramatics are rather absurd, of course, but, when Joan says she'd rather be just friends with Clark Gable than be kept by Neil Hamilton, you've got to admit she's got a point.

The Leech Woman* (U.S. 1959 B&W)

Phillip Terry was Joan Crawford's third husband, which is what makes his role in this schlock horror opus so sublimely ironic: he's cast as an endocrinologist searching for a youth elixir which he'll market to rich old ladies. He knows all about them because he married one for her money: she's Coleen Gray, who is initially presented to us in a frowzy fox fur and dark make-up to make her look old and dumpy. (At the time of the film's production, she was 37. Phillip Terry was 50. The script, however, implies that he's about 35 and she's ten years older.) Their marriage is far from harmonious. Witness some of the overripe dialogue, like when Terry says to her, "You know, I think I like you better when you're sloppy drunk and violent. That's the real you and that's the one I like—the one that hates me and gives me a chance to hate back." Such melodramatic talk may not be worthy of a Joan Crawford movie, but it may have been characteristic of her home life.

Phil and Coleen set off on an African safari, during the course of which they learn that the aging process can indeed be reversed. All you have to do is mix powdered orchids with extracts from the male pineal gland. The rejuvenating effect, though undeniably dramatic, is depressingly temporary. Even so (cumbersome plot mechanics out of the way at last), Coleen becomes a leech woman and her spouse is her first victim.

This is a movie that only a male chauvinist could dream up. It's a blend of lurid sexual titillation ("She *drained* men of their loves and lives!" screams the ad) and cynical sexual politics: "What woman lives, who has passed the prime of life, that would not give her remaining years to reclaim even a few moments of joy and happiness and know the worship of *men!*" as co-star Estelle Hemsley puts it. The film's most outlandish scene is also its most typical: All withered and wizened and back in the States, Coleen pays a visit to the "bad" side of town. She's dripping with jewelry and trolling for fresh victims. She's picked up by a slimy male hustler who takes her to Lover's Lane, where he attempts to choke the life out of her, but she gets him first. The women in this movie are vain and foolish, but the men are something much worse. All the straight males in the film are ridiculously horny, whenever Coleen is high on a fresh pineal fix. As soon as she reverts to old ladyhood, however, they run away screaming, "Don't touch me! Don't touch me!" Even I know this is a caricature.

Les Girls* (U.S. 1957 C)

Here's a film that absolutely screams its gayness. It was recommended for Volume 2 by Danilo Lima de Aguiar, a Brazilian friend of the publisher. The director is George Cukor. The music and lyrics are by Cole Porter. Even the cardboard box the video comes in is lavender.

But the plot, of course, is persistently heterosexual. Like so many 'Fifties musicals, this one takes place in Paris and ends up with everyone happily married. The central issue is whether Taina Elg or Kay Kendall attempted suicide for love of Gene Kelly, whose heart belongs to Mitzi Gaynor. Gay taste is mainly expressed in subtleties of costume, color scheme, and decor: the muted metallic green of Gene's car and the way it complements the monotonous gold-yellow backgrounds; the dresses and the huge, swooping, floppy hats with their classic 'Fifties lines. Late in the film, Gene and Mitzi have a number that comes all the way out of the closet. It's a musical spoof of *The Wild One*. Mitzi's a waitress and Gene's the leader of an all-male, black-leather-clad motorcycle gang. He flirts with her, but then, just when his dreadful Brando impression is becoming unbearable, his boys beckon him back and he takes his leave of her. *Les Girls* is precisely the sort of film my parents would have taken me to see when I was a child. The campiest thing about it is the fact that, in those days, I was firmly convinced that romantic antics such as these were an accurate depiction of what grownups did all day while I was at school.

Liane, Jungle Goddess* (Germany 1956 C)

What are we to make of this 'Fifties jungle girl opus from Germany? It's been more than a decade since World War II, yet Aryanism survives in the form of a busty blonde (Marion Michaels) prancing topless through the jungle with her pet lion cub. ("Beautiful and proud . . . yet more savage than the black jungle she ruled!" maintains the ad.) Stark naked, she swings on a vine while cocktail music swoons and surges on the soundtrack. Down below, Hardy Kruger is stalking her with his camera. "She's just a bit too far away!" he complains, echoing a sentiment no doubt prevalent in the audience.

Under less exotic conditions, he might have been expected to pair off with the pretty doctor accompanying his party. Her arch primness, however, is perhaps a little too civilized and therefore off-putting. ("I am the doctor of this expedition and all the *gentlemen* of this expedition have given their word to forget that I am a woman.") When he gets back to camp, she attempts to divert him with a cup of tea, but he hasn't time. He's just gotta develop those pictures right away!

When the jungle goddess is taken captive, the first thing he gives her to eat is a banana. Next he gives her a mirror, whereupon she immediately commences to primp and pout and preen a la Bardot. When he brings her (and her lion cub) home to Hamburg, it naturally transpires that she's the lost heiress to a huge shipbuilding fortune. Before she assumes her rightful position as a CEO, however, she had better set aside a few of her wild jungle habits. Like, for instance, curling up on the floor by Hardy's bed every night.

Liane is a mother lode of rich camp to be savored by psychotronic film enthusiasts of every sexual persuasion. Think what it could have been with a gender switch! Tarzan and Bomba could learn a thing or two from this saucy minx, at least as regards titillation and entertainment values.

Little Men* (U.S. 1935 B&W)

This B-movie version of Louisa May Alcott's *Little Men* is guaranteed to be gay camp (chicken division). Erin O'Brien-Moore provides an unbearably saccharine performance as Jo. Cloyingly presiding over a cozy

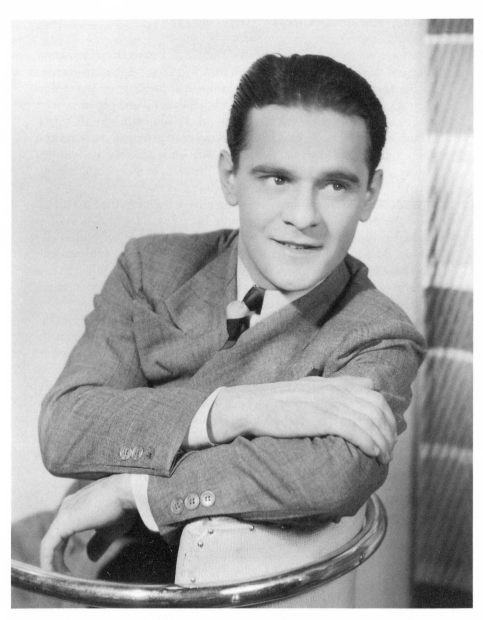

Frankie Darro (1917–1976) in a publicity still from the 1930s film *Tough Kid*.

boarding school, she exudes so much spunk and spirit, you just about want to slug her. "I'll race you to the nursery," she cheerily chirps to co-star David Durand. And, sure enough, she does. She even engages in pillow fights. Frankie Darro, popular movie "tough kid" of the 'Thirties, shakes his head to see such antics. In such a rustic, Victorian setting, his essentially urban, twentieth-century sensibility rudely protrudes like an erect member. But Jo and her stern martinet husband (Ralph Morgan) decide to take him in anyhow. Durand, the eldest pupil, is thrilled at the prospect of having an adolescent his own age to play with. "He can have half my bed and all of my breakfast!" he volunteers eagerly. Darro is pleased with this arrangement. "Come on! Get in!" he urgently whispers at bedtime. Frankie's a bad influence in more ways than one. In the guise of convening a make-believe "powwow," he introduces his classmates to smoking, and I'm not at all sure what kind. "I feel awful funny," remarks a little lad, after his first puff of the peculiar-smelling substance. "I think I worked too long in the sun today." They nearly burn the house down.

Convinced that Frankie needs a more rigorous environment, Morgan packs him off to an institution for wayward youths. There's an interesting exchange of dialogue in the headmaster's office. "He requires a little handling," Ralph cautions the superintendent, who replies in a thick Prussian accent as follows: "Be reassured. He'll have special attention." Frankie finds these attentions so very special, he finally flees the premises. The German disciplinarian misses him sorely, and conveys his sense of loss in a letter to Morgan, who confides to Jo, "He found the boy especially difficult. He would like to work with him further." At which point we wonder just how much further this movie could possibly go.

Like a Horse* (U.S. 1984 C)

As the title so subtly hints, this is a piece of gay male erotica with a heavy emphasis on ample endowments. The director, Matt Sterling, also helmed a thematically related opus called A Matter of Size. Both films feature plentiful footage of men getting spanked.

Like a Horse is a plotless collection of sexual vignettes. In the opener, a wrestling bout evolves into something less competitive (thus approximating the realization of a fantasy which often occurs to me while watching Santo pictures). One segment transpires in a dark alley behind a bar and features a shot of a guy getting poked in the butt while reclining all curled up on top of a garbage can. (Could this be taken as symbolic of the entire genre?) In the final episode, a fellow rubs a magic lamp and, in lieu of a genie, a trio of naked male go-go dancers appear. They are rapidly put to lustful use. The campiest segment has a quasi-Biblical tone: a pair of primeval hunks encounter one another in an idyllic Garden of Eden, where—ahem—they share an apple. The heavens thunder in protest and the sky pours forth rain, which at least serves to wash away the cum stains.

The Lion of St. Mark* (Italy 1963 C)

The Lion of St. Mark is like an opera, except that the people are in better shape. Gordon Scott has been promised in marriage by his father, the doge of Venice, but the bride-to-be is the la-di-da daughter of an aristocrat and Gordon wants no part of her. He'd rather be out with the boys, chasing those pesky foreign pirates who have lately become the terror of the canal (as a matter of fact, one of them is portrayed by Gianna Maria Canale). In direct defiance of his daddy's wishes, he dons a mask and becomes a swashbuckling, buccaneer-battling hero known as "the Lion of St. Mark." When he first encounters Gianna (in a sword-fight, natch), the sexual tension quotient skyrockets. Their love is true, but can the son of the doge find happiness with a common bandit wench who, moreover, is the sworn enemy of all he holds dear?

Melodramatic storylines such as this are merely one of the ways in which movies customarily translate the concept of outlaw sexuality into conveniently heterosexual terms. Nonetheless, I must admit that I find the situation intriguing. With a little more care and style, this costume romance could have been more than just sub-Verdi camp. Gordon looks toothsome in all that velvet finery. Trouble is, he never takes any of it off.

The Living Coffin* (Mexico 1958 C)

The Living Coffin is a peculiar hybrid: a Mexican western (in color!) with Gothic overtones. As so often happens when a masculine genre combines with a feminine one, the end product is homoerotic. We get our first inkling of this from the opening title design: bones bleaching on a desert landscape, under an oddly lavender sky.

Once the action gets underway, it doesn't take us long to notice that the cowboy hero (Gaston Santos) has a nice ass underneath his buckskin britches. The matriarch of the mansion, a disapproving old Puritan, grimaces with distaste when he announces that he's an emissary sent by the urban friends of her young niece, the heroine (Mary Duval), as if anything from the city is automatically degenerate. The hacienda provides the film with a stylized mise-en-scène, full of wide, whitewashed hallways with flickering torches and stark shadows. Such expressive, indirect lighting serves, incidentally, to further highlight the shapely fullness, the globular firmness of Gaston's posterior. The movie's anal preoccupations even extend to the shock scenes: the discovery of a gory male corpse slithering (like a turd) down a tight chimney is framed between close-ups of Gaston's handsome face registering a look of almost blissful horror (pain? or a pleasurable release?). Sad to say, we never actually get to see him buck naked, though the script does give us at least one teasingly tantalizing implication of his nudity. At one point he takes a tumble into a bog while exploring "Skeleton Swamp." Later, when asked where he's been for so long, he explains, "I fell into the quicksand and spent the day washing my clothes in the river." Hmmm. Speaking of clothes, the murderer turns out to be a transvestite. But, as I've indicated, it's the cowboy outfits that really steal the show.

Look in Any Window (U.S. 1961 B&W)

Paul Anka is the terror of suburbia in this cheesy sex melodrama. As the title indicates, he's a Peeping Tom, harassing housewives and scaring children. The poor kid's got a complex, all because his dad (Alex Nicol) is a drunk and his mom (Ruth Roman) is the neighborhood tramp. Paul spends much of the film in a state of seminudity (everyone keeps complaining about how uncomfortably warm the weather is), but I have to confess that I mainly kept my eyes on Ruth Roman, an accomplished scene-stealer from way back. I suppose there are those who would say she was past her prime when she made this flick, but I disagree. We get to see her do the cha-cha in a black lace bathing suit. One scene finds her watering the lawn in what looks like a prom dress. Co-star Jack Cassidy drives up in his sportscar and asks her if she'd like to go on an overnight trip to Vegas with him. She doesn't even stop to turn off the water.

Oddly enough, the kinkiest person in the film is the police detective who's supposed to be tracking down the prowler. "My mother was a lady! You'd never catch her prancing around with everything showing! She never had a dirty thought in her life!" he tells us, while feverishly polishing the barrel of his pistol. "Let me get my hands on any guy that isn't normal; he'll confess!" He spends a good deal of the film trying to get Anka alone so that he can squeeze a confession out of him. Can't say as I blame him.

Love and Kisses   (U.S. 1965 C)

Though *Love and Kisses* may seem to be merely a mediocre movie, it actually provides a subtle comment on the esthetics of mediocrity. During the opening titles we see Ricky Nelson performing the title song. However, while the credits are still in progress, we cut abruptly away from him to inexplicably look out the window of a car traveling through suburban Los Angeles. This disjunctive jump carries us to the picture's principal setting: the spacious, middle-class dwelling where Ricky resides with his Dad (Jack Kelly), Mom (Madelyn Himes), and sister (Sheilah Wells). The decor is rife with chirpy yellows and the green of plastic plants. There are also large splotches of red: a perversely appropriate hue, since this is basically a story about the marriage of two virgins.

Without taking the trouble to obtain parental consent, Ricky weds his steady girlfriend (Kris Nelson, who was also his wife in real life). A clash of emotions (and of colors) ensues when he brings his bride home to live with him. As husbands go, Rick is insufferably stolid, dull, and obtuse. Kris seems blandly coltish. However, she does briefly come alive during a dream sequence which presents her as a stripper in a smoke-filled burlesque joint. Her costume is neon red, naturally. Of even greater chromatic significance is the fact that the dream concludes with Ricky getting a spectacularly bloody nose. Still more sexually in-

RICKY NELSON (1940–1985) was getting towards the end of his "all-American-boy-next door" role on the TV series *Ozzie and Harriet* when he made the film *Love and Kisses* (Universal 1965). Ahead of him was his career as a rock star.

criminating is the nightmare that his sister has, in which she's trying to study a textbook, but she can't, for the simple reason that the pages are all stuck together! The movie comes to a characteristically stylized close when the cleaning lady (Pert Kelton) betrays the essential artificiality of the setting by drawing a theatrical curtain across it. Of course, it's a red curtain.

Love Bites* (U.S. 1988 C)

Love Bites, a gay vampire spoof, is a direct-to-video presentation featuring at least a couple of porno stars and lots of male nudity. Which means that, when the hero brandishes his crucifix, he doesn't get quite the reaction he'd been anticipating. What he hears, instead: "Oh, puh-*leeze*! That fire-and-brimstone shit went out with Tammy Faye Bakker!"

The vampire (Kevin Glover) is tall, handsome, swishy, and sleeps in Care Bears pajamas. Who would have the heart to pound a stake through his heart? Instead, the would-be staker permits himself to be seduced.

"Follow me to my chambers," intones the Count. "Allow me to share with you the release of three hundred and forty-seven years of accumulated passion."

"This won't make me a necrophiliac, will it?" the horny vampire-hunter nervously inquires.

Afterward, the bloodsucker magically becomes mortal, as if having sex has somehow injected him with life. (The softcore sex scene, however, makes it clear that he was the one who was doing the injecting.) The script is not particularly witty. (When the Count is asked why his name is Sanders, he answers, "I like chicken.") But the cast is amiable and attractive. This show has a nice feel for tradition: the theme music is Tchaikovsky's *Swan Lake*, which, of course, was the main title music for the Bela Lugosi *Dracula*, the 1931 campfest that started it all.

Love Has Many Faces (U.S. 1965 C)

Bad movie aficionados have long treasured *Love Has Many Faces* as a priceless gem. It's a film about gorgeous seminude beach boys seducing and exploiting wealthy middle-aged women. I trust that I need not spell out the source of the film's appeal to gay men. Just hearing the theme song (belted out by Nancy Wilson) invariably sets my heart to pounding.

Cliff Robertson and Stefanie Powers stalk through the film in high moral dudgeon. Lana Turner just sort of drifts through in an assortment of Edith Head bathing outfits. The real narrative interest resides in a subplot featuring Ruth Roman and Hugh O'Brian. They meet on the beach (where else?). He flexes his biceps. She gawks appreciatively. This is all very heterosexual stuff, you understand. He asks her if they've ever met before, like on Fire Island, maybe. She asks him if his father was Oscar Wilde. His swimsuit gives a pretty clear picture of what he's got to offer. But, just in case we don't understand, they elucidate it for us.

"What do I like about you?" she asks rhetorically.

"You want me to tell you . . . or show you?" he parries.

Perhaps I should mention that he shares a shack on the beach with Ron Husmann, a novitiate boy toy who's learning the ropes. This is the setting for Hugh's big extortion attempt: he snaps some Polaroid shots of Ruth reclining nude in his bed. Confronted with the evidence, she forks over a check for a thousand dollars—not for blackmail, but for services rendered. "You coulda had it all. . . . I'm blackmail-proof," she explains. "My reputation has long gone." Roman gets every nuance just right, and I doubt that there's a gay man anywhere who can't identify with the scene.

Love Letters of a Portuguese Nun* (Germany 1976 C)

When a movie bears a title as wantonly (and intriguingly) exploitative as *Love Letters of a Portuguese Nun*, we know that we're hot on the trail of camp. I think it's fair to say I've got a nose for these things.

Our heroine is Maria, played by Susan Hemingway. The opening scene finds her clad in green and lavender and romping in the meadow with her boyfriend, Christobel. These innocent antics are interrupted by a priest (William Berger) who, to the accompaniment of what sounds like Bach, drags the straying girl home to her fretful mother.

"I must work to support both of us! My life is that of a washwoman!" Mom protests.

"Very praiseworthy, yet it's not enough," suavely intones the padre. "Your wine is good," he adds.

"May I give you a bottle of it? I prepare it myself."

It's decided that the only way to save Maria's soul is to put her in a convent. Every penny of Mom's life savings (and every bottle of her homemade wine) is still not enough to pay the way; the padre takes it all anyway, of course, as a token of the family's good faith.

Upon arrival at the abbey, Maria is interviewed by the Mother Superior, who, however, specifies, "Always address me as 'Most Eminent Priestess.'"

"I didn't know that," Maria stammers.

"You're just an ignorant peasant!"

"Forgive me," Maria replies, more calmly (and perhaps with a tinge of sarcasm).

"Now you know how to address me."

"Yes, Most Eminent Priestess."

"Are you a virgin?"

"Yes, Eminent Priestess."

"Remove your frock. We must prove that, before you are admitted to this cloister."

"Lamb to the slaughter," titters one of the novices furtively watching from the doorway. The prioress clearly gets off on the ensuing examination, giving Maria's hymen a brutal thrust as she declares its firmness. But that's nothing, compared to the poor child's first confession. Berger cross-examines her regarding her dreams and desires, vigorously masturbating himself all the while. "Were you stimulated . . . excited?" he pants. His groans and moans of orgasm echo outside the confessional; the waiting postulants unsuccessfully strive to contain their giggles. ("Is there something wrong, Padre? Don't you feel well?" Maria innocently inquires.) It is a very long and satisfying confession.

Maria is coaxed into lesbian games by the other girls. Of course, they are caught in the act by that killjoy prioress. "You make friends very quickly," she drily observes. Not that *she's* any paragon of virtue. Seems she's a committed devil-worshiper, as we learn when she undergoes a Satanic ritual that looks suspiciously like an abortion. (She was carrying Berger's child, conceived during a black mass on Walpurgis Night.)

It occurs to me that this order is somewhat lax, perhaps even heretical. Conveniently enough, the headquarters of the Inquisition are located right next door. Maria should give a good yell out the window, rather than resorting to desperate stratagems like writing home to Mom. Of course, the incriminating missive is intercepted. ("The consequences of this letter could have been terrible! Watch it burn, for it's also your soul in hell when you die!") The Grand Inquisitor proves not to be her salvation, either: when at last she complains to him, he pronounces her a witch and sentences her to be burned at the stake.

There is nothing new about any of this. Anti-Catholic screeds about lustful prelates are centuries older than the motion picture camera. Since our enemies these days are found in both the Catholic and anti-Catholic camps, it seems no more than just that we should sit back and enjoy this "love letter," simply as light entertainment.

The Loved One   (U.S. 1965 B&W)

The Loved One, based on Evelyn Waugh's novel and co-scripted by Terry Southern and Christopher Isherwood, is a nihilistic comedy of manners, the manners being those of Southern California. Robert Morse portrays a Britisher confused and corrupted by the American way of life—or, to be more exact, the American way of death, since he ends up working at a mortuary for household pets. This complicates his romance with leading lady Anjanette Comer, an embalmer at a more prestigious institution: Whispering Glades, a cemetery where the elite meet. Both businesses are controlled by the Blessed Reverend Glenworthy (Jonathan Winters), a pious hypocrite who nowadays would no doubt be a televangelist denouncing gays and feminists.

What makes this movie camp is its sublimely outré cast. The fruitiest performance is provided by Rod Steiger, no small feat in a film which includes such off-the-wall talents as Robert Morley, Tab Hunter, Roddy McDowall, and (in the role of a casket salesman) Liberace. (At one stage in the production, the inimitable Jayne Mansfield was also featured, but her scenes were unfortunately excised.) Steiger is cast as Mr. Joyboy, a bleach-blonde beautician in charge of cadaver cosmetology, who occasionally sends Anjanette mash notes pinned to corpses. He lives with his mother (Ayllene Gibbons), a gross behemoth who spends her days in bed watching food commercials on television, her manner as lewdly avid as that of a lecher viewing a striptease. In her final scene, a refrigerator tips over on top of her. This could've been a great part for Edith Massey. I saw this film when I was a senior in high school. It was my introduction to the realm of cinematic grunge humor.

Ludwig (Italy 1973 C)

Ludwig, a three-hour biopic about mad King Ludwig of Bavaria (the European cut is said to run *four* hours), offers us a tantalizing glimpse of what life must have been like for nineteenth-century royalty. Looks very pleasant, indeed. (Never mind that most folks were in misery.) I can't help but think that I should have lived in those days. "But there weren't any films," I can hear you saying. Well, it happens I feel that life itself was like a movie back then.

The atmosphere of this film is comparable to that of an old-fashioned parlor crammed full of overstuffed furniture. As portrayed by Helmut Berger, King Ludwig II comes across as a fastidious old queen, fond of candy and handsome young men. He may not be much of a monarch, but he sure knows how to tip. A principal beneficiary of his largesse is composer Richard Wagner. As played by Trevor Howard, he is neither young nor handsome, but he certainly looks like Wagner.

At one point, His Majesty sends a fan letter to an attractive young actor (Folker Bohnet), inviting him to come stay with him at one of his many castles. (Significantly, this is the actor's reward for having given a superlative performance as Shakespeare's Romeo.) In the movie's prettiest—and campiest—scene, the awestricken fellow is ushered into a subterranean grotto for his initial audience with the king. A waterfall cascades into an underground river stocked with swans. To the accompaniment of music from *Tannhäuser*, Ludwig comes sailing onscreen in a gondola fashioned to resemble a giant sea shell (and looking as though he fancies himself Venus in the famous painting by Botticelli). Together the two men feed the swans.

From here, it's just a hop, skip, and a jump to drunken carousing with the stableboys, a declaration of insanity, and a royal suicide. All very sad, of course, but the director (Luchino Visconti) takes care not to let us get too deeply involved.

M. Butterfly* (G.B. 1993 C)

The presence of Jeremy Irons, that glum embodiment of tortured sensitivity, ordinarily precludes the possibility of camp. *M. Butterfly*, however, is simply too perverse and bizarre to leave out. The setting is Red

China in the mid-'Sixties. Irons is cast as a French diplomat who attends a performance of *Madama Butterfly* and falls head-over-heels in love with the leading lady. Trouble is, she's a man, portrayed by John Lone (who is not particularly convincing in the role of somebody passing as a woman; indeed, with his long, dark hair, he looks more like an American Indian brave). On the Chinese stage, women are invariably played by men. Other characters in the film seem thoroughly aware of this fact, but Irons, stubbornly oblivious, embarks on a passionate love affair with the fellow, fully believing him to be female. Turns out that the opera star is a spy, who's pumping Irons for info on American troop movements in Vietnam. He even convinces Irons that he's pregnant and that Irons is the father. Since, obviously, these two men have had nothing but oral and anal intercourse, this constitutes a major hole in the plot (or, to put it another way, Lone is missing a major hole that would make the story more credible). I realize that the Irons character is supposed to be a hapless patsy, but didn't anyone ever teach him about the birds and the bees? At one point in the narrative, he ponderously intones to Lone, "I'm not what you think I am." *He* should talk!

---

*Macho Dancer** (Philippines 1988 C)

If this film is any indication, there are plenty of great-looking guys in the Philippines. The movie starts right out with a couple of them having sex with each other. One of them is the principal character, a Filipino played by Alan Paule. When his lover, an American soldier, departs for the States, he repairs to Manila, where he supports himself as a call boy. When he seeks a position at a gay night spot, the uncouth manager demands a look at his equipment. ("Hurry up. It won't jump out by itself.") The floor show at this sleazy establishment consists of about a dozen teenage boys sudsing up their crotches and playing with themselves.

The film is consistently absorbing, though perhaps a bit overlong (there's an elaborate subplot about a search for a girl who's the victim of a prostitution ring). This movie has the potential to become a gay cult item. It's not lacking in camp elements, either. Our hero finds employment in a classier joint where he's taken on as a "macho dancer." This means that he and another young man must sinuously writhe together while dressed in nothing but their jockey shorts. Their faces aglow with ersatz ecstasy, they rub up against one another to a disco beat, while soap bubbles dance in the air all about them. Although I dislike the taste of soap, I can imagine few sights more tastefully erotic.

The Mad Ghoul* (U.S. 1943 B&W)

The Mad Ghoul features a cast that spells high-octane camp in capital letters. It's got practically every lower-echelon contract player in the 'Forties Universal stable. The plot is sort of like some wildly improbable soap opera invaded by incongruous horror elements. A talented soprano (Evelyn Ankers) embarks upon a concert tour with her effeminate accompanist (Turhan Bey), with whom she is besmitten. Oh, bother! Here comes her old boyfriend (David Bruce), whom a crazed scientist (George Zucco) has transformed into a killer zombie that subsists upon a diet of freshly stolen human hearts. These bad guys want Turhan out of the way. In a suspenseful sequence they corner him in the alley behind the opera house; he is only rescued by Evelyn's sudden high C as she catches sight of the fiend's looming shadow. The shadow of suspicion is the next to threaten Turhan. "You can never tell about these musicians. A lot of them are pretty queer ducks," observes police inspector Milburn Stone, who also questions Miss Ankers as to how it feels "to share the spotlight . . . with a homicidal maniac!" A comic subplot features a pair of newspaper reporters on unrelated assignments who meet unexpectedly in town after town: Robert Armstrong is a crime columnist trailing the mad ghoul; Rose Hobart is a fine arts editor covering Evelyn's recitals; these two are the first to put two and two together. The soprano's sentimental arias create jarring juxtapositions when contrasted with shots of grave robbery and the theft of the bona fide organ most frequently mentioned in her songs. Expressive camerawork wrings maximum interest from a low-budget, meager production design. Smoothly performed, too, especially by Miss Ankers. There ain't no one who can fret as professionally as this actress, and she's got plenty of cause for alarm here. As for Turhan, one line says it all: "Nothing ghoulish-looking about that guy!"

TURHAN BEY (1920–   ) looks as suave and exotic as ever in this publicity photo from *The Mad Ghoul* (Universal 1943). Accompanied here by EVELYN ANKERS (1918–1985).

Madame X* (U.S. 1965 C)

There is nothing remotely homosexual about this film, save for the fact that a man would have to *be* homosexual to be interested in it. *Madame X* marked the apotheosis of Lana Turner as a camp icon. In the perfect falsity of its pyrotechnics, this wheezingly decrepit weeper formed the appropriate capstone to Lana's career. Plump and matronly, Lana was forty-five years old when she made this film, and she looked every minute of it. But she's cast as a blushing bride approximately twenty years younger than she actually is. In deference to this, she's been surrounded with other middle-aged women who are similarly striving to appear girlish and glamorous. The effect is, to say the least, peculiar. Constance Bennett, sixty-one and virtually at death's door (she died just prior to the film's release), is cast as Lana's mother-in-law. However, because of their elegant costumes and painstaking make-up, the two women look to be about the same age! (Which is to say, no particular age at all.)

The prevailing vagueness extends considerably beyond such simple matters as this. For example, the film has absolutely no sense of period. Indeed, it steadfastly resists the very idea. We are constantly being shown newspaper headlines, but the newspapers are always undated. The only reference point we're provided is the fact that Lana has a child who, by the end of the film, is in his middle to late twenties. Therefore the plot chronology must necessarily include World War II, which, however, goes entirely unmentioned in the script.

Believe it or not, even the music suffers from this overall lack of specificity. After the threat of scandal has irrevocably separated her from her husband and family, Lana has a brief romance with a concert pianist (John Van Dreelen). However, he never plays anything recognizably classical. Like the movie itself, his music is bland, generic, and made-for-TV.

I deliberately refrain from discussing the plot because, in an almost avant-garde sense, the story is quite beside the point. All that we are supposed to care about is the fact that we're watching a bunch of opulent-looking people who move through luxurious surroundings and are dressed in tasteful, pastel clothing (gowns by Jean Louis). Lana is consistently ludicrous, almost all the way up to the bitter end. Then, in the final reel, she manages to pull a rabbit out of her hat: her deathbed reunion with her son (Keir Dullea) is compelling and convincing. This does not mean she's a good actress. What made Lana such a fun actress was the energetically histrionic quality of her performances (in a word, her campiness). One never really knew what she'd do next. The hapless generality of *Madame X* gives her plenty of latitude to do whatever she feels like.

---

*Mademoiselle** (G.B. 1966 B&W, French with English subtitles)

Mademoiselle's title character is the repressed and frustrated schoolmistress (Jeanne Moreau) of a primitive and isolated village somewhere in France. In the very first scene, she releases her sexual tensions by opening the gate of the local reservoir and flooding the entire community. She also dabbles in arson; barn-burnings are her specialty. She poisons the friendly beasts of the field. She can't even walk past a bird's nest without stopping to crush the eggs. This is one mean bitch.

What's driving her bananas is the presence of a lusty itinerant Italian woodcutter (Ettore Manni) in the vicinity. The xenophobic peasants suspect that he's the culprit molesting their farms. They're jealous because he's been porking every woman in town. When he finally gets around to Mademoiselle, she lets everybody think that he raped her. The outraged villagers beat him to death. She leaves town a respected and well-beloved heroine.

This sublimely cynical opus was directed by Tony Richardson (*The Loved One*) and scripted by Jean Genet (*Un Chant d'Amour*). The presentation of the woodcutter testifies to Genet's involvement. Manni strips off his shirt at every opportunity and also has a revealing bath scene. Furthermore, he's consistently linked with phallic objects (his roaring chainsaw, for example). In the movie's most outrageous scene, he invites Moreau to caress his pet snake.

---

*Mame** (U.S. 1974 C)

This, of course, is our old friend *Auntie Mame* dressed up as a musical. It is all too obviously a multimillion-dollar spectacle. I'm astounded that such a vast expenditure of time, effort, and money could result in such a perfectly tedious motion picture. The secret, I think, resides in the casting. The title role has been given to Lucille Ball, who looks absolutely antediluvian and, furthermore, can't sing. (Indeed, her utter lack of musical ability was used as a running gag on the old *I Love Lucy* television series.) What's worse, the entire production has been ostentatiously designed to showcase her as a Great Lady of the Screen. This has the unintended effect of making the movie even more inert. A portrait of her (painted in the swooningly decadent style of Gustav Klimt) adorns her posh apartment in the film. It is considerably more dazzling than her performance.

What this movie could and should have been is hinted at in the splendid hauteur of Beatrice Arthur's performance. With marvelous wit, she has hit upon the novel idea of playing Vera Charles, Mame's dearest chum, as a drag queen. She looks, acts, and talks like a man dressed up as a woman. Indeed, an unprejudiced observer would think that that's what she really was. Contributing to this vivid impression is Arthur's big musical number, which is entitled "The Man in the Moon Is a Lady" and includes such suitably fruity lyrics as "Don't ever offend her! / Remember her gender!" and "The cow that jumped over / cried, 'Jumpin' Jehovah! / I think it's just one of the girls!' " This song, by the way, has almost the same identical melody as "I've Written a Letter to Daddy," which was sung so memorably by Miss Bette Davis in *What Ever Happened to Baby Jane?.*

The supporting cast is large and richly varied. It saddens me to see such diverse talents as Ruth McDevitt and Roger Price appearing in such frustratingly useless capacity.

The Mating Season   (U.S. 1951 B&W)

The Mating Season stars Thelma Ritter and Miriam Hopkins, two cult actresses, each with a sizable gay following. They are cast as a pair of mothers-in-law in this withering comment on marriage and social class (the director is Mitchell Leisen, a kind of sub-Cukor known for his skill with female players). John Lund is an enterprising prole who weds Gene Tierney, the daughter of an ambassador. John's mom is Thelma, who's forced to hitchhike to the nuptials because the bank has just foreclosed on her hamburger stand. She chickens out of attending the ceremony when she learns what a ritzy affair it's gonna be. Instead, she introduces herself to Gene a few weeks later, coincidentally showing up on the day John is bringing home his boss for dinner. The kitchen's a shambles, the turkey's on fire, and the poor kid's overwhelmed. She mistakes

Thelma for hired help and Thelma's only too glad to go along with the gag. Lund lets the error stand, at Thelma's request. She rather enjoys being mistaken for a servant; it lets her help out without seeming to interfere. She can win people over with her hamburgers, while her unschooled grammar passes unnoticed.

This is Ritter's show from start to finish. The corners of her mouth drooping down in a look of perpetual resignation, she is everybody's favorite working-class grandmother. But, though Thelma's performance is the best, Miriam's is surely the campiest. Cast as a bitchy high-society snob, she is overbearing as only she can be. And her flair for lurid melodrama is beyond compare. When she overhears the mother and son having a heart-to-heart chat, she jumps to the conclusion that they've just had sex with each other! ("He was wearing his pajamas! She was wearing her nightgown! They were kissing!") Even the least likely movies have moments of unexpected sensationalism.

The Merry Widow* (U.S. 1934 B&W)

In her role as *The Merry Widow*, Jeanette MacDonald is so shrouded in veils, we half expect her to collide with the furniture. Despite its reputation as a great screen musical and despite its surface text of militant heterosexuality, the film makes furious signals in a gay camp direction. Edward Everett Horton (with a monocle, yet) is Baron Popov (pronounced "Pop-off"). Una Merkel is the Queen. Sterling Holloway is a blonde bellboy in a skintight uniform who attempts, unsuccessfully, to undress the very inebriated Maurice Chevalier. When, finally, Maurice and Jeanette are locked up in a dungeon together, Horton and George Barbier try to act out the love scene they imagine is transpiring within ("I begin to realize that, after all, you are a woman," says Barbier to Horton). The movie is richly entertaining, but it's about as faithful to Lehar's operetta as the characters are to each other.

Messalina Against the Son of Hercules* (Italy 1962 C)

The title is intriguing, but inconclusive. In what sense is she against him? Is she leaning against him? Is she lying against him? Is she rubbing up against him? None of the above, it turns out, since, in this film, Caligula's the one who's on the make for him. The movie begins with the Roman emperor enslaving the inhabitants of ancient Britain. Glaucus (Richard Harrison), a long-lost British son of Hercules, is taken captive in the roundup. Caligula orders that most of the male prisoners be slain. "Not that one!" he shrills, however, upon catching sight of Harrison's firm and shapely haunches. The muscleman also sports a seemingly impermeable pompadour and wears what appears to be a Naugahyde toga. I'm afraid I cannot comment regarding his chest, since he keeps it so chastely covered up, one begins to suspect that there may be something wrong with it. A tattoo, perhaps? A basket of fruit emblazoned with the word "Mother"?

Later, at the arena, amid the gladiators, Cal is disappointed by Son of Herc's disobedience. "Kill! Kill! Kill!" roars the emperor. Glaucus shuts the old queen up by hurling a javelin in his general direction. What's this? An assassination attempt?! Caligula freaks out. Has a fainting fit, in fact. Later, while servant boys dab at his forehead with damp cloths, he decrees that "Killing is much too good for him. He needs a punishment all Rome will remember."

Messalina too is no slouch as a disciplinarian. (She's portrayed by Lisa Gastoni, who looks a bit too long in the tooth for the role of a woman who died at age twenty-six.) One scene finds her flogging her slave girls, including the blonde-haired Hana, true love of Glaucus. Messalina is also partial to milk baths. (This I can only assume. The script fails to specify the nature of the fluid. It looks like water laced with cum.) All appearances (and historical records) to the contrary, she seems sexually frustrated. Out of desperation, she orders that Glaucus be brought before her. "Leave him with me and go away," she curtly instructs the servants. "Do you know the purpose of all this?" she asks the demigod, tauntingly. "You want to play with me before you kill me," he snickers. Though she evidently doesn't have her way with him, she makes him her "personal bodyguard," anyhow.

Having disposed of Caligula, she plots to steal the throne of her husband, Claudius. However, for reasons unclear to me, Glaucus and Hana must first be burned alive. While watching the execution, Messalina and her co-conspirator, Gaius Silius, betray a certain peevishness: "What a waste! With that smoke, I can't see the lovebirds being roasted." "Tell them to stop adding wood!" Fortunately, the auto-da-fé is unexpectedly interrupted by the timely arrival of Claudius and his troops. Messalina takes poison, and the film concludes with kindly old Claudius bidding Glaucus and Hana to go in peace. He might also have urged them to say hello to his nephew, Nero, on their way out.

The Midnight Girl* (U.S. 1925 B&W)

Music hath charms, and so doth camp, and opera hath even more, which is probably why so many homosexuals are opera queens. *The Midnight Girl* begins at the Met, where our hero (Gareth Hughes) occupies a box seat with his fiancée (Ruby Blaine), who has nothing favorable to say about the soprano onstage ("She is passé. Her voice is going—and so am I."). Gareth is indifferent (Ruby's mother complains, "He seems about as ardent as a sick goldfish."). But then he encounters leading lady Lila Lee, cast as "Anna Meridoff, a refugee from Russia's red ruin." She's got the sweetest voice this side of heaven and would seem to be destined for a triumphant career as a diva. First, however, she must serve her apprenticeship as "the Midnight Girl," a cabaret singer who appears each night at the stroke of twelve, swooping about in a bat costume. Thus attired, she naturally draws the attention of co-star Bela Lugosi, a patron of the arts who kisses her hand and promises to exercise his influence on her behalf. Gareth counsels caution: "Do not mar your career as a woman to further your progress as a singer." And, in fact, Lugosi does seem a bit ambiguous: at one point, he asks Miss Blaine to give him "a weenie little kiss"; at another point, Dracula-like, he picks Gareth up in his arms and carries him bodily out of the cabaret. That's sure one way to pick up a guy at a bar.

Mishima: A Life in Four Chapters* (U.S. 1985 C)

Ken Ogata is the actor cast as Yukio Mishima, the great Japanese writer who is also revered as an icon of gay culture. In the opening scene he's wearing a gorgeous turquoise silk dressing gown, but (sigh) he quickly exchanges that for a military uniform. (Mishima's latent Fascism serves, I fear, to keep him somewhat less than fully sympathetic.) In a series of black-and-white flashbacks and to the accompaniment of a hypnotic Philip Glass score, the movie covers the highlights of the author's life. We learn how, as a boy, he got his first hard-on from looking at a picture of St. Sebastian. (A sure sign that he's destined for a martyr's fate or, at the very least, an exciting career in S&M.) We learn that he became a bodybuilder because of a chance remark his lover made while they were dancing together in a gay bar. Ultimately, he is radicalized in a sharply rightward direction, denouncing the corruption of capitalism and the intrusive introduction of Yankee lipstick and nail polish. The movie and the author both come to a gory end, but at least we can savor some pithy bits of wisdom along the way. Like, for instance, the scene wherein Mishima contemplates aging, death, and human longevity: "The average age for men in the Bronze Age was 18. In the Roman era, 22. Heaven must have been beautiful then. Today it must look dreadful." Oh, honey, how true! I'm sure it's simply full of old, saggy-assed queens.

Montana Belle
(U.S. 1952 Released in color. Shown on TV generally only in B&W)

Montana Belle is Jane Russell as Belle Starr. She hooks up with the Dalton brothers when one of them (Scott Brady) saves her from a lynch mob. He escorts her to the rustic cabin where the rest of the gang is holed up. "A squaw!" growls Ringo, a surly Native American, when Jane makes her grand entrance. "Only trouble come with squaw!" Then he spits.

Neither is Jane real enthused about sharing quarters. That evening she washes the dinner dishes; Scott wipes 'em. "I can't stand much more of this!" she grumbles. She and Scott were not really born to do housework.

Soon she's riding and robbing and shooting, planning elaborate bank jobs, and putting together a gang of her own. Once she's got a nest egg, however, she settles down, dyes her hair platinum blonde, and seeks respectability. She even falls in love with a local nabob: puffy, dyspeptic George Brent, who's probably old enough to be her father. In her criminal mode, she disguises herself as a boy. She looks rather odd in this capacity. I mean, if this is a guy, what are those huge growths on his chest?!

The ironies of this film tend to be social and moral, rather than sexual, but that doesn't make them any less campy. Lip service is paid to law and order and to the concept of paying one's debt to society, but we can readily tell where the movie's heart is. How can the outlaws be bad guys when they never stray from their code of honor? What becomes of a town's civic virtue when its most elegant lady turns out to have a price on her head? "Subversive" is perhaps too strong a word to use in connection with this film. Conventionality does triumph, but only just barely, and only by implication.

Morgan the Pirate* (Italy 1961 C)

According to historical records, Captain Henry Morgan appears to have been that true oddity, a heterosexual pirate. As played by Steve Reeves, however, he can't help but be of interest to gay men. Although *Morgan the Pirate* takes place in the seventeenth century, he never misses an opportunity to strip to the waist, revealing his biceps and pectorals. (In fact, during a swordfight, he even shreds the shirt of his opponent.) Thus undraped, he is first discovered being whipped in the slave market of Panama City. He is purchased by the governor's daughter (Valerie Lagrange), who knows a good piece of flesh when she sees it. She, however, bundles him up in silk and satin uniforms. We know that, one way or another, he'll soon have his freedom, and, sure enough, before too long he's sailing the Spanish Main beneath a sword-and-crossbones flag.

In my favorite scene, all his men dress up in drag to deceive the crew of a Spanish ship that they aim to plunder. (One hefty fellow uses grapeshot for falsies.) The ruse succeeds: the Spaniards mistake Morgan's men for a cargo of female slaves being shipped to the West Indies. (Not a very likely story, by the way: female slaves were not much in demand in the 17th-century Indies, one of history's true homosexual paradises.)

These gay doings are staged with unusual solemnity by director Andre de Toth. He brings a real romantic punch to the love scenes involving Reeves and Lagrange. Kisses in this movie pack an almost operatic wallop. The requisite moments of campiness are included, too, of course (Spanish noblewomen, for example, nibbling on hors d'oeuvres while watching a man being drawn and quartered). The opening titles list "the extraordinary participation of Chelo Alonso." She plays a waitress. She does, however, perform a voodoo dance which is rather special. And she sure knows how to caress a newel post when she wants to show she's horny. But the kinkiest thing about this movie is the concept of Steve Reeves playing someone with a wimpy name like Henry.

My Own Private Idaho* (U.S. 1991 C)

My Own Private Idaho, an arty-farty cult film tailor-made for pretentious snobs, is all about a pair of inarticulate, coke-snorting male prostitutes. How could such a quintessentially 'Sixties film be made in 1991?

Our callow heroes (Keanu Reeves and River Phoenix) have sundry dealings with an assortment of middle-aged male customers about whom we are obviously not intended to care. Among them is Udo Kier (*Andy Warhol's Dracula*), who looks commendably well-preserved. Another one is a fussy old queen who insists that you take your shoes off before you set foot in his immaculate apartment. (Joan Crawford was the same way.)

The Keanu Reeves character ends up turning straight. He inherits a bundle of money, gets himself a girlfriend, and turns his back on all of his disreputable homo erstwhile buddies. So at least the movie is true to life. Reeves turns in a flamboyant, quasi-Shakespearean performance that's wildly out of synch with his scuzzy, neorealist surroundings. The River Phoenix character is narcoleptic. He falls asleep whenever he thinks of his mother. I fall asleep whenever I think of this movie.

Mystery of Marie Roget* (U.S. 1942 B&W)

This very, very loose adaptation of a tale by Edgar Allan Poe descends into camp the instant we learn who's playing Marie Roget. Why, it's Maria Montez! Cast as a star of the Comédie Francaise, she's got a glamorous pet leopard and wizened old Maria Ouspenskaya for a granny. Furthermore, she gets to sing a (ludicrously dubbed) French chanson. She's top-billed, but, after only four or five scenes, she gets murdered. Ouspenskaya quickly takes charge of the camp element. "You are chicky rascal," she tells Auguste Dupin (Patric Knowles). "I wun't stand for any more of dis chip sensationaleesm!"

Too late for any objections on that score. Dupin has sneaked into the morgue and made off with Montez's brain. Pretty quirky behavior for someone who's supposed to be the hero of the film. But there are, of course, mitigating factors. You see, the plot hinges on whether Montez kept a diary. Rather than go to the trouble of searching for one, it makes sense to just look at her brain, instead. "Marie had the mind of a criminal," Dupin explains. "A criminal doesn't keep a diary. In the hands of the police, it would be very embarrassing!" This is the brand of scientific logic we'd expect from the Three Stooges, but it nonetheless leads to the murderer's unmasking. A pretty predictable finale. Conversely, the opening scene is surprising. The film starts out with a man in a nightcap and nightgown leaning out of a window and telling the newsboy on the corner to hand-deliver a paper to his bedroom. The little tease, no doubt knowing precisely what's expected of him, claims to be too busy.

The Night Walker* (U.S. 1964 B&W)

"Do you dream of sex? Do you dream of violence?" These shrill inquiries are featured in the coming attractions trailer for The Night Walker, a meditation on the nocturnal subconscious that would stymie most Freudians. The title character is played by Barbara Stanwyck. She's married to a rich, blind, mad scientist (Hayden Rorke) who suspects that she's unfaithful. He records all of her conversations, even when she's talking in her sleep. "My lover is only a dream, but he's still more of a man than you!" she snarls at him, just before he hits her with his cane. Then his laboratory explodes, with him in it. His death leaves Barbara a very wealthy woman, so naturally she goes to work in a beauty parlor. But she keeps right on dreaming: about co-star Lloyd Bochner (the cast listing bills him as "the Dream," and he does look pretty dreamy). He takes her to a chapel for a funereal wedding that's attended by department store mannequins. When the wax dummy in the pulpit asks her if she takes this man to be her lawful wedded husband, Barbara lets loose with one of those sobbing screeches she does so well. The title is a misnomer: Barbara's obliged to run more than she walks. Of course, she turns out to be the victim of a diabolical scheme to drive her out of her mind. All this fuss could have been avoided, if only she was better able to sort out sleeping from waking.

Erotic dreams are a topic with which most homosexuals are intimately acquainted. It's significant that this movie consistently connects them with images of guilt and gore. This exercise in kitschy 'Sixties surrealism ends up an uneasy amalgam of art, camp, and commerce.

99 Women* (Spain 1968 C)

What could be more camp than a women's prison movie? That's easy: a *Eurotrash* women's prison movie. This one starts out with a trio of lasses being transported to the big house. (All three appear to be still dressed in the clothes they were arrested in.) Says one, as the prison looms into view: "The Spaniards built it and christened it . . . Castillo de Muerte!"

"Castle of Death!" translates another, helpfully.

Mercedes McCambridge is Thelma, the wicked warden. She procures nubile prisoners to sate the carnal appetites of her superior (Herbert Lom), the fatso in charge of the men's penitentiary next door. Rosalba Neri is Zoie, the resident dyke. And poor Maria Rohm is the new fish, who, in one memorable scene, is obliged to take on Herbert and Rosalba both.

Lurid flashbacks punctuate the proceedings. One girl reminisces about being gangbanged by a motorcycle club. Another waxes nostalgic about performing exotic dances at a lesbian bar. (We can tell the patrons are lesbians because they're all wearing neckties and business suits.)

Maria Schell is cast as a welfare worker who wants to improve conditions. We can't help but feel sorry for her; she and Mercedes are struggling to maintain their professional dignity under extremely adverse circumstances. "I should like to see the girl later . . . *alone*," says Schell to McCambridge, referring to pretty Ms. Rohm. Mercedes raises her eyebrows on cue and goes running to Herbert, accusing Schell of lesbianism. Since Mercedes spends much of the movie dressed in what looks like a Russian soldier's uniform, this is rather like the pot calling the kettle black.

No Escape* (G.B. 1994 C)

No Escape is a silly sci-fi actioner about prison camps of the future. Prison dramas are invariably replete with sweaty degradation and male-bonding. By placing the plot in the 21st century, the moviemakers have a pretext for upping the ultraviolence all the more. The warden resembles Louis B. Mayer (this may or may not be significant). He presides—

albeit via long-distance—over a tropical Devil's Island where the convicts are, to put it mildly, unsupervised. You've heard of Amazon women? Well, these appear to be Amazon men. They caper through the jungle virtually naked, their faces grotesquely painted and masked, as if for a *National Geographic* special. No form of dastardliness is beyond them. Even cannibalism is hinted at. They are utterly bestial and much of their time is spent ranting incoherently. Their leader is Stuart Wilson, a handsome actor accustomed to performing in more genteel entertainments (he's probably best known for his *Masterpiece Theatre* appearances). The cast of the film is entirely male; there isn't a woman in sight. Perhaps as a consequence, the plot nervously steers clear of sex. Still, with all the references to wet dreams and water sports, we know that *something* must be going on. Inherently gay, intrinsically camp, *No Escape* is nonetheless the perfect film for audiences that like to see a guy catch a burning arrow in his mouth in the middle of a yawn.

---

*The Oscar** (U.S. 1966 C)

This sordid wallow in 'Sixties sleaze was a camp classic from the day of its release. The film is derived from Richard Sale's novel about cutthroat competition for a Best Actor Oscar. Stephen Boyd is cast as Frankie Fane, an amoral opportunist who will do just about anything to win. Homosexual interest resides in the thoroughness with which the book's abundant gay references have been systematically excluded from the screenplay. In the movie, Fane is up against real-life 'Sixties superstars such as Burt Lancaster, Richard Burton, and Frank Sinatra. Save for a single brief exception, these guys are never glimpsed. In the novel, on the other hand, the competitors take an active part in the storyline. They are as fictitious as Fane, and one of them—a Britisher named Brett Chichester—is gay.

In both the book and the film, Frankie is temporarily disconcerted by the revelation of a scandal from his past. In the book he was an athletic model, nude photographs of whom appeared on a pack of gay pornographic playing cards. In the movie he was the emcee of a strip show starring Jill St. John. Quite a contrast.

Adding insult to injury, the script perversely and persistently underlines its own heterosexuality. At times this becomes downright obsessive, as when, for example, a group of TV executives discuss Frankie's potential as the star of a weekly series:

"I don't think we need to worry about Fane being a man."

"He looks like a *real* man."

"Hell, he's a man, all right!"

The supporting cast includes a number of real-life Oscar winners. Surprising that they'd stoop to this swill. Then again, maybe it's not so surprising. The campiest line of dialogue is when co-star Tony Bennett exclaims, in a tone of outraged innocence, "Prostitution?! What have *we* got to do with prostitution?!" I wish someone would tell him.

On Approval* (G.B. 1944 B&W)

Clive Brook scripted, produced, and directed this cute, quaint little comedy in which he has a bathing scene and claims to sleep in pink pajamas. Had it been anyone other than Clive Brook, I might almost have been interested. Leading lady Beatrice Lillie shares my lack of enthusiasm. "If you had a little more brain, you'd be in an asylum," she remarks to him waspishly. At one point he hands her his hat and umbrella, whereupon she flings them off the porch with peremptory dispatch. Moments later, she gives his nose a nasty, really agonizing tweak.

She and Roland Culver are shacked up at her castle in Scotland. No hanky-panky, mind you; they simply wish to discover whether their personalities are compatible for marriage. Googie Withers and Clive tag along—partly out of curiosity, partly to act as chaperones, and partly to follow suit, trying each other out "on approval." Poor, meek little Roland is utterly appalled by Ms. Lillie's termagant qualities, which, as I've indicated above, are amply demonstrated herein. And Googie, meanwhile, is rapidly disillusioned by Clive's chauvinistic need to be waited on hand and foot. Particularly since they're *her* hands and feet; the servants, scandalized by the dual immorality of two unmarried couples sharing the same habitation, have by this time fled the premises. The Victorian ambience is charming and lends the film a richness of visual appeal. Victorianism is also what makes the film camp: like *The Importance of Being Earnest* (discussed in Volume 1), *On Approval* is an exercise in absolute, unmitigated archness.

BEATRICE LILLIE (1894–1989), comedienne and actress was called "the funniest woman in the world." Shown here in a publicity photo of 1938.

The Painted Veil* (U.S. 1934 B&W)

Greta Garbo, in *The Painted Veil*, is billed simply as "Garbo." Furthermore, this name, in huge letters, remains onscreen throughout the opening titles, which are superimposed over it. One can't help wondering how the other players felt about this. (Not that these other players are anything to reckon with. In this picture Garbo has her choice of stodgy Herbert Marshall and moon-faced George Brent.)

The film is a serious distortion of the fine novel (by W. Somerset Maugham) from which it is derived. There's so much padding, the movie is half over before it even arrives at the point where the book begins. The setting is China. Greta Garbo is cast as the wife of a doctor (Herbert Marshall). He discovers that she has allowed herself to be seduced into a passionate affair with an outrageous flirt (George Brent). To punish her, he drags her with him to a remote town so stricken with cholera that the peasants are dropping dead in the streets. The campiest moment comes earlier, when Brent takes Garbo to see a Chinese religious festival that looks remarkably like an Oriental Ziegfeld Follies, complete with dragons and chorus girls (the latter waving scarves) descending a mammoth staircase together. One wonders what Maugham must have thought.

Paradise Plantation* (U.S. 1994 C)

After an hour or so at *Paradise Plantation*, we commence to wonder who's minding the farm. The owner, I suppose, though we never lay eyes on him. We *do* get to know his son, and that quite intimately. We discover him in his bath, where he's beating off while fantasizing about a farmhand loading bananas aboard the banana boat. (The name of the boat is the "Rambo.") He's surprised in his ablutions by a pair of lustful strangers who carnally use and abuse him. The setting is South America—Brazil, to be exact. None of the guys speak English, but it doesn't really matter, since the dialogue mainly consists of grunts and groans, the universal language of sex. The camera angles are extraordinarily imaginative. (Credit should go to director Kristen Bjorn, who also did the photography.) The main theme is a guitar fantasia based on a melody from *Tosca*. The best erotica, I've noticed, looks to the classics for inspiration.

Passing Strangers* (U.S. 1976 B&W, but the last half is in color)

What's this?! A gay porno flick with a plot and character development? A fuck film with tenderness and romance and a genuine sense of caring? Sounds like something from a bygone age.

Actually, *Passing Strangers* lacks that prurient feel which characterizes porn. It's like some little, low-budget art movie that just so happens to incidentally contain scenes of explicit gay sex. The storyline presents us with a couple of guys (a closeted teen and a streetwise cruiser) who meet via a personal ad in the *Berkeley Barb*. The film is pure 'Seventies, through and through. The director, Arthur J. Bressan Jr., has a real gift for telling a story and conveying a sense of character through cinematic means. Ironically enough, this works against the film succeeding as erotica. I didn't feel like I was watching guys have sex. Instead, since I'd already gotten to know them and care about them as people, I felt like I was simply watching a new development in their relationship.

Only part of the film is in color (a homage to *The Wizard of Oz*?). It occurs to me that cum photographs poorly in black-and-white. On the other hand, it looks more esthetic and less earthly.

Pearl of the South Pacific (U.S. 1955 C)

Pearl of the South Pacific has a story that's strictly from hunger. Says so right in the credits: "Story by Anna Hunger." Virginia Mayo and Dennis Morgan find a secret island where black pearls can be had. The beaches are athrong with happy, bongo-playing natives straight from the Copacabana. They worship an idol that looks like a Polynesian version of the Pillsbury Doughboy. The son of the high priest is shapely, succulent Lance Fuller, who's been promised in marriage to Lisa Montell, the daughter of a tribal chieftain. But Lance wants to go off and see the world. At any rate, he wants to see more of Virginia, who has memorized the Beatitudes so as to pass herself off as an innocent missionary lady. The drama which ensues has little to offer in the way of moral uplift. It does, however, contain the most flagrantly phony octopus of the 'Fifties (a decade renowned for its unconvincing octopi). And Fuller never once puts on a shirt.

Parrish* (U.S. 1961 C)

Early on in *Parrish*, Karl Malden sees an attractive middle-aged woman and her dreamboat son. "Who are they?" he asks Hampton Fancher. Hampton replies, "I don't know," but we, of course, *do* know: they're Claudette Colbert and Troy Donahue. Claudette has come to work for Dean Jagger as a paid companion for his wayward offspring, Diane McBain. The setting is a tobacco farm in Connecticut. Two of the field hands are Madeleine Sherwood and Sylvia Miles; when they catch sight of pretty boy Troy, they just about rape him where he stands. Connie Stevens (destined to be his frequent screen cohort) has a tad more class, but not a whole lot, and we don't see much of her after Colbert takes her straying son aside and gives him a lecture on the perils of loose women. Fortunately for this movie, he eventually takes refuge in the Navy, and we get to see a stimulatingly stirring montage of his maritime experiences. Troy wears an exciting assortment of sailor suits, and even gets assigned to a submarine on an Arctic expedition. At the end of his hitch, he goes back to the farm.

"Well, you've left your boyhood behind you, hmmm?" inquires Dean Jagger, insinuatingly.

"Yes, sir. One night under the ice at the North Pole," replies our hero. (I'll bet he found ways to keep warm.)

Aside from these moments (and some dewy close-ups of Troy, his blonde pompadour an architectonic marvel), this movie might as well be a documentary on the care and nurturing of tobacco plants. I never knew carcinogens required such tender, loving attention.

The Phantom Empire* (U.S. 1935 B&W)

The Phantom Empire is a bizarre meditation on the clash of alien cultures. "Cultures" is perhaps too strong a word; "alien," on the other hand, maybe isn't strong enough. This twelve-chapter serial begins at Radio Ranch—an aptly named establishment, since it's from here that leading man Gene Autry terrorizes the airwaves with his unspeakably

Troy Donahue (1936–   ), handsome hunk and heartthrob of the 1950s.

flat renditions of cowboy ballads. However, thousands of feet below all his barns and bunkhouses, there's a lost civilization known as "the Scientific City of Murania," ruled by the glamorously bitchy Queen Tika (Dorothy Christy), who is constantly calling people "Fools!" and "Imbeciles!" and ordering that they be dragged off to either the "Chamber of Death" or the "Cavern of the Doomed." She hates Gene Autry because he attracts too many tourists to Radio Ranch and she's scared they'll discover her lost civilization. So she's constantly having Gene kidnapped and he's constantly escaping so that he can get back to the surface in time to sing a number or two on his show. If he misses, even just one time, the bank will foreclose the mortgage and he'll lose Radio Ranch!

Gene is understandably ill at ease in Murania. Ever the advocate of sunshine and wholesomeness, he bravely denounces the undergrounders for their perversely decadent lifestyle. The queen maintains that her civilization is dedicated to the advancement of intellect (a peculiar argument, since she's always accusing her countrymen of terminal stupidity). Then she has him taken away to be executed. A "radium bomb" is dropped on him. The queen, however, suffers a change of heart and orders him brought back to life. The presiding physician protests that Gene is dead. With regal hauteur, Queen Tika replies, "No one is dead in Murania unless we do not wish to revive him."

She proves to be as good as her word. By now, she's got a new worry: her subjects are revolting against her. ("I never heard a queen scream," gloats one of the revolutionists. I sometimes wish that I could say likewise.) Gene and the queen forge an alliance to quell the insurgency. Muranian rebels are even now storming the palace gates! The fiercely contended conflict rapidly escalates. The bad guys avail themselves of a disintegrator ray. The city is doomed! Autry implores Tika to flee with him. He invites her to walk by his side in the daylight of Depression era America. She flatly refuses, on the grounds that, for her, "It would be a living death!" Murania melts and evaporates, like the substance of a dream from which the sleeper has awakened. In her throne room, Queen Tika sits serenely awaiting her fate. Her head held high to the bitter end, she wavers and blurs and finally fades away. Gene overcomes his grief and is last seen back at the microphone, yodeling another chorus of "Uncle Noah's Ark."

Lost civilizations are customarily explored by some intrepid, romantic, impassioned adventurer. At the very least, we expect someone with a measure of intelligence and sophistication. Gene Autry looks like he'd be more comfortable at a suburban barbecue. The singing cowboy he portrays is so mellow as to be soft, so bland as to be sissified, and, furthermore, is much given to falling into sudden swoons. In the course of the plot, he twice sees fit to exchange clothes with an overpowered blackguard: first with a renegade airplane pilot, and then with a captain of the Muranian Thunder Guard. (I can't help wondering what it's like to have a man at such a disadvantage that you can take all his clothes off.) At one point Gene attempts to pass himself off as a typical citizen of Murania. He ambles down the main boulevard of the kingdom, toting a bulky bundle to hide his face and thus conceal his identity. He chances to pass a swishy pair of male Muranians (both of them clad in elegantly flowing capes). One of them, noticing Gene traipsing by, turns to the other and says, "Things have come to a sorry pass when a Muranian must labor. What do you suppose has happened to his robot?"

Said robots, by the way, look like they're made out of stovepipes and milk buckets. The charm of low-budget sci-fi lies in its phoniness. However, I'm perfectly able to suspend my disbelief. Indeed, if there's such a thing as reincarnation, I'd like to come back as Queen Tika.

Pink Narcissus* (U.S. 1971 C)

There is room in the realm of camp for experimental, non-narrative cinema, a genre to which Pink Narcissus belongs, though the film often teeters precariously on the brink of gay porn. Such balancing acts, in my opinion, automatically qualify a film as art.

The movie begins in a moonlit jungle so patently artificial, I'm sure that Maria Montez would have felt perfectly at home there. Our hero (darkly voluptuous Bobby Kendall) has more costume changes than she ever had. Each of his ensembles includes extremely tight britches. One scene finds him in the guise of a toreador. This turns out to be a fantasy which occupies his mind while having sex in a T-room with a blonde biker in a black leather jacket.

Bobby's bachelor pad includes an impossibly glitzy mirrored boudoir. (The street outside is populated with homoerotic icons: cowboy, construction worker, sailor, hustler, etc.) The furnishings and accessories are simply too divine for words. Bobby picks up his sequin-covered phone and starts to dial a number. Then he decides to just jack off, instead, meanwhile contemplating a distant volcano. (A close-up of his nipple looms like Mt. Vesuvius.)

The scenario hurtles us back and forth through time and space. The most frankly erotic scene transpires in the court of an Eastern potentate. A naked belly-dancer with a hard-on gives a whole new meaning to the term "jiggle." The scene concludes with the picture's only cum shot.

The bold (some might call them lurid) colors of this film are uniformly oversaturated. The music is mainly by Mussorgsky. The film as a whole is a gloriously inspiring exercise in bad taste. Gay men with good taste have no business reading this book.

Poison* (U.S. 1991 C)

Poison, a homoerotic art picture directed by Todd Haynes, was a subject of controversy at the time of its release, mainly because it was partially funded by the National Endowment for the Arts. But even Jerry Falwell would have to admit they got good value for their money. This low-budget movie looks like a million bucks, is a thoroughly professional production, and never even once strikes a false note. For our purposes, it's also of interest because it has all the makings of a gay cult film.

The basic structure is borrowed from Griffith's *Intolerance*. We cut back and forth between three different stories. Each of these has its own symbolic language, which, with varying degrees of obliqueness, pertains to AIDS. The most oblique, and also the most basic, is called "Hero": a simulation of a television documentary about a seven-year-old boy who shoots his father and ascends into heaven. The themes explored herein are of primal significance: the rebellion against patriarchy and the general destructiveness of traditional male roles. We were all of us children once. And many of us didn't get along very well with our fathers.

The campiest of the narratives is called "Horror": a perfectly realized parody of a late 'Fifties/early 'Sixties B-grade horror film. A researcher distills the liquid essence of the human sex drive, then mistakenly ingests it, confusing it with his coffee. Of course, he's quickly transformed into a leprous sex killer, whose kiss is virulently infectious.

The most powerful story, entitled "Homo," portrays the convolutions which characterize sexual relations in a French prison. Violence and sex and macho posturing are here inextricably linked. The missing factor is love. In this skanky environment, love is a guilty secret and a source of shame. Love between men is the poison that haunts and terrifies the entire world. The nuclear family feels particularly threatened by it. Love and death—love and disease—have become synonymous in the new world order. Who, we might ask, is poisoning whom? This is a film that offers no answers, but raises some extremely provocative questions.

Powertool* (U.S. 1988 C)

Powertool is a prison picture starring Jeff Stryker, noted gay erotic icon. Of course, upon his arrival at the big house, one of the first things he's told to do is to remove his clothes.

"Spread those cheeks! I said spread 'em! Spread 'em wide!" orders the guard, whose oh-so-butch uniform looks just a tad too neatly tailored for credibility.

"You like lookin' at that asshole, don't ya?" sneers Jeff, his insolence verging on the sublime.

"Listen, jerkoff! I can make your life here heaven or hell! The choice is yours." Stryker makes his choice, and the consequences are heavenly.

Stryker has a tendency to be somewhat garrulous during intercourse. ("Ah love fuckin' this tight purty li'l ass!") He looks a bit like a pumped-up Elvis Presley. Sounds like one, too. His line of conversation, however, does grow repetitious. I wish I had a nickel for every time he says, "Tighten that ass!" I do like the fact that the first big sex scene is followed by a shot of inmates mopping the floor. I've always felt that boys should learn to clean up after themselves.

The director is a comparative newcomer named John Travis. The dialogue delivery of his cast may leave something to be desired, but at least the creaking of the bedsprings sounds convincing. This movie gives us more plot to chew on than is provided in other Stryker vehicles (In Hot Pursuit, etc.). I appreciated the soap-operatic melodrama of the conclusion: released from jail, Stryker goes home and discovers his male roommate fucking another man! Deeply offended, he turns right around and leaves, presumably never to return. I must say I find his sense of moral outrage difficult to fathom. I mean, his own behavior in the hoosegow was hardly a model of fidelity and chastity. Why should the roommate be held to a Penelope-like standard of conduct that nobody else in the movie adheres to?

Problem Girls (U.S. 1953 B&W)

Problem Girls lives up to its name. The hero and narrator (Ross Elliott) informs us that he's a hardened veteran of World War II who fought in the jungles of Burma and survived a stretch in a Japanese prison camp. And yet he avers that the "most dangerous period" of his life was the term he spent teaching at a place called the Manning School for Girls.

The first person to greet him on campus is a student played by Beverly Garland. "This is a girls' school!" she points out. "You have no business here!" Meanwhile the headmistress (Helen Walker) is berating an inebriated colleague. "Don't give me any of your professorial platitudes, you disgusting old sot!" Helen scolds. "I won't have you seen this way! You're a disgrace to the position you hold here!" His position is halfway between sitting and reclining when Ross comes tapping at the door. Before letting him in, Helen offers some last-minute directives: "Straighten up! Wipe your mouth! You're slobbering!"

She describes to Ross the distinctiveness which characterizes the student body: "Most of our girls are here because they proved embarrassments in their homes." In point of fact, there are a good many households that would indeed be embarrassed by outbreaks of arson, kleptomania, and the other girlish peccadillos depicted herein. Girls who become especially problematic are hung by their wrists from the ceiling of the shower room and subjected to drenching downpours of ice-cold water. In her role as the presiding sadistic tyrant, Walker chews the scenery like a bush-league Bette Davis. It all works up to a camp crescendo of sorts, when the limpwristed piano instructor pounds out a performance of "The Mephisto Waltz" by Franz Liszt, the diabolical cadences of which are seen to inspire a jealous lesbian catfight to break out in the audience!

The Purchase Price* (U.S. 1932 B&W)

This may not be one of Barbara Stanwyck's best-known films, but it's certainly one of her most entertaining. She plays a torch singer in a night club and she's fixing to ditch her gangster boyfriend (Lyle Talbot). So she changes her name to Francine La Rue and moves to Montreal.

BARBARA STANWYCK (1907–1990) in a publicity photo from the 1930s.

One of Talbot's henchmen traces her there, so she figures she'd better scramola. Her next stop is Elk's Crossing, North Dakota, where a gauche, snuffly farmer (George Brent) is looking to buy himself a wife.

The train ride to North Dakota is instructive. Barbara listens to the other mail-order brides exchanging wisecracks:

"You know what they say about men with bushy eyebrows and a long nose?"

"Oh, Queenie! I can tell you've been married before!"

The wedding is like Emily Post's worst nightmare. The justice of the peace chews tobacco and spits in the flower pots. The witnesses are the village idiot and a fat housewife stirring a bowlful of cake batter. Midway through the ceremony, a dogfight erupts in the front yard.

Turns out that Barbara was not George's first attempt at feminine companionship. She learns this when she discovers a hairpin in his bed. He confesses that he once had a live-in housekeeper: "She was an Indian squaw. She weighed 250 pounds and she smelled. Took me two weeks to get rid of the bedbugs after I got rid of her." ("How awful!" Barbara laughs. And, of course, how racist!)

Life is tough on the prairie. Talbot shows up and wants to take Barbara on a luxurious world tour, but she'd rather stick with George, even though he treats her like a beast of burden. The worse he is to her, the more she loves him; it's that kind of movie. I saw this film on TV when I was in grade school. (Somehow I'd misremembered it as being a Claudette Colbert picture.) Watching it on video was like being reunited with an old and slightly disreputable friend.

Quantrill's Raiders   (U.S. 1958 C)

This movie shows how far and how unexpectedly homoerotica can penetrate. By the late 'Fifties, even a juvenile B-grade western wasn't immune. Steve Cochran's shirt gets ripped open in a fight and, sure enough, it stays ripped open for the balance of the pic. (He's wearing suspenders at the start of this donnybrook, but they strangely disappear in the course of the battle. Perhaps one of the bad guys swiped 'em.) Steve gets tied up in a chair, which means there are several full-color bondage shots of his nipples and hairy chest-flesh straining against the cords. And then there's the matter of his pants: tight, white, clinging, form-fitting, plainly displaying the most intimate contours of his lower body. Both the good girl and the bad girl throw themselves at him, and we can see why. (The bad girl, incidentally, wears hoop earrings and a peasant blouse, but the gingham-clad good girl gets him.) Steve's revealing attire was emphasized in publicity stills promoting this film. One of these photos has been on display in my bedroom for well over a decade.

Queen Bee* (U.S. 1955 B&W)

This classic camp bitchfest is a prime example of Joan Crawford doing the sort of thing she always did best. Though disguised as a soaper, it's actually almost a horror movie, and she's the monster. The plot structure is pure Gothic romance: a sweet young innocent (Lucy Marlow) comes to stay at a gracious Southern mansion that's populated with a clan of snarling neurotics. Presiding over this ménage is Crawford, who *seems* to be a perfectly charming, devoted wife and mother. In fact, however, she's a sweetly malevolent, slyly manipulative gorgon of absolute selfishness and downright vicious vindictiveness. Her face is made up like a Kabuki mask; she looks like a dragon lady in a comic book. As for her gowns (by Jean Louis), they're all bedecked with trains and veils and capes, as if she were a vampire (instead of just a vamp). Her manner, meanwhile, is that of a real, real *mean* grade school principal.

Everybody's intimidated by her. No one can manage to do anything about her. She even bamboozles a professional psychiatrist. ("Really, that Dr. Pearson! He's so absurd! He actually trembles when I talk to him. You'd think he'd never seen a beautiful woman before.") She's driven her husband (Barry Sullivan) to drink. Years ago, she stole him away from Fay Wray, who has since gone mad. Now she's doing her level best to steal John Ireland away from Betsy Palmer, who's cast as Barry's sister. But John's not having any. "You're like some fancy kind of disease," he tells Joan. "I had it once; now I'm immune." (This is the sort of thing that people routinely say to one another in campy melodramas.) Because Joan is so mean to her, Betsy hangs herself in the stables. When informed of this development, Joan gets to do a full-fledged mad scene, smearing cold cream all over the mirror on her dressing table.

I'm telling you, Crawford's such a bitch in this picture, Ireland and Sullivan actually have a spat over which of them gets to kill her. When one of them finally does, we're sort of sorry to see her go. After all, she's the most interesting character in the movie. By a long shot.

Rock Hudson's Home Movies* (U.S. 1992 C)

As the title indicates, this is a film that overtly takes gay camp as its subject. Essentially, it's an assemblage of snippets from classic Rock Hudson vehicles of the 'Fifties and 'Sixties, taken out of context and put together in such a way as to bring out their gay subtext and thereby relate the secret saga of Hudson's covert life and career. Hudson provides narration from beyond the grave (the voice belongs to actor Eric Farr). The film is particularly strong in its depiction of Rock's less than satisfying relationships with women. We watch as his amatory ambiguity and emotional equivocation stymie such diverse leading ladies as Dorothy Malone, Lauren Bacall, Martha Hyer, Jane Wyman, Liz Taylor, Julie Andrews, and, of course, especially, inevitably, Doris Day.

The fictive Rock of this movie speculates that the Hollywood powers-that-be were actively seeking to "out" him by placing him in questionable onscreen situations. And I must admit that the wealth of documentary material presented herein would seem to confirm this view. Confronted with such profusion, it's hard for me to select my favorite clips. There's Jennifer Jones blithely urging Rock to go downtown and find himself "some gay young playmate." There's Rock's whole face lighting up as he hears a starlet enthuse that "Hamburg is the gayest city in Germany." There's Rock making a promise to Kirk Douglas: "I'll cum for you at sundown." ("I'll be waiting for you," Kirk replies.) There's also a freeze-frame of Rock looking at his perennial "best friend" Tony Randall with naked, blatant, undisguised lust.

I find I can readily identify with Mark Rappaport, the maker of this film. His mission—to distill the gay content from seemingly "innocent" films—is basically the same as mine. To compile this movie, he must have sat through dozens of old Rock Hudson pictures, approaching each one with the question, "Does this have something I can use?" (Reader, I must confess that my approach is the same.) But it grieves me to note that he somehow overlooked one of *the* most homoerotic moments in the entire Hudson canon: the fight scene in *Back to God's Country* (1953) that has him endlessly rolling around on the floor with Steve Cochran!

ROCK HUDSON (1925–1985) in a publicity photo (with Gena Rowlands) from the 1962 film *The Spiral Road* (U-I).

Ruthless People* (U.S. 1986 C)

Ruthless People is a suitably depraved reworking of the famous O. Henry story, "The Ransom of Red Chief." Its greatest depravity is probably the casting of Ms. Bette Midler in the Red Chief role. She happens to be kidnapped on the very day when her scheming husband (Danny DeVito) intends to do away with her. DeVito refers to her as a "squealing, corpulent little toad." He despises everything about her ("I hate the way she licks stamps!"). It's a rare film that portrays heterosexual married life so frankly.

At least initially, she gets along with her captors about as well as she did with her spouse. She describes to one of them (Judge Reinhold) the colorful experiences awaiting him in prison: "You'll be so popular, making all kinds of new, close friends . . . big, ugly, *hairy* friends! Not that you'll ever see what they look like, 'cause you'll be facing the other way!" He apparently takes her at her word: at the climax of the film, he's so desperate to avoid arrest, he drives his car off a pier into the Pacific.

One of the campiest things about this film is the decor of Ms. Midler's mansion. The style is 'Eighties New Wave. Or should I call it 'Fifties ultramodern? At any rate, the overall effect is to make it look as though she and DeVito are residing inside of an animated cartoon.

The other campiest thing about this flick is Midler herself. She howls, she whines, she brays, she rolls her eyes and generally makes a spectacle of herself. This is not an exceptionally funny comedy and it runs out of gas midway through. But Bette is clearly a performer who's able to do a lot with a little.

Salo* (Italy 1975 C)

Salo, Pier Paolo Pasolini's film of de Sade's *120 Days of Sodom*, transposes the action (I hesitate to call it a plot) to Mussolini's Italy in the waning days of World War II. A bunch of Fascist big shots retire to a country estate with a group of adolescents they've abducted. The kids are to be degraded, raped, tortured, and ultimately killed. Also on hand are an assortment of elderly prostitutes, elegantly gowned and coiffed, who jolly things along by telling pornographic stories.

A goodly amount of screen time is devoted to eating shit. (Just keep

telling yourself: "It's only Swiss chocolate! It's only Swiss chocolate!")
A banquet of turds is prepared to celebrate the "wedding" of a middle-aged male official and a likely-looking young lad. "Nothing's worse than a breath without odor," says the horny old fart, as he force-feeds feces to the bridal-begowned boy.

It is difficult to find camp or cult elements in what is essentially a catalogue of atrocities. The point seems to be that the Fascists are so sensually jaded that only the most unspeakable depravities can turn them on. Believe it or not, the generally grim proceedings are punctuated with moments of levity. Like when the bad guys get themselves up in drag of a ridiculously unconvincing sort: frumpy 'Forties ensembles, complete with gala chapeaux. Thus attired, they ascend a grand staircase to yet another "marriage" ceremony, this one presided over by what appears to be an Art Deco Aztec priest.

Salome's Last Dance* (G.B. 1988 C)

We mustn't neglect to include Oscar Wilde. This typically febrile Ken Russell production has Wilde (Nickolas Grace) visiting a palatial whorehouse that caters to each and every inclination. In his honor, the staff and patrons stage a performance of his latest play, *Salome*. The title role is enacted by a chambermaid (Imogen Millais Scott). John the Baptist is portrayed by Lord Alfred Douglas, Wilde's lover (Douglas Hodge). He is flogged by dominatrices clad in topless leather attire. When he spits in Salome's face, she slobbers it up as if it were nectar. When Herod says he hears a great wind, a Roman ambassador farts loudly and slave girls immediately spray the area with perfume. The prophet is beheaded by a huge, naked Nubian. ("You don't think it was a mistake casting the soldiers from the rough trade, then?" the brothel-keeper nervously asks the playwright, after the show.) Imogen Millais Scott gives a splendid impression of a servant girl impersonating a princess. A genuinely nasty surprise ending suggests that Russell aims to draw a parallel between the brittle esthetic decadence of high Victorian England and the cruel barbarities of ancient Roman times. The music is mainly Debussy and Rimsky-Korsakov, with Grieg's "In the Hall of the Mountain King" seeing service as the Dance of the Seven Veils. Surprisingly, there's not so much as a note of Richard Strauss.

Salon Kitty* (Italy 1976 C)

In Volume One we examined Visconti's *The Damned* starring Ingrid Thulin and Helmut Berger. Now let's take a look at the trash version, which has the same two stars, but a different director (Tinto Brass). This opus pushes decadence as if it were going out of style. It starts right out with Ingrid Thulin (clad in what can only be described as hermaphrodite drag) crooning a cabaret song which includes the following lyrics: "Why be glum / when you could be gay? / Once around / should suffice, / if you just slip / a little 'versa' / into your vice." She is Madame Kitty, proprietress of a whorehouse in Hitler's Berlin. Berger is cast as an ambitious ss officer who takes over her business, the better to get the goods on his rivals and superiors. The film's most outrageous scene takes place in a huge gymnasium, where he has his highly disciplined— and naked—stormtroopers audition a bevy of prospective prostitutes to the musical accompaniment of a military band. Sex as calisthenics! (A suitably joyless Hitlerian concept.)

Ken Adam's production design is a triumph of art deco style. Vital to this decor is Helmut Berger himself, with his boyish death's-head of a face, his pain-filled eyes, his aquiline nose, grim set lips, sibilant voice, and mincing mannerisms. One scene has him showing off his huge wardrobe of elegant dresses. Not that he'd ever try one on, but he *does* have a lot of costume changes (sometimes within the course of a single scene, like when he switches from a sequin-spangled superhero union suit to a spiffy uniform of shiny black leather). His gaudiness suggests that he's supposed to be the premier glitter queen of the Third Reich. It should come as no surprise that the character he plays ends up getting assassinated in a steam bath. The joke is that, according to the script, he's supposed to be a heterosexual.

Scorpio Rising (U.S. 1963 C)

Kenneth Anger's *Scorpio Rising* manages to cram a good deal more campy decadence into its 28 minutes than do many of the full-length films discussed in this book. Its iconography of boots, chains, and motorbike exhaust pipes will strike a resonant chord in the heart of any man who shares my fondness for 'Fifties juvenile delinquency epics. (*The*

Wild One, starring Marlon Brando, is quoted.) Needless to say, the imagery is drenched in homoeroticism. Gay porno palaces have run this film, and I doubt that any of the customers felt shortchanged.

The title character is partial not only to Brando, but also to James Dean, *Mad* magazine, Lucky Strikes (he lights a match with his teeth!), Siamese cats, and newspaper comic strips (today the mix would undoubtedly include drawings by Tom of Finland). In short, a man after my own heart. The movie seems to compare the type with Christ. Found footage from a Sunday school Biblical flick is skillfully interwoven with the action . . . to the accompaniment, I might add, of my all-time favorite Top 40 pop song: "He's a Rebel" by the Crystals. "Well, just because he doesn't do what / everybody else does, / that's no reason why / I can't give him all my love!" the girl group ecstatically warbles, while Jesus is performing a miraculous healing onscreen. The fun continues with a visit to an East Village Halloween party which culminates in a homosexual orgy. Through the magic of clever editing, the Messiah seemingly offers a gentle reproof when the shindig threatens to be getting seriously out of hand. The casual blasphemy of it all comes to a suitable grand finale: astride a donkey, Jesus seems to participate in a motorcycle race. The Religious Right would not be amused. (*I* was amused, however.)

The classic rock music score is a highlight for baby-boomers like me. Bobby Vinton croons "Blue Velvet" while an otherwise naked man puts on a pair of tight Levis. The camera watches lovingly as the belt is buckled. Rebel that I am, I prefer to watch belts being unbuckled.

Scorpio Rising is part of Anger's "Magick Lantern Cycle," which includes the other shorts which comprise his cinematic output: the evocatively titled *Puce Moment* (wherein a silent movie goddess rigs herself up for an afternoon outing), *Kustom Kar Kommandos* (a boy, a car, and a powder puff), the aptly named *Fireworks* (in which a penis abruptly turns into an exploding Roman candle), *Inauguration of the Pleasure Dome* (with Anais Nin as the goddess Astarte), the psychedelic *Lucifer Rising* (with UFOs soaring through the skies of ancient Egypt), and *Invocation of My Demon Brother* (if you feel that some of these titles sound vaguely diabolical, I guess I'd be just about the last one to disagree with you).

Sebastiane* (G.B. 1976 C)

Sebastiane, Derek Jarman's film (in Latin dialogue with English subtitles) about the famed Christian martyr and Catholic saint, begins with a bona fide Roman orgy. Naked young men with huge dildos squirt a solo male dancer with what looks like a goopy mixture of milk and oatmeal. If only all religious epics could be this inspiring.

The balance of the film transpires at a remote and desolate military outpost, where Sebastian suffers persecution for the one true faith while his fellow soldiers satiate themselves with various coarse amusements. ("You're worse than a girl, Adrian. Don't you want to lose your virginity? Or have you got piles?") The proceedings are saturated with gay sex, much of it filmed in lyrical slow motion. Indeed, I don't think I've ever seen an "art" film that came so close to being a gay porno flick. Politically useful, too: it serves to remind us that homosexuality was no big deal in the ancient world. All the current controversy regarding gays in the military rings rather hollow when we realize that, in the Roman army, it was simply taken for granted that soldiers stationed far from feminine companionship would, as a matter of course, have sex with each other.

There's a lot of sound and fury before the title character finally gets tied to a post and shot full of arrows (an image photographed in lush, oversaturated colors, as befits the subject of so many celebrated paintings). All the boys have the hots for Sebastian, but he, of course, remains pure. However, he does entertain us with a performance of the exceedingly graceful dance which made him a court favorite of the Emperor Diocletian.

This film was the official British entry at the Locarno Film Festival. (Says so right on the video box.) I'll wager that Maggie Thatcher was less than delighted.

Serial Mom* (U.S. 1994 C)

Serial Mom, a clever and elaborate murder comedy written and directed by John Waters, raises some uncharacteristically serious questions. Namely, in an era when serial killers invariably get the big media treatment, why should the rest of us have to put up with scofflaws who consistently break the rules of courtesy that right-thinking Americans hold so dear? The irony and injustice of it all have quite simply overwhelmed poor Kathleen Turner, cast as a perky suburban housewife who commences to deal out capital punishment for gum chewers and people who won't wear seatbelts. Not to mention people who don't recycle and who fail to rewind their rented videotapes. (She also makes obscene telephone calls to Mink Stole, who swiped her parking spot one day at the shopping mall.)

Kathleen's m.o. is nothing if not inventive. She sneaks into the men's latrine and runs a guy through with a fireplace poker while he's zipping up at the urinal. (A homosexual witness spots her while he's peering through a glory hole.) The cops attempt to trail her, but she misroutes them handily; while she's slaughtering the neighbors, they're barging in on a guy who's beating off to a Chesty Morgan video. When she's finally apprehended and brought to trial, she serves as her own defense counsel, utterly demolishing a police detective witness by revealing that he reads a porno magazine called *Chicks with Dicks*. The verdict is Not Guilty. Moments after it's handed down, however, she beats one of the jurors (Patricia Hearst) to death with a telephone receiver for wearing white shoes out of season. Nearby, a portrait of Spiro Agnew looks on enigmatically.

Evidence of a gay cinematic sensibility is readily apparent: the opening scene presents us with references to Village People, Pee-Wee Herman, and Betty Page. The proceedings are slathered all over with Hitchcockian background music, as though we were watching a "real" suspense movie. The clearest homage to Hitchcock, however, is a murder scene obviously inspired by a classic episode of his television series (the one in which a wife bludgeons her husband to death with a frozen leg of lamb). To top it all off, the film includes a clip of the greatest "serial mom" of them all: Joan Crawford lopping off heads in *Strait-Jacket*.

The Servant* (G.B. 1963 B&W)

The Servant is fairly typical 'Sixties "art house" product, with a distinguished pedigree (script by Harold Pinter, based on a novel by Robin Maugham) and a notably strong homoerotic subtext. Dirk Bogarde is cast as the vaguely sinister valet and general factotum in the household of James Fox, an insufferably pompous Sloane Ranger type. An hypnotic fascination is supposedly exerted by the subtly kinky relationship

DIRK BOGARDE (1921–   ) looks possessively at his co-star JAMES FOX (1939–   ) in a rather homoerotic shot from *The Servant*, directed by Joseph Losey from a novel by British gay author Robin Maugham.

which evolves between these two (it's mainly a matter of camera angles), but I thought they both seemed pretty fey right from the start. I mean, Dirk is hired strictly on the basis of his abilities as a cook and interior decorator. We know things are getting pretty campy when James comes home in a sleetstorm and finds Dirk ready and waiting for him with a nice, warm footbath (gotta personally peel the socks off Master's tired tootsies first, of course).

Dirk's most urgent priority is to get rid of Fox's fiancée (bitchy, snooty Wendy Craig). Toward that end, he summons his own "sister": a miniskirted Sarah Miles, who is obviously Trouble with a capital T. She is, theoretically, the new maid. Yes, the plot takes on a surface veneer that's heterosexual, but it's merely a ploy and a stratagem to make Mr. Fox more dependent on Mr. Bogarde. Before too long, these guys are sipping absinthe together and playing cozy games of hide-and-go-seek. We're supposed to be overwhelmed by the pervasive mood of evil decadence. I just felt like I was watching a bunch of people with bad hangovers.

Sex Garage* (U.S. 1972 B&W)

Fred Halsted's *Sex Garage* gets underway with a girl bringing her car in for a tune-up. Somehow she ends up giving the mechanic a blow job. (I confess I was taken aback to find heterosexuality lurking in this well-known gay porn film.) Meanwhile, back home, her husband is jacking off in the shower. We soon find out what he's fantasizing about. When he shows up at the garage, his wife beats a hasty and embarrassed retreat, whereupon he swiftly takes her place at the mechanic's crank. He even puts on her discarded panties. Then along comes a hirsute motorcyclist, who apparently wants his oil changed. A three-way rapidly takes shape. The climax is uniquely, fundamentally, and quintessentially American: the biker quite literally makes love to his machine, shooting his wad all over it.

The two masturbation scenes both make use of the same musical background: Bach's "Jesu, Joy of Man's Desiring." An unfortunate choice, I think. I don't believe in going out of one's way to offend. Then again, we can hardly expect Halsted to be a paragon in matters of musical taste. In *L.A. Plays Itself*, his most celebrated work, he interrupts Bartok's *Music for Strings, Percussion and Celesta* at one of its most dramatic moments, just to stick in a bit of standard fuck music.

The Shanghai Gesture* (U.S. 1941 B&W)

The Shanghai Gesture, a curiously decorous excrescence of would-be decadence, mainly transpires at a gambling casino operated by Mother Gin Sling (Ona Munson). In the Broadway play on which the film is based, the character was known as Mother Goddam. Bette Davis once expressed an interest in playing the part. The role is more than campy enough to suit her: this "mother" drips gaudy costume jewelry and has her hair arranged in absurd and exotic curlicues—more a semblance of an Oriental garden than a coiffure. Gongs precede her; a wizened amah (Maria Ouspenskaya) trails submissively behind her.

The plot is easily summarized. Mother Gin Sling seeks to avenge herself on the long-ago husband who sold her into whoredom. Now he's a titled, fabulously wealthy and powerful fat-cat tycoon (Walter Huston) with a spoiled, petulant, beautiful daughter (Gene Tierney). With the help of a handsome Eurasian ne'er-do-well (Victor Mature, in a burnoose and fez), Mother Gin Sling reduces the girl to an alcoholic slut and compulsive gambler. Then she discovers that Tierney is not only Huston's daughter, but also her own. (Since there's never any mention of Huston having a second wife, the audience is way ahead of her on this one.) Thoroughly disgusted by the creature she's created, she quickly proceeds to shoot the girl dead.

Everyone natters on and on regarding the unwholesomeness of the atmosphere (Tierney claims she can close her eyes and literally smell the evil), and that impression is amply seconded by the suitably overwrought music score. But this sort of drama simply couldn't be pulled off persuasively in 1941; the times were too prudish, the censors too vigilant. The gambling den is photographed as if it were the innermost circle of hell, but, in fact, it rather resembles La Scala, the famous opera house in Milan. There is a jarring moment when Huston and Mike Mazurki (cast as a beefy, brawny coolie) seem to be cruising one another. Indeed, Huston's flirty smile is downright lewd. But the only real decadence resides in close-ups of Victor Mature (as "Doctor Omar"). His eyes and lips are commendably large and voluptuous. His brows arch suggestively. He makes a convincing seducer in this otherwise far-fetched fable. He incarnates the sordid poetry glimpsed but fleetingly in the script itself.

She* (U.S. 1935 B&W)

She is a white queen of unparalleled beauty and unfathomable age, ruling a lost civilization of unbridled savagery and cruelty. The role is delineated by Helen Gahagan, who later went into politics (she was an early victim of Richard Nixon's redbaiting tactics). The film is based on H. Rider Haggard's novel, published in 1887. Back in those days, these Saturday matinee antics were considered tremendously mystical and avant-garde. By now, on the other hand, queens of lost cities are rightly and generally regarded as camp.

Randolph Scott and Nigel Bruce are explorers seeking a magic flame which bestows eternal youth. (Helen Mack tags along to do the cooking.) In the book they travel south, to Africa. In the film they head north, to the Arctic Circle and an undiscovered country which is warmed by volcanic fires. Presiding over this realm is Gahagan as She-Who-Must-Be-Obeyed. Scott is the reincarnation of her lost love. She's disappointed that he doesn't remember her, though it's been more than five hundred years.

Her subjects mainly consist of seminude tribesmen given to staging religious ceremonies which somewhat resemble Busby Berkeley production numbers. "Who gives you leave to think contrary to my will?!"she fumes at one point. Later she makes arrangements to have Mack served up as a human sacrifice. She-Who-Must-Be-Obeyed is a lot like the exotic sirens and temptresses later delineated by the incomparable Maria Montez. She also prefigures (in temperament, at least) some of the domineering females played by divas like Crawford, Davis, etc. It's all very well to say we admire strong women, but movies like *She* tear the masks away: what we *really* like is imperious bitchery.

Sign of the Gladiator (Italy 1959 C)

In *Sign of the Gladiator* Anita Ekberg gets to strut her stuff as Zenobia, proud and imperious queen of Palmyra. She looks like she's having a wonderful time. So does Chelo Alonso, who plays a wicked seductress in the service of the Persian empire. Chelo does a show-stopping belly dance. Ekberg, meanwhile, wears huge golden breastplates when she leads her Palmyrans into battle. The gladiator to whom the title refers is Georges Marchal, who wins the heart of the queen. He's a Roman, unfortunately; Anita spears him when she finds him fighting on the wrong side. Ah, well. We already knew that Zenobia was not overly fond of lovemaking. (According to Gibbon: "She never admitted her husband's embraces but for the sake of posterity. If her hopes were baffled, in the ensuing *month* she reiterated the experiment." Italics his.) My favorite moment of perversity came earlier: a banquet scene wherein a slobby diner wipes his hands on the long golden hair of a slave girl.

At one point there's a subjective shot, from Marchal's viewpoint, of a bad guy taunting him with a cool glass of water. One seldom finds these nice cinematic touches in a peplum. That's because the audience would rather be looking at the seminude Marchal, bound and spread-eagled in the hot sun.

The Silver Cord (U.S. 1933 B&W)

In *The Silver Cord* Laura Hope Crews provides the definitive portrait of a smothering mother. This dame is a *real* Mommie Dearest. The film is based on a play by Sidney Howard and we are able to clearly see where the acts fall. In the first act it's plainly evident that she's sowing the seeds of discord between her two sons and the women they love. In Act Two she succeeds in persuading the younger, weaker son (Eric Linden) to break off his engagement to Frances Dee, who promptly tries to call a cab and go to the local hotel. Mindful of what people would say if that were to happen, Mom yanks the phone right out of the wall. Then she turns to Miss Dee and reproachfully says, "You're the only person in the world who's ever forced me to do an undignified thing. I shall not forget it." In the third act, matters come to a head (as matters often do in third acts). The predatory, snake-tongued, subconsciously incestuous hag tries to break up the marriage of her elder son (Joel McCrea) to a "lady scientist" (a biologist played by Irene Dunne). The movie's campiest moment comes earlier, when Frances, attempting to get to town on foot, falls through the ice of a nearby pond and is drowning. Joel and Eric hasten to rescue her, while their mother, always brimming with tender maternal concern, hangs out a window and shrieks, "If only those boys don't catch pneumonia! Dave, you're not dressed! Robin, get your coat! Are you *crazy*?!"

Sins of Rome* (Italy 1954 B&W)

Nothing quite like a good peplum for those of us who enjoy watching the madcap antics of a bitchy femme fatale. *Sins of Rome*, Riccardo Freda's certifiably insane version of the Spartacus legend, presents us with Gianna Maria Canale as Sabina, wicked temptress of ancient Rome. Need I tell you she's got the hots for our hero, Spartacus (Massimo Girotti)? And she thinks she can get him, too. "After six months with me," she gloatingly promises him, "you'll be a *man*!" Of course, he's only got eyes for Ludmilla Tcherina, her personal slave girl. With splendid hauteur, Gianna orders her sandals laced up by the sullen but servile Ludmilla, reminding her that "My feet are much more important than all your foolish thoughts, and even than your existence!" Said existence is somewhat at risk, since hell hath no fury like a disappointed seductress. Evil lights sparkle, glitter, and dance in Gianna's eerie, cat-like eyes as hungry lions interrupt the classical ballet that she has staged as a diversion in the midst of the gladiatorial games. Ludmilla, needless to say, is the prima ballerina. Spartacus comes bounding to the rescue. He and Gianna climactically confront one another. "We don't have anything in common," the revolutionary slave leader points out to the debauched aristocrat. Seems like sort of an understatement.

This movie is like some brutal, gargantuan opera—very much in the Fascist style, but with an anti-Fascist message. And with a beefcake visual subtext. Girotti is a hairy, sweaty, muscular hunk of manhood, photographed in a frankly, unashamedly homoerotic style. Check out the extraordinary intimacy of the massage scene at the gladiator school, early on. We can almost feel the firmness, the warmth of the well-muscled bodies. Equal time is provided for softer flesh: I mustn't neglect to mention the somewhat more decadent massage scene involving Vittorio Sanipoli as the cowardly Rufus, who dictates his memoirs as his remarkably white and hairless chest is being stroked and caressed by slave girls. Director Freda, a former art critic, has a decent respect for the unathletic.

Skin Deep* (U.S. 1983 C)

Skin Deep is a gay porn flick (by director Tom De Simone) with a love story plot that's conventional: a writer (skinny, pale, blonde, diminutive, ascetic, soft-spoken, sensitive) falls hard for a hustler (big, dark, hairy, musclebound). Most of us can relate to that, can't we? At one point the writer romantically envisions his stud as a male Marlene Dietrich. It's a fantasy sequence: the screen image fades to black-and-white and the bodybuilder comes parading down a staircase, a cigarette dangling from between his fingers while German cabaret music tinkles on the soundtrack. It is, I think, a moment that genuinely qualifies as an apotheosis of gay high camp.

John Rowberry, author of *Gay Video: A Guide to Erotica* (G.S. Press 1986) calls *Skin Deep* "without question, the great gay erotic film of all time . . . creatively photographed and perfectly paced."

Slaves in Bondage* (U.S. 1937 B&W)

Say, didja ever wonder how white slavers manage to capture their victims? Well, listen up! "I was walking home from church and . . . and he drove up and told me that Mother met with an accident and . . . and she wanted me right away!" That's how it happened to poor Mary Lou (Louise Small). Lucky for her, she was able to jump out of the car and get away. So you just better be careful, next time you're walking home from church!

The principal heroine of this exploitation flick is the flamboyantly untalented Lona Andre, who looks kind of like Gene Tierney disguised as Sylvia Sidney. Her close-ups are so frequent, various, and gratuitous, there must have been a special clause about them in her contract. She's employed as a manicurist at a barber shop which is owned and operated by a woman named "Belle Harris" (Florence Dudley), who, of course, is actually the secret manager of all of the local whorehouses. Aiding and abetting this procuress is a henchman/pimp named Nick, who is played by John Merton, a chunky favorite of mine and the villainous veteran of innumerable B-grade westerns. He frankly enjoys slapping the girls around ("The customer is always right!"). They, in their turn, have a good time casting aspersions on his manhood ("Hi,

Nick! Say, my powder puff's worn out! When ya gonna get me a new one?"). In the "Oriental Room," we find a couple of lanky, lingerie-clad lovelies who like to spank one another ("Not too hard, now!"). These sure don't look much like "slaves" to me. Kinkier still is the comic relief: a pair of male contortionists who get into some pretty unseemly positions ("C'mon, Hal! Hold still!"). Their "human wheel" looks suspiciously like a sixty-nine to me. Too bad that they always wear two-piece business suits while performing.

Sodom and Gomorrah* (Italy 1962 C)

There's just no way this movie could ever live up to the expectations implicit in its title. From the start, we know that we're in for a huge disappointment. The film begins with a slow pan across the remains of what must have been an extremely decorous drunken debauch. Overdressed chorus girls are sprawled on every available surface.

The film depicts the struggle of the Hebrew leader, Lot (Stewart Granger), to maintain the purity and faithfulness of his people during their lengthy sojourn in the land of Sodom. The cultural tensions are by no means eased when he weds one of the local girls (Pier Angeli). His biggest problem is getting her to dress in burlap (traditional housewifely garb in those days). Meanwhile his very own daughters are feeling tempted to try on more feminine attire. They're enticed by the rich colors, soft fabrics, and daring décolletage favored by those kooky Sodomite fashion designers. Clothes are such a hassle, even at the dawn of recorded history.

Anouk Aimee looks uncannily Crawfordish in her role as the Queen of Sodom. The script implies that she's having it off with a sneery-faced Asian dancing girl. Anouk has a profligate brother who is portrayed by Stanley Baker. His lusts are carefully designated as being heterosexual, but there's no denying he looks the very incarnation of masculine sex appeal. Hot pants, high collars, plunging necklines, and exquisitely trimmed facial hair are extraordinarily flattering to this actor.

The director is Robert Aldrich, who frankly revels in all the cruelty and destruction (including, of course, the climactic annihilation of the title cities). He later helmed *What Ever Happened to Baby Jane?* and *The Killing of Sister George*, projects to which he brought a somewhat more gay-friendly sensibility.

Song of India* (U.S. 1949 B&W)

In *Song of India*, Turhan Bey and Gail Russell are cast as an Indian prince and princess who set off on a jungle excursion. These are thoroughly modern Indians: before departing the palace, Gail asks Turhan to pose for home movies she's taking. When she tells him to smile, he flashes a dazzling grin so adorably asshole-ish, it's a wonder her camera doesn't break. ("Your fillings show!" she complains.)

The pair go tootling off to the Forbidden Jungle, so called because hunting is not permitted and, presumably, because Sabu cavorts there in a diaper. Gail and Turhan are trapping animals for zoos, which seems fairly innocuous. Sabu, however, despises their dilettantism. He releases the animals, which pisses Turhan off. The scene, by the way, transpires at night; Turhan's silk pajamas are lovely.

Gail sweet-talks Sabu into promising not to free any more animals. This annoys the men of his village, who spit on the seat of his loincloth when his back is turned. His virility questioned, Sabu kidnaps Gail. Turhan responds by threatening to burn the village and execute every third one of its male citizens. (It would seem that the Prince is not as thoroughly westernized as he thinks.) The situation is complicated when it becomes apparent that Sabu is of royal blood, also. "Only one man can rule this state," says Turhan, unfastening his belt. On the brink of a cliff, he and Sabu have a knife fight, which is interrupted by a wounded tiger . . .

Repressed homosexuality exacts a terrible toll, does it not?

Song of Scheherazade (U.S. 1947 C)

Biopics about classical composers are camp at its mystical, transcendental best. *Song of Scheherazade* purports to be the story of Nikolai Rimsky-Korsakov, who is played by Jean-Pierre Aumont, Mr. Maria Montez himself. (They were married in '43, four years before this film's release.) It's a little-known fact that Rimsky-Korsakov served with distinction in the Russian Navy. The film portrays his days as a humble cadet. The opening scene finds him aboard a ship, standing at attention for the morning inspection. The captain is Brian Donlevy, who is given a truly stunning entrance, stripped to the waist (his barrel chest glistening with sweat) and smoking a cigarette in a long and elegant holder (a nice touch, that). Brian gives the young men in his charge a thorough going-over. He coyly inquires of Jean-Pierre, "What kind of a sailor are you? Don't answer. I know only too well." The background music in this scene is taken from R-K's opera, *The Golden Cock*.

The ship drops anchor off the coast of Morocco. It is here that Nikolai encounters a beautiful dancing girl named Scheherazade (Yvonne De Carlo), who inspires him to compose some of his most romantic music. His crewmates are amazed to discover him thus be-smitten. ("Look! I don't believe it! It's Nicky with a *girl!*") He even fights a duel in defense of her honor. The chosen weapons are whips. Grinning orgasmically, the two men have at one another. "They'll kill each other!" cries Yvonne in alarm. The soundtrack, meanwhile, thunders with the *Russian Easter Overture*. It's the kinkiest scene in the movie.

As if all this weren't enough, Yvonne has a mother (named Conchita) who is played by Eve Arden. Indeed, the two women dance a wild fandango together to the tune of Nikolai's *Capriccio Espagnol*. Eve gives Jean-Pierre the once-over. ("I *adore* the Navy!" she enthuses.) She even throws a party for him and his shipmates. ("Get my smelling salts!" she instructs the maid. "I might wish to faint later.") Toward the end of the movie, Yvonne disguises herself as a sailor and slips aboard Jean-Pierre's ship in hopes of getting a free ride to Russia. Brian Donlevy is determined to flush her out. "Down with your pants!" he shouts at his men. "All of you! Down with your pants!" You'll be discouraged to hear that Yvonne gives herself up before the promised spectacle can occur.

---

*Song of the Loon** (U.S. 1970 C)

Many gay men of my generation (or older) have a nostalgic fondness for Richard Amory's "Loon Trilogy." These gay western novels, seemingly forgotten nowadays, were hugely popular in their time and formed a vital part of the late 'Sixties gay culture. They are well-written, highly entertaining books and well worth tracking down (though I'm not sure where you would look to find them). I still have my battered paperback copy of *Song of Aaron*, the second novel in the series. "Adults only," it says on the cover. "Not for sale to minors," it says on the back (just in case there's any misunderstanding). These admonitions seem rather quaint, since Amory's style is really not much more explicit than that of the average bodice-ripper paperback published for the ladies' romance market of today.

In mood and flavor, these books are strongly reminiscent of the spaghetti western movies that were popular at roughly the same time. The protagonists, however, are not what you'd call the strong, silent type. Quite the contrary. These cowpokes habitually use cutesy nicknames to refer to their genitals. Furthermore, these are *singing* cowboys. Their lyrics, I hasten to add, are not the kind Roy Rogers could ever feel comfortable with. ("His laigs was long and his hips was lean. / He was hung like a stallion and twice as mean.") Similarly, the Native American characters are not "wild" in quite the customary sense. Tsi-Nokha, a brave of "gentle and peaceful" demeanor, is given to making pronouncements such as the following:

> I am looking for a white man, a tall man, tall as the Douglas fir, with a smile like an April sky. His hair is the color of October corn, and his cock—it is like the Umpqua River, when the snows have melted.

It's plain to see that this is material that could radically expand the boundaries of the traditional Hollywood western. But *Song of the Loon*, a movie based on the first book in the trilogy, is clearly an independent production, the work of a bunch of gay hippies operating on a shoestring. Still, in its simple earnestness, it conveys the spirit of Amory's prose. It's fun to watch these pretty lads traipsing through the wilderness. And the scenery itself is breathtakingly gorgeous (it could have been even more gorgeous, if only the cheap Eastman Color had better withstood the passing decades). The principal character is a handsome blonde named Ephraim (Morgan Royce), whose charms have made him the talk of the forest. All the brawny woodsmen and intrepid Indian braves are chattering like magpies about his "corn-colored hair and blue eyes." "You are my brother. . . . I would show you happiness," gushes Singing Heron to Ephraim, who rewards him with a bashful smile and a demurely downcast gaze. The sex scenes—softcore, of course—are photographed in negative. (A furious flourish of artiness? Or a deliberate obfuscation to placate the censors?) Despite the 1970 release date, this is what the neocons would call a very 'Sixties film. "The Indians use many powerful medicines," Cyrus, the burly trapper, coyly explains to Ephraim. "And Bear-who-dreams uses all of them, all of the time." The climax is reached when the bad guys, Calvin and Montgomery, a pair of no-goods who can't come to terms with their true homosexual natures, punch each other out in the dusty street outside a saloon. Sex, drugs, and violence! I guess that just about covers all the bases.

So's Your Aunt Emma!* (U.S. 1942 B&W)

Films about the fight game invariably contain homoerotic elements. Add ZaSu Pitts to the formula and you've got yourself a gay camp classic. Hers is the title role in *So's Your Aunt Emma!*, a B-grade opus entirely designed as a showcase for her ambiguous talents. This makes the film an anomaly in the context of her career, which was mainly devoted to sweet-little-old-lady supporting parts: lady's maids and small town spinsters, all of them vaporously vague and dithering. Aunt Emma attends a prizefight and winds up managing one of the contending palookas. She even shows his trainer how to give the kid the right kind of massage (I think I can relate to this). Matters are complicated when the bad guys mistake her for "Ma Parker," a notorious hoodlum. They think she's packing heat. Indeed, they fear she's got a rod concealed in her umbrella. The misunderstanding permits her to wander ludicrously out of character: going along with the gag, she warns a mobster (Tristram Coffin) that her "trigger finger starts to itch." The concluding scene has her coming home to her dykish, domineering sisters. She calls them "silly jerks" and then announces, "From now on, I'm the big cheese in this rat trap and you're taking orders from me!" Improbably enough, the women go frantically scurrying for safety. A more convincing gun moll is found in the supporting ranks: horror movie cult actress Elizabeth Russell, cast as Zelda, Coffin's hardcase girlfriend.

South Sea Sinner (U.S. 1950 B&W)

South Sea Sinner finds Shelley Winters and Liberace washed ashore on a romantic, tropic isle. This concept, I need hardly mention, promises camp of an almost mind-boggling purity and richness. Shelley is in her slinky early 'Fifties sex siren mode (the pounds came later; if she and Lee had made this film in 1960 instead of 1950, the hilarity quotient would be at least a hundred times higher). She plays a blowzy saloon singer, sort of along the lines of a road company Sadie Thompson. She makes her entrance in a bare-midriff outfit, wearing feathers, crescent-moon earrings, and a sneer. "Buy me a man if you can!" she sings, while Lee pounds out enthusiastic support. (He's her accompanist.) Liberace is the wise old queen in this movie, calmly playing Chopin while a tavern brawl rages all around him. Shelley, however, proves herself to be his philosophical equal. "Don't believe everything you read," she sagely advises Macdonald Carey. "Even when you read it in a woman's face!" But Winters and Carey are not a match made in heaven. She gets all flustered whenever he uses big words, like "introvert" and "virtuoso." He brings her to a high society bash where the swells treat her like dirt, but Lee saves the day by playing 'em a concerto. (The orchestra, though plainly audible, is nowhere to be seen. Perhaps they were stashed out on the patio?) This is a remake of a Dietrich picture (*Seven Sinners* from 1940). Shelley is no Marlene, I'm afraid. But the sight of her singing "It Had to Be You" makes her a Great Lady of Camp, even so. Especially with Lee tickling the ivories.

The Spider Woman* (U.S. 1944 B&W)

The Spider Woman is a campy villainess played by Gale Sondergaard. Going by the name of "Adrea Spedding," she's the brains behind the wave of "pyjama suicides" which are plaguing London and which have stymied Scotland Yard. She's a svelte, veiled presence, at once angular and sinuous, with a captivating manner, crisp, elegant diction, and a rich, theatrical voice. The redoubtable Sherlock Holmes (played, of course, by Basil Rathbone) considers himself equal to her challenge. The introduction of distaff dirty work into the stuffy, stodgy, clubby, homoerotic ambience so typical of the Sherlock Holmes series serves to create an amusingly chauvinistic effect. Let's listen in as Sherlock and Dr. Watson (his semi-retarded ward, it would sometimes seem) discuss the perplexing case at hand:

"Indubitably, these murders are the work of a well-organized gang, and directing them is one of the most fiendishly clever minds in all Europe today."

"Any notion who?"

"I suspect a woman. Any tobacco around this place, Watson?"

"In that pack there. A woman? You amaze me, Holmes. Why a woman?"

"Because the method, whatever it is, is peculiarly subtle and cruel . . . feline, not canine."

"Poppycock!" Inspector Lestrade interjects. "Canine, feline, quinine! When a bloke does himself in, that's suicide."

"Unless the bloke is driven to suicide," Holmes points out, "and in that case it's murder."

"Driven . . ." Watson ponders the word. "That sounds like a woman, doesn't it?"

The film is surreal in its nifty, nasty nightmarishness. There are pygmies and tarantulas and a weird, mute little tyke who walks with a spasmodic hop and catches flies. He tosses a poisoned candy wrapper into Holmes's fireplace, thereby filling the apartment with deadly fumes. Since the case concerns spiders, the investigation leads our heroes to a cozy, but unpleasant little establishment which is designated as follows by the sign out front: "Matthew Ordway, Rare and Exotic Insects." (I guess it's true what they say: no matter what it is you want to buy, you can be sure there's a shop someplace that sells it.) But the best scenes are those that involve the Sondergaard character's stunning talent for audacious deceit. She and Sherlock really seem to enjoy bullshitting each other. The merry chase finally draws to a close at a phantasmagoric carnival arcade, amid a sinister miasma of gypsy fortunetellers and mutilated Kewpie dolls. The climax finds Holmes going 'round and 'round on a conveyor belt in the shooting gallery, trussed up behind a pasteboard placard of Hitler (the others represent Hirohito and Mussolini; "Hit 'em where their hearts ought to be and hear the hollow sound!" shouts the barker), while Watson unknowingly takes aim at him with a rifle and a nearby calliope blasts out a frenzied rendition of von Suppé's "Poet and Peasant" Overture. (Whew!) The Spider Woman's fiendish scheme is undone by Watson's lousy marksmanship. No matter. The denouement offers further assurance (as if any additional demonstration were necessary) that no man, no matter how wise or homosexually inclined, can hope to be a match for a crafty femme fatale like Gale Sondergaard.

The Spider Woman Strikes Back (U.S. 1946 B&W)

Sherlock Holmes is conspicuously missing from this bovine (as opposed to arachnoid) sequel. Gale Sondergaard is once again cast as the Spider Woman, who now goes by the name of "Zenobia Dollard." She resides in a gracious Southern mansion, but it looks kind of dreary and dismal, mainly because she keeps the lights turned off. You see, she wants the neighbors to believe that she's blind. Toward this end, she engages the services of Brenda Joyce, a paid companion whose principal duty appears to be reading poetry aloud to her. Sondergaard plies her with

GALE SONDERGAARD (1899–1985) vamps it up in a scene from *The Spider Woman Strikes Back* (Universal 1946).

glasses of drugged milk. ("I stopped drinking *milk* when I was a child," Brenda protests. "Then it's high time you started again. Adults need milk, too," Gale coos in reply.) Once Brenda has dropped off into a deep, deep sleep, Gale comes creeping into her bedroom to siphon off a pint or so of her blood, with which to water the rare South American orchid she keeps in the basement. "You're such a fine, healthy girl," she ghoulishly enthuses. "You know, I'm becoming more and more dependent on you!"

All this crypto-lesbianism is working toward an improbably prosaic purpose. In her secret laboratory, Gale grinds up the petals of her vampire orchid, in order to distill from them an untraceable poison with which—get this—she murders cows. Yes, you read that right. She's endeavoring to drive the local dairy farmers off their land, which she then intends to buy for back taxes. This isn't a movie; it's a 4-H Club lecture.

---

*Stella Dallas** (U.S. 1937 B&W)

There are two schools of thought about *Stella Dallas*. The traditional view is that it's a camp classic of the soap opera genre. Revisionists, however, feel that it's a bona fide cinematic masterpiece which skillfully makes the most of an admittedly maudlin storyline. I belong to the latter group, but I can still perceive and appreciate the film's abundant camp elements.

This is a movie about social class, America's dirty little secret. Barbara Stanwyck delineates the title character, a working-class woman (her mother is portrayed by Marjorie Main, the perennial "Ma Kettle") who marries above her station and spends the rest of her life paying for it. Stella's middle-management spouse (John Boles) has a tendency toward stuffy dullness. Stella, on the other hand, is obviously coarse, to the point that we literally cringe whenever he takes her anywhere. Stella insists on attending a dance at the country club as soon as she gets home from the hospital after the birth of her child. (Apparently it's considered demure to keep to one's bed a while longer.) At the party, she encounters the man who's destined to be her downfall: Ed Munn, a damp fart of a fellow, much given to strong drink and practical jokes. (He's played by Alan Hale, father of Alan Hale, Jr., who was the Skipper on *Gilligan's Island*.) He and "Stell" hit it off immediately. Her husband emits a genteel shudder and, shortly thereafter, retires from the scene: business takes him to New York, where he chances to meet a former sweetheart (Barbara O'Neil), now a well-bred widow of impeccable taste and social standing.

Stella wants "position," too, if only for the sake of the daughter she's been left to raise. The girl is named Laurel (Anne Shirley; like Stanwyck, she was Oscar-nominated for her role in this film). She takes after her father, but is fiercely loyal to her mother. In the first of several heart-breaking scenes, Stella throws a lavish birthday party for the child, but none of the guests show up , and it's all because Stella and Ed were seen being boisterous on the train to Boston. Ed brings about an even worse disaster when he shows up drunk on Christmas, right in the middle of a visit from Laurel's father, who, up until that point, had seemed to be considering a reconciliation. The climactic coup de grâce comes during another train journey, when Stella and Laurel, each in her separate sleeping berth, happen to overhear passengers gossiping about Stella's clownish appearance and behavior.

By now a divorce is impending, so that Boles and O'Neil will be able to wed. In a scene that's so expertly acted, it could wring tears from an audience of arbitragers, Stella goes to their mansion and pretends not to want her child any longer. She's willing to relinquish custody rights simply because she's incapable of providing Laurel with the proper "advantages." An amicable arrangement seems imminent, but then a hitch develops: Laurel refuses to leave Stella; the mother-daughter bond is too strong.

Desperate, Stella goes running to Ed Munn, by now a pathetic alcoholic residing in a fleabag rooming house. She talks him into marrying her (he proposed, long ago), then goes home to Laurel, triumphantly announcing that Ed is in and Laurel is out. This is the campiest scene in the film. Stella puts on a ragtime record and brazenly lights up a cigarette, whereupon we're given a reaction shot of Laurel looking like she just caught sight of the Creature from the Black Lagoon. The effect may be laughable, but it's also the carefully calculated payoff of a long build-up.

Needless to say, Laurel flees, choosing social "success" and all that goes with it. The grand finale—Laurel's wedding, with Stella standing outside in the rain, peering through a window—is, of course, a lachrymose cliché, though undoubtedly powerful in its time. I might add that the groom is Tim Holt, who starred in another drama of mother love and social class: *The Magnificent Ambersons* (1942).

The Story of Esther Costello   (G.B. 1957 B&W)

"Did you see the way she drives the car? Like a man!" exclaims one of the picturesque Irish peasants at the outset of *The Story of Esther Costello*. I knew right away he must be talking about Joan Crawford and, sure enough, he was. Joan's is not the title role, however; that belongs to Heather Sears. Joan is cast as a wealthy American do-gooder who's persuaded to adopt the eponymous Esther, who is deaf, dumb, and blind as a result of a tragic childhood accident (she played with a grenade). With uncharacteristic patience, Joan gradually teaches the girl how to communicate. At this point, the movie seems like an educational picture about the rehabilitation of the handicapped. But then it turns into a traditionally lurid Joan Crawford soap opera.

Joan and her charge make inspirational appearances at women's club luncheons and Catholic school assemblies. Someone suggests they should start collecting donations for a charitable fund. Then who should show up but Rossano Brazzi, Joan's no-good estranged husband. He engages the services of a high-powered huckster (Ron Randell), who turns what had been a pure-but-modest enterprise into a bustling big business. Before you know it, there are Esther Costello dolls, Esther Costello candystriper clubs, and mass fund-raising rallies worthy of Leni Riefenstahl. Brazzi is skimming off bucks by the thousand. Joan is just glad to have a husband again. But then he kills the goose that lays the golden eggs: dazzled by Esther's youthful, virginal innocence, he rapes her. The shock is so traumatic, it restores her sight, speech, and hearing. Joan comes to her senses, too. She grabs a gun and shoots him. Unfortunately for her, she does the deed while they're driving through a tunnel, so she gets killed, too.

The only thing that mitigates against this shameless melodrama's stature as a camp classic is the dignity, intensity, and brilliance that Heather Sears brings to her pivotal role. Joan's part is sort of subordinate. Sure is juicy, though.

Strait-Jacket*   (U.S. 1964 B&W)

As a movie, *Strait-Jacket* is no better than adequate. As myth, however, it's something else again. For homosexuals, this is a remarkably resonant film. Few images could be more iconic than that of Joan Crawford as the ultimate castrating mom: an axe-murderess who carries a weapon which has a handle that seems to grow longer with each successive reel. Add to this the fact that she's all dolled up in 'Forties finery, including a shoulder-length hairstyle and a flashy, flowered dress. Her mouth is a livid, lipsticked slash. To complete the ensemble, she sports a set of charm bracelets which clank and tinkle ominously whenever she's hefting her hatchet.

The film gets underway with ingenue lead Diane Baker reminiscing about her childhood. Talk about a primal scene! Diane saw her Dad screwing an old girlfriend while Mom was out of town. Worse yet, she also saw Mom arrive home unexpectedly, catching the pair in flagrante delicto with bloody (but predictable) results. These inauspicious events are presented to us in flashback. We get to see Joan sashay off the train (past a sign which says, "Watch Your Step"), flick a cigarette butt over her shoulder, and brazenly stride off into the night. As the narration puts it, she's "very much a woman, and very much aware of it." Stumbling upon the adulterous situation at home, she chops off the heads of both fornicators and is consigned to an institution for the criminally insane. The murders, rather rash under any circumstances, seem particularly bizarre owing to the relative chastity of early 'Sixties screen conventions: the illicit lovers are fully clothed and reclining on top of the covers.

But now twenty years have gone by, Diane is all grown up, and the doctors are finally ready to let Joan out of the loonybin. At this point, the film turns into a catalogue of life's awkward moments. Taking Mom on a tour of the family farm, Diane blurts out utterly tactless remarks about slaughtering hogs and butchering chickens. On two occasions, somebody claims to be "just dying" to meet somebody. Taking Joan on a social outing, her brother (Leif Erickson) tries to put her at ease by saying, "Just remember we're going to a party, not a funeral."

Matters take an even more pathological turn when Joan buys a wig and puts on her old duds. Hubba hubba! There goes that song again! She looks like a painted-up transvestite or—to put it more accurately—a cartoon character intruding and impinging on the live action of the other actors. Diane has cause for regret when she brings her fiancé (John Anthony Hayes) home to meet Mother. "*Well*!" Joan enthuses, swaying her hips as she's bearing down on him. "You didn't tell me he was *that* good-looking!" The mortifying scene which follows is like something straight out of *Stella Dallas*. Or *Mildred Pierce*.

Few are surprised when decapitated corpses start turning up again. In these later murder scenes, however, it's significant that we don't get a good look at who's doing the pruning. Also significant is the fact that every female in the film is inexplicably hostile to Joan, with the notable exception of solicitous daughter Diane, who, oddly enough, is the only one who might have cause to be nursing grudges and harboring resentments. Such incongruities arouse suspicion, and our suspicions are confirmed. The movie ends with the implication that mother and daughter will go off to live happily ever after in the county asylum.

Sudan (U.S 1945 C)

"You have no secrets from me. You love a *queen*!" So says Andy Devine to Jon Hall in this absurdly amusing fairy story. The queen, of course, is Maria Montez, but she's traveling incognito (a queen in the closet, so to speak). This time out, she's in ancient Egypt. As an actress, however, she's at rather low ebb. Her lines are so garbled, it sounds like she must have learnt them phonetically. She does her various dance numbers heavily veiled, probably so that a stand-in might perform the more difficult moves. When she discovers her father lying dead with an arrow in his back, she manages to display nothing more than a vague perturbation. At one point she's kidnapped by slavers. As their branding iron makes contact with her pampered royal flesh, she looks . . . like she's suffering from a mild gastric upset.

But what of it? We love these movies, not for their histrionics, but for their flash, their color, their febrile exoticism. One scene has Turhan Bey propelling Maria down the Nile on a barge. I can conceive of few images more deliciously campy than this. And the costumes! Maria and the bad guy (George Zucco) appear to be trying to outdress one another. (Indeed, a few of George's ensembles put hers to shame. I particularly liked his gold satin headdress.) Turhan is introduced to us in a tailored burnoose that makes him look like a nun. I can't imagine a prettier postulant. And, with its richly melting tones of blue and golden orange, I can't imagine a prettier campfest than this one.

Sudden Fear* (U.S. 1952 B&W)

Sudden Fear presents us with Joan Crawford in the role of a successful Broadway playwright who's in love with a younger man. (The concept would seem to have been inspired by *All About Eve*, which featured

Bette Davis as a successful Broadway actress who's in love with a younger man.) His name is Lester and he's played by Jack Palance. They meet when she has him fired from the cast of her latest play because she doesn't feel he's handsome enough. Owing to his pasted-on, Mephistophelian eyebrows, we can't help but agree with her. But then they meet again on a cross-country train trip during which Jack engages Joan in a game of stud poker. By the time they get to San Francisco, she's got him playing bridge, her game of choice.

They wed, but then along comes Gloria Grahame, Jack's old flame. Initially, her intention is to blackmail him regarding some unspecified scandal which transpired on Fire Island. (In Cherry Grove, perhaps?) Thanks to a dictaphone machine which was carelessly left running overnight, Joan discovers that Palance and Grahame are plotting to kill her. She resolves to get them before they can get her.

This movie won Joan an Oscar nomination, probably on the basis of several lengthy wordless passages in which she mainly acts with her huge, bulging eyes. Camp interest resides in the absurdly violent fantasy sequences. Joan imagines Jack smothering her with a pillow, shoving her off a skyscraper, and setting her up for a spectacular auto mishap. Then she imagines herself shooting Jack dead and pinning the deed on Gloria, who is dragged away to the gas chamber, screaming. A pervasive mood of dark deceit marks *Sudden Fear* as a film noir. Jack and Joan have numerous scenes in which they address one another lovingly while inwardly hating each other's guts. Hey, I know a lot of marriages like that!

---

*Tabu** (U.S. 1931 B&W)

Tabu begins at such an insistently homoerotic pitch, we momentarily think that we're dreaming. Seminude native boys energetically spear fish, while waves splash photogenically all around them and Wagnerian music (an obvious ripoff of "The Ride of the Valkyries") surges in the background. Next these likely-looking lads laughingly romp beneath a waterfall. But then they go watch their girlfriends frolic down by the old swimming hole. So much for *that* fantasy.

We are on the island of Bora-Bora, somewhere in the South Seas. The hero, just like his cohorts, is clad in a clingingly skimpy loincloth which, in scene after scene, he appears to have deliberately tucked into his butt-crack. His fiancée is (rather peremptorily) set aside for dedication to the gods. She is now Tabu. The lovers flee to a more civilized island where the influence of the white man has eclipsed the power of paganism. Unfortunately, they are followed by an elderly high priest, a baleful presence who aims to kidnap the girl and skewer the boy in his sleep. Nearby is an oyster bed, rich in pearls, but it's guarded by a great white shark so huge, it makes the one in *Jaws* look like a minnow. The place is Tabu. But the boy dives there anyway, outswims the shark, and grabs a pearl sufficiently large to buy him and the girl passage on a boat to some far-off land. Little does he know that, in hopes of averting the wrath of the gods, the girl has resigned herself to her fate and has willingly set sail with the high priest. The boy swims after them in hot pursuit, but is overcome by exhaustion and drowns. So perish those who take taboos too lightly.

The director is F. W. Murnau, an acknowledged master of Germanic expressionism and a shining light in the firmament of gay culture. *Tabu* was his final film. Even so, I fail to see why this rather hokey little drama is regarded as a great screen classic. When, little more than a decade later, Maria Montez made movies like this, everyone considered them glitzy trash.

---

*Tam Lin** (G.B. 1969 C)

Roddy McDowall directs Ava Gardner in a swinging 'Sixties romance! No, *Tam Lin* really isn't as crass as all that. In fact, it's an artsy, evocative effort, with Ava designated the Queen of the Fairies. Her court, however, consists of a rather tedious crew of flower children. She's their wealthy patron, den mother, and playmate. And the palace favorite is her consort, Ian McShane, who, before the movie is many minutes old, falls head over heels in love with the local vicar's daughter (Stephanie Beacham). It's not nice to ditch Ava Gardner, especially when she's the Queen of the Fairies. And it's even worse to ditch her in favor of a younger woman. Ava threatens him, drugs him, finally chases him through a swamp. Ever wonder how the New Age came to have such a bad rep? The propaganda started way back in '69, with movies like this.

Gardner is actually quite remarkable, looking simultaneously beautiful and ancient, at times like a cruel Princess Turandot, at times like a bird of prey. The film itself tries desperately hard to be hip, yet all it really goes to show is that we haven't come very far since the days of Theda Bara and *A Fool There Was*. Like that venerable opus, it's based on a poem (this one by Robert Burns). Apparently, McDowall's intention was to craft a ghostly, haunting sort of movie, full of vague menace and suggestive subtlety. What he came up with instead, however, was a worthy addition to that campiest of genres, the older-woman-and-younger-man melodrama.

---

*The Terror of the Steppes** (Italy 1964 C)

The Terror of the Steppes is sort of like a western, except that it takes place in Central Asia. Strictly speaking, it's not a peplum, but it qualifies as camp, due to its homoerotic intensity and extravagantly overstated sadism.

The film starts out on the right foot with sweaty, bare-breasted male dancers performing in tight zebra-skin trousers, while the soundtrack throbs with sub-Khachaturian ballet music. A little later on, a tribal chieftain decides to toughen up his warriors. "Too much soft living has made women out of them! Use your whip to rouse their courage!" So the guys all strip to the waist for a ritual flogging. Our muscular hero (Kirk Morris) arches his back photogenically as he tastes the lash. He's also got a wrestling scene in which the crimson-clad buns of his opponent are thrust and jutted into the camera lens at every opportunity. Kirk is caught between a pair of women: a demure redhead and a villainous brunette. The latter gets shot in the bosom with arrows (*three* of them, arranged in perfect symmetry!). This is obscene, but even more lewd is the fact that the sadistic, misogynistic archers are supposed to be the good guys!

---

*That Certain Woman** (U.S. 1937 B&W)

This pathetic tearjerker would have been camp, no matter who was in it. The fact that it stars Bette Davis automatically places it in the high camp stratosphere.

The plot merits a detailed synopsis, if only to show how much gratuitous masochism can be crammed into ninety-three minutes. Davis is cast as the widow of a gangster who was killed in the St. Valentine's Day Massacre. (This has nothing to do with the story; it merely establishes that she's a woman of unfortunate repute.) Since then, she's put her-

BETTE DAVIS (1908–1989) in the famous opening scene from *The Letter* (Warner 1940), arguably her greatest film, and one which has taken on gay cult status.

self through business school and has become a dependable, hard-working secretary. Her married boss (Ian Hunter) is secretly in love with her, but she only has eyes for a wastrel playboy (Henry Fonda), whose father (Donald Crisp) is a tyrannical tycoon. She and Fonda elope, but Crisp breaks things up, has the marriage annulled, and drags his straying son back home. Bette has Fonda's baby, but keeps it a secret. Fonda marries Anita Louise, but cripples her for life in an automobile accident. Hunter—Bette's boss, remember?—is fatally stricken with some unspecified disease and drags himself to Bette's apartment so he can die there. (Never mind that this will ruin her reputation; he's not supposed to be thinking clearly.) His wife follows him there and, as he breathes his last, Bette takes the wife's hand and places it in his for a final farewell, whereupon a nearby newshound snaps a front-page photo which makes it look as though the two women are struggling over the corpse. During the course of the ensuing scandal, Fonda and his family learn the truth about Bette's baby. Anita, in her wheelchair, visits Bette and begs her to run off with Fonda so that he can finally have the child which—sniffle, sniff—Anita can never give him. This is a major bid for the Sappy Self-Sacrifice Sweepstakes Award, but Bette pins her ears back by turning the child over to her and Fonda, no strings attached. Anita is so overcome with gratitude, she conveniently expires, thus clearing the way for a happy ending. The script is so shameless, it actually dares to have Davis say, "I believe I'm like those unfortunate gals you read about in the dime novels." She don't know the half of it.

That Night in Rio   (U.S. 1941 C)

That Night in Rio features some utterly gorgeous gowns by Travis Banton. Alice Faye shows up in an evening dress of shiny gold material with a spectacular ruby necklace and she looks absolutely stunning. Co-star Carmen Miranda is clad as kaleidoscopically as always, with typically fruity headgear and, in one scene, a bright lavender handbag. The cast also includes Maria Montez. Furthermore, she and Carmen actually have a scene together! The mind reels. I blink my eyes in disbelief. I didn't know the screen could hold this much camp without exploding.

Maria dallies with Don Ameche, but beats a hasty retreat soon after Carmen sneaks up behind her. Thanks to the wonders of trick photography, there are two Don Ameches in this movie. "You grass-in-the-snake!" Carmen hisses at one of them, the very one who later gets into trouble cruising at the stock exchange. He flirtatiously waves at a suave, mustachioed gentleman, who turns out to be a trader. Waving at the stock exchange, it seems, is like waving at an auction: Don ends up with fifty thousand shares of stock he never intended to buy. Sometimes it just doesn't pay to be friendly.

Theodora, Slave Empress* (Italy 1954 C)

Theodora, Slave Empress, directed by Riccardo Freda and starring Gianna Maria Canale, is the sort of movie project that Maria Montez might well have turned down, on the grounds that it's too far-fetched and melodramatic. It's even more operatic than *Sins of Rome*, a Freda opus from the same year. Indeed, some of the costumes look like leftovers from a production of *Boris Godunov*. (The rest resemble the sort of pop star frippery that Bob Mackie used to design for Cher.)

The film takes the form of a flashback, with the emperor Justinian (Georges Marchal) reminiscing about his relationship with the title character (portrayed by Ms. Canale). He gushes, "It was Byzantium—garish, dazzling, mysterious Byzantium—that brought us together, united us in an undying devotion." While blue-haired Africans accompany her on the lyre, Theodora prances around in a practically nonexistent bikini. This serves to get Justinian's attention. He romances her incognito, offering her a necklace which she spirits away before he can even manage to steal a kiss. Enraged, he has her arrested. (She attempts to hide in a cage filled with lions, but Justinian's men have more nerve than she figures.) She's sentenced to have her right hand chopped off, then consigned to a dungeon to await her fate. "Do not fasten them tightly, please," she implores the jailer who is putting on her shackles. "My bones are fragile," she explains. He is burly, half-naked, and easily bribed. She tempts him with her golden armlet. (I guess he wants to try it on, although his bulging biceps are going to make it a tight fit.) Later his eyes are put out for helping her to escape.

She doesn't remain a fugitive for long. At the hippodrome she challenges the emperor to a chariot race. She's in male attire at this point, but, in the heat of competition, her disguise falls off. He's charmed when she beats him, even going so far as to ask her out for the evening. (She prepares for the orgy by bathing in what looks like a giant coffee cup.) Her mama beams with pride, but her jealous sister (Irene Papas) casts her lot with the bad guys. ("You'll be envied by every

ARTHUR TREACHER (1894–1975) gives TYRONE POWER (1913–1958) the eye in a scene from *Thin Ice* (20th Century Fox 1937).

courtesan in Byzantium," they promise her.)

With almost unseemly dispatch, Justinian makes Theodora his empress. The dialogue in their love scenes virtually defines purple prose. ("With the passing years I discovered your true worth, and the passion that enslaved me was replaced by a great tenderness.") But nothing lasts forever, least of all wedded bliss. Justinian has a notion that his bride still carries a torch for one of her former beaux. And, as usual, he overreacts. When he catches them together in her boudoir, he pulls a Joan Crawford (attired, I might add, in a silver lamé dressing gown that would have looked good on her). He excoriates Theodora mercilessly ("Trull! Slut!" he calls her). Remember the jailer whose eyes were put out? He is sent to garrote our heroine. This climax is staged by Freda as a macabre coup de théâtre, with a phalanx of soldiers impassively blocking the desperate woman's escape while her blind nemesis stumbles inexorably closer.

A rather sadistic film, though not, I might add, as sadistic as the actual historical facts. It isn't Freda's most surreal movie (that distinction belongs to *The Horrible Dr. Hichcock*, a Gothic romance about a necrophile), nor is it his most nonsensical (*The Witch's Curse*, discussed in Volume One, takes that honor), but it is his most deliriously flamboyant. True, the politics are awfully convoluted and rather difficult to follow. But, hey, that's why they call this stuff Byzantine, right?

Thin Ice* (U.S. 1937 B&W)

Thin Ice transpires at an Alpine ski lodge. All the other resorts have snow, but here, as one Swiss villager complains, "pansies are blooming!" And, sure enough, Tyrone Power shows up to attend a diplomatic conference. He is cast as a handsome prince, attended by his trusty British valet (Arthur Treacher). "My skis, Nottingham! My skis!" Tyrone frets. "What *have* you done with them?!" Tyrone has everyone in a dither, and he knows just how to keep them that way. "I would give anything to get that boy alone for five minutes," sighs the Belgian ambassador (Maurice Cass). I can well imagine.

Musical highlights include Joan Davis (accompanied by her all-girl orchestra) singing "I'm Olga from the Volga." Sonja Henie skates to Borodin's Polovetsian Dances. (Someone at 20th Century Fox apparently believed that skating should be accompanied by Russian music; in *Happy Landing* she skates to Rimsky-Korsakov's *The Snow Maiden*.)

At one point we're shown a newspaper headline implying that Power is obligated to marry Henie. Tyrone's actual feelings, however, are subtly conveyed by the heading on the column nextdoor: "Gay Dancer Preferred." Yes, those are the best kind. (That's why they call it a preference, I guess.) This movie seems to be sending its audience semaphore signals that Power is gay. Even the uninitiated can read them.

These Bases Are Loaded* (U.S. 1982 C)

"Let's hit the showers!" That, of course, is the opening line of dialogue in These Bases Are Loaded, a notably athletic porno movie. Down in the locker room, an after-the-game circle jerk gets underway. The film consists of flashbacks, as various participants fantasize regarding their past indiscretions. The first of these interludes is partially photographed through a fish tank. The second transpires on a waterbed. (Is director William Higgins developing an aquatic motif?) Only five flashbacks are included. Is that supposed to indicate that the other guys on the team are straight? Probably not, judging from their behavior during the big climactic orgy in the exercise room. This gymnasium, by the way, has deep-pile wall-to-wall carpeting. I do hope the janitor's got a good supply of rug shampoo.

The Thorn* (U.S. 1974 C)

The Thorn, a.k.a. The Divine Mr. J, is all too clearly the work of a bunch of hippies trying to make a movie. The plot satirizes the life of Christ. The aim, of course, is to utterly appall as many Christian fundamentalists as possible. The blasphemy is a tad too pretentiously heavy-handed. God is portrayed as a very bad Harpo Marx clone. John the Baptist is a creepy old flasher. The Virgin Mary is Bette Midler in her film debut and with all of her trademark mannerisms already in place. She gives birth to the Christ child after being seduced by Gabriel, a lecherous rabbi disguised as an angel. The three kings are three queens, two of whom have a disputation while trying to decide which star they should follow to Bethlehem. Consider the alternatives:
"Judy Garland!"
"Mick Jagger!"
"Mae West!"

"Jim Morrison!"

"Bette Davis!"

"Mary Boland!"

"Who's she?"

"Oh, next thing you know, you'll want to know who's Bette Midler . . . or *what's* Bette Midler."

It's easy to comprehend why Ms. Midler's present-day publicists would like to pretend that this film was never made.

Thoroughly Modern Millie* (U.S. 1967 C)

Thoroughly Modern Millie is a nostalgic musical comedy that takes place in 1922, just a year before Hitler's beer hall putsch and the advent of *Weird Tales* magazine. The setting is American (New York, to be precise), which makes us rather puzzled as to why the principal roles are played by Britishers (Julie Andrews, James Fox, and Beatrice Lillie). From a gay standpoint, the historical period is interesting because it represents one of the few fashion moments when women sought to look like young boys. Furthermore, John Gavin (the second male lead) is cast as a Babbitty businessman, but is photographed as if he were Lana Turner (at this point I should note that the film is a Ross Hunter production). Bea Lillie is cast as a white slaver. When she encounters poor, prissy Mary Tyler Moore (the second female lead), Bea wants nothing so much as to feed her a poisoned apple, trundle her off in a laundry hamper, and ship her away to Big Mary's Tart Shop in Peking. Lord only knows why. I mean, even the insidious Chinese have standards, after all. Then again, when Mr. Fox gets himself dolled up in really bad drag, Ms. Lillie wants to shanghai him, as well. When someone points out that Fox is somewhat less than a fox, she crisply replies, "Oh, she's not much, but, in a dark corner on the late, late shift . . ." Yes, quite.

Tie Me Up! Tie Me Down!* (Spain 1989 C)

Midway through *Tie Me Up! Tie Me Down!*, a sex comedy directed by Pedro Almodovar, we're confronted with a spoofy TV ad so utterly tasteless, it epitomizes the best of modern camp. Intended to contrast the spendthrift ways of Spaniards with the canny financial practices of, say, Germans, for example, we're presented with a pair of happy Hitler youths signing up for a retirement plan. It's a heterosexual couple, of course, but they both sport swastika armbands.

The film itself offers us Almodovar's subversive take on the Stockholm syndrome. A former mental patient (Antonio Banderas) kidnaps a movie actress (Victoria Abril) in hopes of forcing her to fall in love with him. Since this is a lighthearted farce, he succeeds. (She's a dope addict; what turns the tide in his favor is when he gets beat up while buying her some smack.)

There's abundant evidence of a gay sensibility at work. The camera seems indecently preoccupied with the tightness of Antonio's jeans. At one point he steals and wears a female wig (he pretends he's a rock star). One of the thugs who works him over is a homosexual sadist who gets off on it. The monster in the horror film Victoria is making is a masked muscleman dressed in S&M regalia. Too bad there's just no way we can get around the fact that what we're watching is essentially a heterosexual love story.

To Please a Lady* (U.S. 1950 B&W)

In *To Please a Lady* Barbara Stanwyck is cast as a tough-as-nails newspaperwoman. Roland Winters begs her to please, please stop picking on him in her column. She ignores him; she's too busy trying on new shoes. Later on, she's mildly perturbed when he blows his brains out in despair.

She's also been journalistically needling Clark Gable. He's a gruff old race-car driver and her complaints about his sportsmanship (or lack of it) get him barred from the track. "When I meet up with her again, she'll know about it!" he growls. He tries to wipe that smug little smirk off her face by giving her a good, hard slap, but the smile stays in place as if it were glued there. Then he grabs her and kisses her, apparently attempting to overcome her with his denture breath. But, this being a movie, she instantly falls in love with him, instead.

The final scene finds him all banged up from an accident. A bitchy nurse brandishes a huge hypodermic. He ain't impressed and he tells her so, in a line that brings down the curtain: "It'll take a bigger one than that . . ." I know the feeling. But how big a one does it take to please a lady?

Torch Song* (U.S. 1953 C)

Torch Song has Joan Crawford as a Broadway musical star who cries herself to sleep nights o'er an unrequited love for her blind accompanist (a lumpish, somewhat befuddled Michael Wilding). This comes as a surprise, since her imperial arrogance has reduced all her other colleagues to nervous wrecks. She is also coarse; we know this because she uses vulgar words like "stink" and "girdle." Dogs growl at her. She even sounds cranky handing out drinks at a party. This makes the dulcet singing voice that's been dubbed into her mouth seem all the more unbelievable. When she performs the big "Two-Faced Woman" number in blackface, we think she's hit the nadir of tastelessness, but then she carries it one step further: she whips off her brunette wig, revealing the dyed auburn hair underneath. It clashes with the make-up.

Here's how Wilding sums her up: "Your mouth belonged to an angel, but the words that came out of it were pure tramp." We sense that everyone in the movie is aching to call her a bitch. Unfortunately, people in movies weren't allowed to use that term in 1953.

The Tramplers* (Italy 1966 C)

"He's got a peering gaze that could melt glass," writes a Gordon Scott fan in South Carolina. This propensity of Gordon's is amply demonstrated in *The Tramplers*, a spaghetti western which the correspondent recommends highly. Gordon sports a Stetson in this opus. The hat casts a shadow on his face that sets off the smolder in his eyes real purty-like. His days as a Son of Hercules are behind him, but he fills out his jeans right nicely. He's still a physically perfect specimen. If he's no longer Goliath, that's merely because of the fact that, by 1966, the peplum was passé and horse operas were suddenly all the rage (with, I might add, a decided emphasis on opera). His beautiful body is all bundled up. By way of compensation, the movie presents us with a pair of alternate sex objects: James Mitchum and Franco Nero.

Camp in the spaghetti western genre resides in baroque and eccentric details. This movie has a weird emotional intensity—perhaps I should call it a purple passion—reminiscent of bizarre Hollywood oaters like *Duel in the Sun* and *Johnny Guitar*. Joseph Cotten is cast as Gordon's pa, a kind of ultra-patriarch straight out of the Old Testament. His name is "Temple," which may have symbolic significance: this guy is so chauvinistic, he sequesters all of his womenfolk on the upper floor of his mansion. (His wife is permitted to come halfway down the stairs to greet Gordon when he returns home from the Civil War.) When one of his daughters elopes with Franco Nero, Cotten is so mortally offended, he has one of his crooked shirttail relations throw dynamite at them. Gordon hurls it right back at the owlhoot. There's a huge explosion; all that's left is a big hole and a cowboy boot with the foot still in it. Mitchum goes away for two months and comes back minus an arm. The film offers absolutely no explanation whatsoever for the missing limb. The final gundown is staged as a kind of Civil War in miniature, literally pitting brother against brother.

The prevailing esthetic is that of the horror genre. If you don't believe me, simply take note of the lighting, the camera angles, the set decoration, and, above all, the eerie instrumentation of the music score. This incongruous Gothic mood is a fixed characteristic of Italian westerns. I think it has something to do with the way in which the nineteenth century is perceived through European eyes. A contributing factor is the pervasive feeling of geographical dislocation (just about all of these films were lensed in Spain). *The Tramplers* is so Gothic, Joseph Cotten even gets to go insane at the end. Cotten acts rings around the rest of the cast. Still, I sure don't mean to sell Gordon short; this is his best performance and probably also his best film.

The Triumph of Hercules   (Italy 1964 C)

The Triumph of Hercules is better-than-average beefcake, with moderately opulent production values, lush color, a fair-to-middling music score, and plenty of gory violence, fiendish tortures, hand-to-hand, man-to-man, chest-to-chest combat, and good, sweaty, muscular male-bonding. Hercules is portrayed by Dan Vadis. He's got a body that just won't quit, but his heavy lantern jaw and close-set eyes seem to suggest that his most appropriate line of dialogue would consist of a single word: "Duh-h-h." (Then again, he's not supposed to be a genius. At one point he thoughtlessly demolishes an entire village while searching for his ladylove.)

The plot is concise, coherent, and reasonably interesting. Ever so subtly, it plays upon the semiconscious psychic associations connecting money with shit. Not for nothing are misers called anal retentive! The wicked witch, for example, resides in a cave that is almost obscenely anal: dripping with shiny, glittering slime and abundant with noxious fumes and vapors. She traps one of the good guys by turning the ground on which he stands into quicksand. Hercules then must rescue him. The sight of these two seminude he-men grappling with each other while covered with muck is "dirty" in more ways than one. Or two. Or three. We are introduced to a king of Assyria who, we're explicitly told, defecates in a chamber pot made of gold. Furthermore, the principal bad guy (son of the wicked witch) has at his disposal a small platoon of bald-headed Frankenstein monsters; these are apparently made of that same precious metal. In fact, however, they look like shit, both literally and figuratively.

---

*The Undersea Kingdom** (U.S. 1936 B&W)

Before we commence to examine *The Undersea Kingdom*, we'd best forget every precept and principle of logical dramaturgy. This twelve-chapter serial is sheer surrealism, albeit primitive and utterly naive. A tidy cross-section of 'Thirties humanity—including a distinguished scientist, a courageous and curvaceous girl reporter, a spunky little boy, a lunatic, and Ray "Crash" Corrigan—visit the lost continent of Atlantis, which is located beneath a glass dome at the bottom of the sea. The locals wear robes and togas and all manner of comic-strip regalia, much of it apparently cut from cardboard. A civil war is in progress. One of the contending factions is led by an Oriental despot (Monte Blue) who wants to bring about a series of earthquakes that will gradually submerge North America. Opposing him is a benevolent dictator (William Farnum) whose principal pleasure in life is watching half-naked gladiators roll around together in the dust. (The most peculiar thing about this serial is the fact that, despite the title and despite the aquatic decor, we actually see very little water.) Both sides of the conflict are equally and inherently Fascistic, engaging in ritualized hand salutes and worship of the male body beautiful. In Atlantis, proper military attire always leaves chests and legs bare. Under such circumstances, hand-to-hand combat takes on a whole new added dimension.

The chaotic plot never really jells into something susceptible to summary; it remains an incomprehensible mélange of Space Age robots, Bronze Age chariots, and bathing-suited hunks. The ceremonial trap-

RAY "CRASH" CORRIGAN (1902–1976) shows off his musculature in *The Undersea Kingdom* (Republic 1936).

pings and the sense of Wagnerian vista are articulated with all the logic of a child's fever dream. The pervasive homoeroticism ripens into sadism. Supine and spread-eagled, Ray "Crash" Corrigan is lashed to the front of an armored tank. "Go ahead and ram!" he bellows defiantly, his warm, sun-bronzed flesh recumbent on cool metal and securely bound with tightly knotted rope. Grimacing orgasmically, the driver (Lon Chaney, Jr.) is only too glad to comply.

Unfortunately, coitus interruptus is virtually axiomatic to the serial format. Anything and everything "almost" happen, but nothing ever quite does. An episode is always structured to conclude with some dire effect which the onset of the following segment invariably mitigates, nullifies, or even utterly contradicts. Thus, all across the genre, we're confronted with what amounts to a sort of intrinsically ritualized masturbation. When Monte's remarkably phallic-looking attack vessel finally soars to the surface of the ocean, American naval guns blast it to smithereens while the soundtrack thunders with a martial quotation from Liszt (*Les Preludes*). Atlantis is destroyed in an inundating deluge. With all exoticism exorcised, the stage is set for a conventionally heterosexual denouement: Crash and the blonde reporter go marching off to the marriage license bureau, along with all survivors so inclined.

Urinal* (Canada 1988 C)

Urinal starts out as a gay/lesbian sci-fi/fantasy, then segues in and out of being a documentary. Six gay artists—Frida Kahlo, Sergei Eisenstein, Yukio Mishima, Langston Hughes, and Canadian sculptresses Frances Loring and Florence Wyle—plus one fictitious character (Oscar Wilde's Dorian Gray) investigate police surveillance of public toilet sex in present-day Ontario. Among other things, they learn that small town intolerance and bigotry are just as prevalent now as they were in the days of Sinclair Lewis. Predictably, the men and the women disagree and bicker regarding the "morality" of sex in public places. Eisenstein (Paul Bettis) takes us on a tour of the latrines in question. The background music for these visits includes Mussorgsky's *Pictures at an Exhibition*, "The Volga Boatman," and "Lara's Theme" from *Doctor Zhivago*. However, it's "Somewhere Over the Rainbow" that Eisenstein is singing when Mishima surprises him in the shower. ("I thought I'd shower with you to save water," Yukio explains.) Except for a feeble ending, this film is actually quite a cultish diversion.

Valentino* (G.B. 1977 C)

Ken Russell is the undisputed master of elegant bad taste. Has he ever made a film that didn't qualify as camp of one kind or another? *Valentino*, his biopic of the silent era screen idol, finds Russell at the height of his powers and with a massive production budget to back him up. In his recreation of the Roaring 'Twenties, he summons up a fully realized world, lovingly depicted down to the last Art Deco detail. And, incidentally, in so doing, he presents us with a movie that really looks like a *movie*.

In time-honored style, the film begins with its subject lying in state at a plush mortuary; his life is revealed in flashbacks. He's portrayed by Rudolf Nureyev, and, in light of his recent real-life death from AIDS, it is ghoulishly ironic that we initially see him in the guise of a corpse. Equally ironic, in a way, is the fact that, when we first see him alive and kicking, he's engaged in a passionate tango with a man (turns out to be Nijinsky, played by Anthony Dowell). We see quite a lot before the film runs its course. Nureyev even has a scene of full frontal nudity.

The supporting cast is suitably colorful. Leslie Caron is cast as Alla Nazimova, the lesbian actress who introduced Valentino to his bisexual bride (played by Michelle Phillips). Huntz Hall, the former Bowery Boy, is cast as Jesse Lasky, the boss of Valentino's studio. William Hootkins plays Fatty Arbuckle as a Jazz Age Rush Limbaugh. He has the best—or, at any rate, the nastiest—line of dialogue, addressing a drunken terpsichorean with the words, "Hey, sister! You dance like my ass chews gum!"

Valentino is presented as a gentle, ambiguous, guileless soul who wants nothing more than to buy a farm and grow oranges. The film examines the iconic fascination which his screen image held for so many, many women—and the corresponding bitter resentment this kindled in the hearts of men who take pride in being "clean-living, red-blooded Americans" (as the script terms them). This movie builds a case against the typical beer-swilling, flag-waving macho male. In a sense, *Valentino* is a surprisingly political picture. And it says just what I wanna hear.

RUDOLF NUREYEV (1938–1993) poses in his elaborate costume and powdered wig for his role as Monsieur Beaucaire in Ken Russell's *Valentino* (UA 1977).

*Valley of the Dolls** (U.S. 1967 C)

Back in the mid-'Sixties ('67 or thereabouts), almost every gay man I knew was reading *Valley of the Dolls*, Jacqueline Susann's trashy best-selling novel about doped (and dopey) starlets. We all trooped off to see the movie version, too. It is, of course, a camp classic of glitzy Hollywood excess. Nowadays, when I watch the film on video, its sheer wretchedness embarrasses the hell out of me. ("I *liked* this shit, once upon a time?!") I know, however, that there exists a core group of gays who have remained steadfastly loyal to this kitsch masterwork. The camp quality mainly resides in two members of the large cast of characters: Neely O'Hara (played by Patty Duke and ostensibly modeled on Judy Garland) and Helen Lawson (an Ethel Merman clone delineated by Susan Hayward).

Miss Duke chews the scenery something awful, apparently operating under the firmly held conviction that the only way to play an out-of-control personality is to deliver an out-of-control performance. At one point, Neely marries a fashion designer who's reputed to be homosexual. ("Ted Casablanca is not a fag, and I'm the dame who can prove it!") This movie is so sexually backward that, perplexingly, men who are designated gay are only permitted to have sex with women. Neely divorces Ted (Alex Davion) after she discovers him fooling around in the swimming pool with a girl.

The role of Helen Lawson proved difficult to cast. Ironically enough, Judy Garland was hired; then she was fired. There was nothing wrong with her performance; she simply didn't show up for work half the time. Susan Hayward was a less than satisfactory replacement, since her singing had to be dubbed. She has just one number: a certifiably insane piece of work entitled "I'll Plant My Own Tree." ("It's *my* yard / so I will *try* hard / to welcome friends I have yet to know.") It is, in a sense, a show-stopper.

Duke and Hayward have only a single scene together, and, of course, it's the camp highlight of the film. Appropriately, it transpires in a ladies latrine, and I should note that Susan is clad in a perfectly hideous spangled pantsuit. "You get out of my way," she growls at Patty, " 'cause I've got a *man* waitin' for me."

"That's a switch from the fags you're usually stuck with," Patty pertly replies, to which Sue delivers the perfect squelch: "At least *I* never married one!" Patty retaliates by snatching off Susan's flaming-red wig and

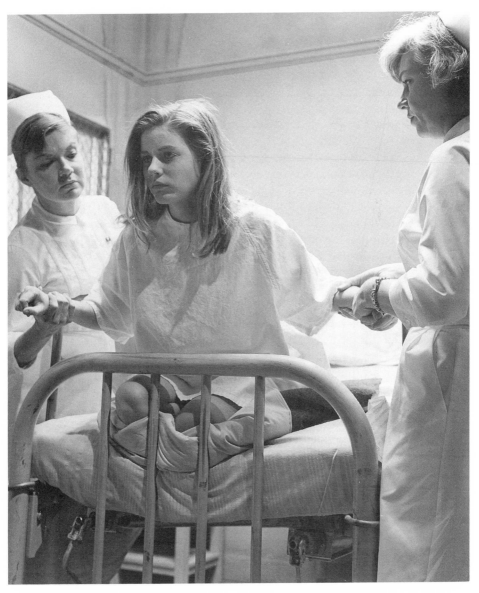

Patty Duke (1946–) appears to be in a drug-induced haze in this still from *Valley of the Dolls* (20th Century Fox 1967).

hurling it into a toilet, which she then attempts to flush, but only succeeds in clogging it. At moments such as this, the movie lurches precariously into John Waters territory. It intrigues me to imagine how Judy might have played this scene. *Valley*, had she completed it, would have been her final film, and it might have brought her career to a conclusion which, though far from distinguished, could have been truly spectacular.

---

*Venus in Furs** (Italy 1969 C)

Venus in Furs is based on the well-known novel by Leopold von Sacher-Masoch, whose name has become eponymous for an entire species of sexual perversity. The book is an elegant, subtle, and sophisticated work of nineteenth-century erotic literature. The film stars James Darren, best known for his role as "Moondoggie" in the *Gidget* pictures.

The setting of the movie is contemporary—the late 'Sixties, in other words. "I really dug that chick," says Darren, regarding the title character. "It was buggin' the life out of me!" She is Maria Rohm, and, before the film is fifteen minutes old, she's getting flogged by a bunch of decadent jet-setters (a radical alteration, since, in the book, it is she who wields the whip). Darren witnesses this tableau. "Man, it was a wild scene," he comments. "Like, if they wanted to go that route, it was their bag."

Incredibly, this incompetent film does manage to convey at least a sense of its source novel's fetishistic intensity. In one scene Darren strips off his clothes while an assortment of nineteenth-century portrait paintings seem to look on in a beatific rapture. A pair of lesbians get it on while a gay male couple watch, and while somebody else scatters feathers all over the room. (Sacher-Masoch neglected to include any lesbian scenes in his book. The movie more than corrects this oversight.) And then there's the part where Dennis Price has a fatal coronary brought on by frustrated lust. He literally dies from too much looking. The audience should take this warning to heart.

Victim   (G.B. 1961 B&W)

Were it not for the lurid subject matter (the harassment and persecution of British gays before the laws were liberalized), this would seem a somewhat jejune thriller, but *Victim* does deserve a certain cult status for being one of the very first films to explicitly be "about" homosexuality. Dirk Bogarde hunts down the blackmailers who drove his young boyfriend (Peter McEnery) to suicide. The film is both a measure of how far we've come and a reminder of how little times have changed. Much of the dialogue, I regret to note, is as pertinent now as it was in 1961. The brains behind the blackmailing ring turns out to be a spinsterish bookstore clerk who's a British edition of Anita Bryant. "They're everywhere!" she rages with regard to homosexuals. "Someone's got to make them pay for their filthy blasphemy!" A straight friend of McEnery's attempts to console him by saying, "Well, it used to be witches. At least they don't burn you." In a very real sense, the Religious Right still sees us as the most insidious kind of witch.

When the screenplay indicated that the object of all this blackmail fuss was a photograph, I quite naturally assumed that it showed McEnery and Bogarde having sex. Or, at the very least, kissing. I laughed out loud when it merely proved to be a picture of the two of them bidding one another a tearful farewell. Incredibly (and rather absurdly), the film intends us to admire the Bogarde character because he's remained "pure" and has never once given in to his natural impulses. Bogarde can be justly proud of this film for the role it played in changing public attitudes. But it's nonetheless something of an embarrassment.

Voodoo Island*   (U.S. 1957 B&W)

A Boris Karloff horror movie with lesbian action?! When a reader in Nova Scotia wrote and told me about this, I thought it sounded weird in more ways than one. The rather underdeveloped plot has Boris leading an expedition to Voodoo Island. Accompanying him are Beverly Tyler (his pert-'n'-pretty secretary), Jean Engstrom (a lezzie interior decorator who wants to put the ol' make on Bev), Rhodes Reason (the brawny pilot who brings them to the island), and a zombie (the only survivor of a previous expedition). The laughs begin before they've even left the airport (the public address system consists of a female Japanese voice making announcements like this: "Prease report to Gate 4. Your prane is ready for boarding."). Rhodes Reason is so studly, his name in the film is Gunn. His sense of direction, however, is somewhat confused: he's constantly making passes at the lesbian, who's a good deal older than he is and who, furthermore, is so frosty, her last name is Winter. She goes skinnydipping in a lagoon and gets suffocated by woman-eating carnivorous plants. When these same plants grab Beverly, the aptly named Mr. Gunn is so flustered, he shoots at them. (Fortunately, he soon realizes that a machete is a more appropriate weapon.) Boris seems to relish his own bad acting, and the movie raises an interesting question: since zombies have no volition and can only do what they're told to do, how do they go to the bathroom?

Week-end in Havana* (U.S. 1941 C)

Week-end in Havana is a rather peculiar musical, in the sense that the characters are mostly unsympathetic. Alice Faye is a peevish, tawdry shopgirl vacationing in Havana. There she encounters lounge lizard Cesar Romero, who grins incessantly, wears a white tropical suit, and looks sort of like Charlie Chan, only slimmer. He dances divinely and makes a stab at romancing her, but it's all too clear that his heart isn't in it. Her alternate escort is John Payne, who, despite the high-gloss sheen in his hair, resembles nothing so much as a troubled little boy. "Would it make you any happier if I made love to you?" he asks her, then looks extremely worried that she might say yes. When they sing a duet, I couldn't help but notice that her voice is deeper than his.

Cuba appears to be overrun with gangsters and gamblers. John takes Alice on a tour of the sugar cane fields, where the peasants are busily engaged in backbreaking labor. "The cane is cut with machetes," he blandly informs her. "Oxen are still used to till the fields and haul the cane to railroad cars." No wonder there was a revolution!

Camp interest is mainly centered on Carmen Miranda, doing what she always does best: namely, singing in Portuguese so fast that even a Brazilian can't understand her. The gigolo played by Romero proves to be hot for her; probably, and quite understandably, he's mistaking her for a drag queen. Clad in an ugly orange dress and a clashing hot pink chapeau, she announces that she intends to pull all of Alice's hair out. Later she tells Cesar she's going to tear off all of his clothes. If only

CARMEN MIRANDA (1909–1955) in a typical camp publicity still.

Carmen made good on her threats, this might have been a much more lively movie.

Walk on the Wild Side   (U.S. 1962 B&W)

It has never been fashionable to admire this film, but I still like it, just the same. The critics gave it dreadful reviews, though everyone agrees that Saul Bass's opening title design (an alley cat prowling the gutters of New Orleans) is bodaciously imaginative. I should also mention that Elmer Bernstein provides a music score that's remarkably beautiful.

The movie starts out by telling us it takes place in the early 'Thirties. It's a good thing they let us know, since the clothes are strictly 1962. Laurence Harvey journeys to New Orleans in search of his true love, who's portrayed by Capucine. Little does he suspect that she's now a prostitute in the French Quarter's most notorious whorehouse and that, furthermore, she's also the pampered favorite of the lesbian madame (Barbara Stanwyck). This is all a bit much for an innocent young swain to absorb, a fact which Barbara hastens to point out ("Tell him about the mud you've rolled in for years!"). She does her best to bust things up, which, of course, tends to make Capucine a mite cranky. ("I want to sit drinking with a man, not with you!" she snaps at Stanwyck.) Barbara is compelling in her uncharacteristically Crawfordish role. Her retinue of hangers-on is a veritable freak show. The bartender is played by veteran cowboy actor Donald "Red" Barry. To keep the girls in line, she's got a sadistic henchman played by Richard Rust. She's also got a husband (Karl Swenson) who lost both his legs in an accident and rolls around town on a skateboard. She flinches every time he touches her. We get the feeling she flinches whenever *any* man touches her. One scene is a virtual lesbian lament: "Love is understanding and sharing, enjoying the beauty of life without the reek of lust! Don't talk to me about love!" she snarls at Swenson. "What does any man know?!"

The cast also includes Jane Fonda, who's a good actress, but I don't like her. Capucine, on the other hand, is a poor actress, but I do like her. Barbara Stanwyck we can all agree on; she's a fine actress and everybody likes her.

What's the Matter with Helen?* (U.S. 1971 C)

There's really no need to review this film in the usual sense. Since it's quite evidently a conglomeration of gay camp elements, all one has to do is enumerate them. Debbie Reynolds and Shelley Winters portray a pair of middle-aged women who open a talent school for tots in Depression era Hollywood. (The two women met, grotesquely enough, as a result of their sons having collaborated on a murder a la Leopold and Loeb. Debbie even talks of hiring Clarence Darrow for an appeal.) We know we're in suspense/horror territory (the title alone is sufficient indication), but the trappings are half Busby Berkeley, half Nathanael West. 'Thirties glamour goddesses are constantly invoked, with an almost grating insistence. When, for example, Debbie is presented with gardenias, she can't resist mentioning that these flowers are "Joan Crawford's favorite." Midway through the proceedings, there is a musical revue featuring a little girl who performs an elaborate impression of Mae West.

The cast of the film includes a pair of cult figures in cameo roles: Timothy Carey (as a panhandler) and Yvette Vickers (as a stage mother). There's also a guest appearance by Agnes Moorehead as a radio evangelist modeled on Aimee Semple McPherson. The scenario has an explicitly gay subtext: the thing that's the matter with Helen (Ms. Winters) is the fact that she's flipping out because of her repressed lesbian tendencies.

My only complaint about this film is its unexpectedly brutal climax, which seems unnecessarily cruel in light of all the cozy decadence leading up to it. The narrative structure bears a strong resemblance to that of *What Ever Happened to Baby Jane?*, which is hardly surprising, since both plots were concocted by the same author: Henry Farrell.

Where Love Has Gone* (U.S. 1964 C)

Where Love Has Gone is a kind of film à clef based on a Harold Robbins roman à clef that was clearly inspired by a certain well-known scandal involving Lana Turner. Of course, since any resemblance to persons living or dead is purely coincidental, this is a story about a sculptress, not a movie star. Susan Hayward gets to play the coveted central role,

SUSAN HAYWARD (1918–1975) lets go with a vengeance at an insipid painting of her mother (Bette Davis) in this scene from the melodramatic *Where Love Has Gone* (Paramount 1964).

with Bette Davis doing a stellar turn as her mother. "Somewhere along the line, the world has lost all its standards and all its taste," declaims Bette, in a line much quoted by critics at the time of the film's release.

They even bitched about the art direction, this time out. Bette's mansion is furnished in a kind of golden russet color scheme that goes well with the flaming red coiffures of Hayward and ingenue lead Joey Heatherton (cast as Hayward's daughter and accused of slaying Mom's latest gigolo). Davis is a control freak who (we learn in flashbacks) ruined Susan's marriage to Michael Connors, mainly by buying the newlyweds a house with a decor reminiscent of an early 'Sixties dentist's office. The crowning touch: a puke pink portrait of La Davis looking like Lucrezia Borgia. Small wonder that Connors starts hitting the bottle and Sue starts cattin' around. (Her agent, played by DeForest Kelley, has convinced her that the only way to create great art is to have lots of good sex. Sounds reasonable.) "I've heard about them! I've laughed about them! I've even joked about them! But I never thought I'd end up married to one! *A rich hooker!*" Connors hollers, in a line very prominently featured in the film's coming attractions trailer.

Though Susan gives her a run for her money, Davis is the one who steals the show. This movie is an excellent showcase for the peculiar way she has of breaking even the simplest sentence down into several individual lines ("Well, Luke. What a pleasant. Surprise."). It's no wonder that, in the climactic scene, Hayward loses patience and finally yells at her, "Will you shut up for once?" And the presence of 'Sixties icon Joey Heatherton is the proverbial frosting on the cake. Thanks to her, this movie qualifies for inclusion in not one, but two beloved camp genres: the trashy soap opera and the teenage bad girl movie.

White Cargo* (U.S. 1942 B&W)

This is the one where Hedy Lamarr makes a stab at playing a jungle Jezebel. Covered from head to foot with dusky pancake make-up, this sultry siren slinks all over Africa in an assortment of skimpy, tight-fitting garments. Her opening line of dialogue is famous: "I am . . . Tondelayo!" She casts her spell on Richard Carlson, who goes to hell in a hand-basket. She marries him because he can give her "much silk and many bangles." But she always wants more, more, more. ("You've got enough junk *now* to open a shop!" he grouses.) Perversely enough, he married her to make Walter Pidgeon jealous. The camera loves Hedy in this flick, even if nobody else does. Notice the gorgeous close-ups of her gloating as the two guys are punching each other out over her.

White Savage   (U.S. 1943 C)

White Savage, a South Seas romance, unites Maria Montez with all three of her customary male co-stars. (*Re*unites, I should say; this quartet had made its debut a few months earlier in *Arabian Nights*.) She portrays a sultry princess who becomes enamored of an Australian fisherman. He is Jon Hall. Sabu is cast in his usual role as a quaint, good-natured, seminude sidekick. The always-breathtaking Turhan Bey gets to play somebody called Tamara, a name so glamorous that I'd always mistakenly believed it was reserved for females.

The villain of the piece is Thomas Gomez, who, because this is a 1943 release, is identified in the script as being German. He corrupts poor Turhan, who takes to strong drink, games of chance, and wearing loud Hawaiian shirts. Jon and Princess Maria "meet cute" when he casts his line and the hook gets caught in the fabric of her sarong. This situation is unbecoming to the dignity of her royal office. Jon explains to her that he hunts sharks for a living because the male of the species is rich in vitamin A. Maria has never heard of vitamin A, but she knows what she likes. "You may go now," she tells her servants, when Jon comes calling. "This may develop into a private matter."

Jon also flirts with Sabu, but this, of course, is merely horsing around. "Funny face," he calls him.

Turhan is Maria's brother. She reproaches him for embracing Western vices and he reproaches her for embracing "a tramp with fish scales on his hands." (He's as bitchy as she is, in other words.) The bad guys are buried in a timely earthquake so violent, it shakes the coconuts right off the trees. All ends happily for Jon and Maria. Now, if Her Majesty could only manage to get used to those fish scales on his hands . . .

The White Warrior*   (Italy 1959 C)

The White Warrior marks the only appearance of Steve Reeves in the oeuvre of Riccardo Freda, the least macho and most unathletic of the sword and sandal directors. The film is a historical romance with

JON HALL (1913–1979) has a brief Encounter of the Third Kind with MARIA MONTEZ (1918–1951), Princess of a South Sea island, in this scene from *White Savage* (Universal 1943).

peplum elements. It takes place somewhere in the Caucasus Mountains sometime around 1850. The source material is *Hadji Murád*, a short novel by Leo Tolstoy. The (to put it mildly) audacious concept of starring Steve Reeves in a story by the author of *War and Peace* and *Anna Karenina* could only have originated with Freda.

Despite the seemingly unpropitious narrative circumstances, Steve has plenty of chances to take off his clothes. There's a wrestling scene. There's a kinky bondage scene which finds him spread-eagled upon a very Victorian-looking hospital bed. This leads up to a torture scene in which he is whipped and his naked flesh singed with red-hot pincers. There are also a couple of clothed scenes in which he bear-hugs guys hello.

Pretty earthy stuff, but, with Freda at the helm, we can count on its being deliriously estheticized. The most impressive sequence arrives midway through the film: an ambush shortly after dawn, with Russian soldiers in white tunics slinking through morning mist and diagonally slanting rays of sunlight. The photography is by Mario Bava, which means we can groove on plenty of lurid, garish lighting effects and outré color combinations. Steve's sonorous dubbed-in voice is provided by skinny Reed Hadley, which in itself makes for a mildly discombobulating juxtaposition. From a camp standpoint, the most notable scene is a peasant celebration, featuring some Italian's dizzy idea of what Tartar folk music sounds like. The movie culminates in a mad collision of camp and high style, with Steve galloping his horse through a crowded ballroom right in the middle of a Strauss waltz! It is, I would say, a moment more typical of Freda than of Reeves.

---

*Woman's World** (U.S. 1954 C)

The best and easiest way to subvert right-wing propaganda is to regard it as camp. *Woman's World* is a handy guide to the "proper role" of women in the Eisenhower era. Clifton Webb owns a motorcar company, and he's decided to choose the next general manager, not on the merits of the candidate so much as the merits of the candidate's spouse. "May the best wife win," as he puts it. We're supposed to like June Allyson, the smarmy little homemaker from Kansas City. "Every time I look up at those tall buildings, I'm afraid they're gonna fall on me!" she gushes on her first day in New York. We're supposed to abhor her principal competitor: Arlene Dahl, who's aflame with ambition and dripping with sophisticated elegance. She throws herself at Clifton, apparently unaware that he doesn't like girls. (He even wipes his mouth after kissing her!) Clifton maneuvers her husband (Van Heflin) into ditching her, and then awards him the job. As for June, she and her hubby just can't wait to get back to their happy and charming home—and their three delightful children—in the Midwest. Clean-living, right-thinking folks like them just naturally know their place. Webb delivers the closing benediction: "It's a wonderful world—a great, big, wonderful woman's world, because men are in it." Who should know that better than him?

Yellowstone Kelly   (U.S. 1959 C)

This notably homoerotic western has big Clint Walker shacking up with Edd Byrnes in a cozy little cabin way up in the high country of Montana. They sleep in the nude, their brawny chests left uncovered (the blankets aren't quite long enough). A distant howl echoes through the pines. Edd asks nervously if maybe it's a wolf and, for just a moment, we're absolutely sure he's gonna go scampering across the room to hop into bed with Clint. Instead he recites the Lord's Prayer. This is a far cry from Jeff Stryker, but it must have warmed the hearts of many a homosexual back in 1959.

Youth Aflame*   (U.S. 1945 B&W)

This utterly uproarious vintage j.d. flick is especially notable for its subplot involving a do-gooder policewoman named Mrs. Clark (Mary Arden) who wants to establish a "jive club" where the local young folk may congregate in safety, free of pernicious influences. ("We could have a milk bar!" Mrs. Clark enthuses. "And all the dairies are willing to donate!") Little Peggy (Julie Duncan), her hair fetchingly beribboned, is a proud first-nighter at this bland hangout. ("Look at Peggy over there. This is her first time out. Her mother thinks all men are monsters and pleasure evil.") But then—woe is us!—some miscreant spikes the punch and the joint is promptly raided. Peggy's mom thrashes her soundly, whereupon the crestfallen miss attempts to throw herself off a bridge. Mrs. Clark talks some sense into her:

"Only quitters do that, dear. Everything seemed all right when I took you home last night."

"Oh, please don't make me go home, Mrs. Clark! Please! I can't! I can't go home!"

"Peggy!" Tenderly taking her into a warm embrace, Mrs. Clark tentatively opens the girl's blouse, exposing the angry welts.

"It doesn't hurt now," Peggy asserts. "Mother didn't understand. Please don't make me go home, Mrs. Clark! Please!"

"This'll all be straightened out, Peggy," Mrs. Clark assures her, clutching her all the tighter. "You're going to have a *new* home. And you *do* have something to look forward to, dear. I'm going to see you have friendship and love."

Need I mention that Mrs. Clark favors a mode of clothing that's rather severe, matronly, even somewhat butch? I think all I really need to add is the telltale line of dialogue that she utters at the conclusion of a teen committee meeting: "And now you kids all pile into my car and I'll drive some of you home." I would guess that the difference between "all" and "some" equals the number of sweet young things who end up trapped at Mrs. Clark's house.

You'll Never Get Rich* (U.S. 1941 B&W)

You'll Never Get Rich is a musical comedy on the subject of military service and basic training. The songs are by Cole Porter, a man who clearly savored seeing vast legions of virile young men cooped up together in bunkhouses. In this film, it's Porter who doubtless deserves the credit for the obscenity of Fred Astaire strutting around in a uniform, singing about how he's "Shootin' the Works for Uncle Sam."

These patriotic musicals invariably carry a right-wing ideological freight. *You'll Never Get Rich* unintentionally tells us more about the army than we're meant to know. I deem it significant that Astaire, the sensitive artist, spends most of his time in the guardhouse. In the real world, someone like him might not survive such incarceration. The climactic number is a fantasia of guns and flowers, with Astaire and Rita Hayworth tripping the light fantastic atop a Sherman tank. That's entertainment, so they say. Readers of this book will readily notice that it's also camp.

RITA HAYWORTH (1918–1987) from an early publicity photo when she was at the height of her beauty.

Zachariah* (U.S. 1971 C)

Zachariah is a hippie western featuring performances by an assortment of rock groups. "Head" movies like this were fairly common in 1971. Nowadays, of course, such a film seems desperately outré. The prevailing sense of humor is readily apparent: the gold shipment travels in a crate labeled "Gold of Acapulco." The gay subtext is equally clear, even in the very first scene, which has the title character (John Rubinstein) encountering Don Johnson, who wears a leather blacksmith's apron and little else.

"What are you lookin' for?" Johnson inquires.

"A friend," replies Rubinstein. "Got a light?"

Don and John become such good friends, they qualify as the film's romantic couple. What makes Zachariah so desirable is the fact that he's such a fast draw. (Only in westerns are men celebrated because they shoot their load quickly. In real life it's quite another story.) He sends away for a nice, smooth, shiny pistol, which (as he puts it) arrives in "a plain brown wrapper." But, as soon as he straps it on, he's got nothin' but trouble. He can't even go into a bar without some redneck asshole coming up to him and saying, "Well, well, well. Look what the tough little boy has in his pants! I'm gonna kill you, you little fag!"

The only overtly sexual scene is straight: Rubinstein goes to bed with Belle Starr (Pat Quinn). But she talks like Mae West and, what's more, the boudoir mood music is provided by a naked, all-male band (the New York Rock Ensemble). At any rate, Rubinstein soon returns to the arms of Don Johnson, who, I must admit, looks a hell of a lot better *now* than he did in 1971. That choirboy look he had when he was a kid doesn't appeal to me.

INDEX

This is an index of all the performers mentioned in this book who might conceivably be considered of camp or cult interest, particularly as regards gay audiences. For maximum information value, I have listed every film I've reviewed in which a given performer appears, *whether or not* that performer is actually mentioned in the review.

Aimee, Anouk
  *Sodom and
  Gomorrah*
Alante, Lewis
  *The Boys of
  Cellblock Q*
Allyson, June
  Woman's World
Alonso, Chelo
  Morgan the Pirate
  Sign of the Gladiator
Ameche, Don
  Greenwich Village
  That Night in Rio
Anderson, Dame Judith
  The Furies
Andre, Lona
  Slaves in Bondage
Andrews, Harry
  *Entertaining Mr.
  Sloane*
Andrews, Julie
  *Thoroughly Modern
  Millie*
Angeli, Pier
  *Sodom and
  Gomorrah*
Anka, Paul
  Girls Town
  Look in Any Window
Ankers, Evelyn
  The Mad Ghoul
Ann-Margret
  Kitten with a Whip
Arden, Eve
  Cover Girl
  Song of Scheherazade
Ardisson, Giorgio
  *Hercules in the
  Haunted World*

Arthur, Beatrice
  Mame
Astaire, Fred
  Dancing Lady
  You'll Never Get Rich
Atwill, Lionel
  Balalaika
Auer, Mischa
  Destry Rides Again
Aumont, Jean-Pierre
  Song of Scheherazade
Autry, Gene
  The Phantom Empire
Bacall, Lauren
  The Cobweb
  Woman's World
Baker, Carroll
  Andy Warhol's Bad
Baker, Diane
  Strait-Jacket
Baker, Stanley
  *Sodom and
  Gomorrah*
Ball, Lucille
  Mame
Banderas, Antonio
  *Tie Me Up! Tie Me
  Down!*
Bankhead, Tallulah
  *Die! Die! My
  Darling!*
Bara, Theda
  A Fool There Was
Bates, Ralph
  *Dr. Jekyll and Sister
  Hyde*
Baxter, Anne
  Carnival Story
  *Walk on the Wild
  Side*

Beacham, Stephanie
  Tam Lin
Bendix, William
  Greenwich Village
Bennett, Constance
  Madame X
Bergen, Polly
  The Caretakers
Berger, Helmut
  Ludwig
  Salon Kitty
Berger, William
  *Love Letters of a
  Portuguese Nun*
Beswick, Martine
  *Dr. Jekyll and Sister
  Hyde*
Bey, Turhan
  Arabian Nights
  The Climax
  The Mad Ghoul
  Song of India
  Sudan
  White Savage
Birell, Tala
  Isle of Forgotten Sins
Blaine, Vivian
  Greenwich Village
  If I'm Lucky
Bogarde, Dirk
  Death in Venice
  The Servant
  Victim
Bogart, Humphrey
  Dark Victory
Bondi, Beulah
  The Furies
Borg, Veda Ann
  *Isle of Forgotten
  Sins*

Bowie, David
　Just a Gigolo
Boyd, Stephen
　The Oscar
Boyer, Charles
　The Cobweb
　The Garden of Allah
Brady, Scott
　Montana Belle
Brazzi, Rossano
　The Story of Esther
　Costello
Brent, George
　Dark Victory
　Montana Belle
　The Painted Veil
　The Purchase Price
Brian, David
　The Damned Don't
　Cry
Brook, Clive
　On Approval
Browne, Coral
　Auntie Mame
　The Killing of Sister
　George
Bruce, David
　Jungle Hell
　The Mad Ghoul
Bruce, Nigel
　Becky Sharp
　Gypsy Wildcat
　She
　The Spider Woman
Burr, Raymond
　Crime of Passion
Burton, Wendell
　Fortune and Men's
　Eyes
Byrnes, Edd
　Go Kill and Come
　Back
　Yellowstone Kelly
Calhern, Louis
　Athena
Canale, Gianna Maria
　Goliath and the
　Vampires
　The Lion of St. Mark
　Sins of Rome

Theodora, Slave
　Empress
Capucine
　Walk on the Wild
　Side
Carey, Timothy
　What's the Matter
　with Helen?
Caron, Leslie
　Valentino
Carradine, John
　Blood and Sand
　The Garden of Allah
　Isle of Forgotten Sins
Carstensen, Margit
　The Bitter Tears of
　Petra Von Kant
Chandler, Jeff
　Female on the Beach
Cherkasov, Nikolai
　Ivan the Terrible,
　Part II
Chevalier, Maurice
　The Merry Widow
Christine, Virginia
　The Cobweb
Christy, Dorothy
　The Phantom Empire
Cochran, Steve
　Carnival Story
　Copacabana
　The Damned Don't
　Cry
　Quantrill's Raiders
Coffin, Tristram
　So's Your Aunt
　Emma!
Colbert, Claudette
　Cleopatra
　Parrish
Comer, Anjanette
　The Loved One
Como, Perry
　If I'm Lucky
Connors, Chuck
　Death in Small Doses
Connors, Michael
　Sudden Fear
　Where Love Has
　Gone

Cooper, Gary
　Design for Living
Corrigan, Ray "Crash"
　The Undersea
　Kingdom
Cotten, Joseph
　The Tramplers
Coughlin, Kevin
　The Gay Deceivers
Crawford, Joan
　Berserk
　The Caretakers
　The Damned Don't
　Cry
　Dancing Lady
　Female on the Beach
　Laughing Sinners
　Queen Bee
　The Story of Esther
　Costello
　Strait-Jacket
　Sudden Fear
　Torch Song
Cregar, Laird
　Blood and Sand
Crews, Laura Hope
　The Silver Cord
Cushing, Peter
　Land of the Minotaur
Dahl, Arlene
　Woman's World
Dall, John
　Atlantis, the Lost
　Continent
Dallesandro, Joe
　Killer Nun
Darren, James
　Venus in Furs
Darro, Frankie
　Little Men
　The Phantom Empire
Davis, Bette
　Dark Victory
　That Certain Woman
　Where Love Has
　Gone
Davis, Joan
　Thin Ice
De Carlo, Yvonne
　Song of Scheherazade

Dee, Frances
  The Silver Cord
Dee, Sandra
  Imitation of Life
Demarest, William
  Jupiter's Darling
Depp, Johnny
  Ed Wood
Dietrich, Marlene
  Destry Rides Again
  The Garden of Allah
  Just a Gigolo
Donahue, Elinor
  Girls Town
Donahue, Troy
  Imitation of Life
  Parrish
Donlevy, Brian
  Destry Rides Again
  Song of Scheherazade
Donohoe, Amanda
  The Lair of the White Worm
Donovan, Casey
  Boys in the Sand
Dors, Diana
  Berserk
Duke, Patty
  Valley of the Dolls
Dullea, Keir
  Madame X
Dunne, Irene
  The Silver Cord
Eburne, Maude
  Ladies They Talk About
Eddy, Nelson
  Balalaika
  Dancing Lady
Egan, Richard
  The Damned Don't Cry
Ekberg, Anita
  Fangs of the Living Dead
  Killer Nun
  Sign of the Gladiator
Ellis, Antonia
  The Boy Friend

Ewell, Tom
  The Girl Can't Help It
Farrow, Mia
  Hurricane
Faye, Alice
  That Night in Rio
  Week-end in Havana
Fonda, Henry
  That Certain Woman
Fonda, Jane
  Walk on the Wild Side
Ford, Constance
  The Caretakers
Forsythe, John
  Kitten with a Whip
  Madame X
Foster, Preston
  The Harvey Girls
  Ladies They Talk About
Fox, James
  The Servant
  Thoroughly Modern Millie
Fuller, Lance
  Pearl of the South Pacific
Gable, Christopher
  The Boy Friend
Gable, Clark
  Dancing Lady
  Laughing Sinners
  To Please a Lady
Gahagan, Helen
  She
Garbo, Greta
  The Painted Veil
Gardner, Ava
  Tam Lin
Garland, Beverly
  Problem Girls
Garland, Judy
  The Harvey Girls
Gavin, John
  Imitation of Life
  Thoroughly Modern Millie
Gaynor, Mitzi
  Les Girls

Gilbert, Billy
  Arabian Nights
  Destry Rides Again
  Week-end in Havana
Girotti, Massimo
  Sins of Rome
Gish, Lillian
  The Cobweb
Glover, Kevin
  Love Bites
Gomez, Thomas
  The Climax
  White Savage
Gough, Michael
  Berserk
  Caravaggio
Grahame, Gloria
  The Cobweb
  Sudden Fear
Granger, Stewart
  Sodom and Gomorrah
Grant, Hugh
  The Lair of the White Worm
Graves, Peter
  Death in Small Doses
Gray, Coleen
  The Leech Woman
Greer, Michael
  Fortune and Men's Eyes
  The Gay Deceivers
Guttman, Amos
  Drifting
Hale, Alan
  Stella Dallas
  Thin Ice
Hall, Anthony
  Atlantis, the Lost Continent
Hall, Huntz
  Valentino
Hall, Jon
  Arabian Nights
  Gypsy Wildcat
  Sudan
  White Savage
Halsted, Fred
  Erotikus

Hardin, Ty
  Berserk
Hardwicke, Sir Cedric
  Becky Sharp
Harrison, Richard
  Messalina Against the
  Son of Hercules
Harvey, Laurence
  Walk on the Wild
  Side
Hayden, Sterling
  Crime of Passion
Haydn, Richard
  Jupiter's Darling
Hayward, Susan
  Valley of the Dolls
  Where Love Has
  Gone
Hayworth, Rita
  Blood and Sand
  Cover Girl
  You'll Never Get
  Rich
Heatherton, Joey
  Where Love Has
  Gone
Hemingway, Susan
  Love Letters of a
  Portuguese Nun
Henie, Sonja
  Thin Ice
Hersholt, Jean
  Dr. Christian Meets
  the Women
  The Painted Veil
Hobart, Rose
  The Mad Ghoul
Holloway, Sterling
  Dancing Lady
  The Merry Widow
Hopkins, Miriam
  Becky Sharp
  Design for Living
  Hollywood Horror
  House
  The Mating Season
Horton, Edward Everett
  Design for Living
  The Merry Widow
Hudson, Rochelle
  Island of Doomed Men

The Night Walker
  Strait-Jacket
Hugueny, Sharon
  The Caretakers
  Parrish
Hunter, Tab
  The Loved One
Huston, Walter
  The Furies
  The Shanghai Gesture
Ireland, John
  Queen Bee
  Salon Kitty
Irons, Jeremy
  M. Butterfly
Jackson, Glenda
  The Boy Friend
  Salome's Last Dance
Jergens, Adele
  The Cobweb
Jewell, Isabel
  Go West, Young
  Man
Johnson, Don
  Zachariah
Joyce, Brenda
  The Spider Woman
  Strikes Back
Jurgens, Curt
  Just a Gigolo
Ka'ne, Dayton
  Hurricane
Karlen, John
  Daughters of
  Darkness
Karloff, Boris
  The Climax
  Voodoo Island
Kaufmann, Christine
  Bagdad Cafe
  The Last Days of
  Pompeii
Keel, Howard
  Jupiter's Darling
Keith, Brian
  Dino
Kelly, Gene
  Cover Girl
  Les Girls
Kendall, Bobby
  Pink Narcissus

Kendall, Kay
  Les Girls
Kerr, John
  The Cobweb
King, Perry
  Andy Warhol's Bad
Knowles, Patric
  Auntie Mame
  Mystery of Marie
  Roget
Kohner, Susan
  Dino
  Imitation of Life
Krabbe, Jeroen
  The Fourth Man
Kruger, Hardy
  Liane, Jungle
  Goddess
Kruger, Otto
  Cover Girl
La Rocque, Rod
  Dr. Christian Meets
  the Women
Lamarr, Hedy
  The Female Animal
  White Cargo
Landau, Martin
  Ed Wood
Lansbury, Angela
  The Harvey Girls
Lee, Christopher
  Hercules in the
  Haunted World
Lee, Lila
  The Midnight Girl
Liberace
  The Loved One
  South Sea Sinner
Lillie, Beatrice
  On Approval
  Thoroughly Modern
  Millie
Locke, Richard
  Kansas City Trucking
  Co.
  Passing Strangers
Lone, John
  M. Butterfly
Lorre, Peter
  Island of Doomed
  Men

Losch, Tilly
  The Garden of Allah
Louise, Anita
  That Certain Woman
Lugosi, Bela
  The Midnight Girl
MacDonald, Jeanette
  The Merry Widow
Madison, Guy
  The Beast of Hollow
    Mountain
  Go Kill and Come Back
  Jet Over the Atlantic
Main, Marjorie
  The Harvey Girls
  Stella Dallas
Malden, Karl
  Gypsy
  Parrish
Mansfield, Jayne
  The Girl Can't Help It
March, Fredric
  Design for Living
Marchal, Georges
  Sign of the Gladiator
  Theodora, Slave
    Empress
Marshall, Herbert
  The Caretakers
  The Painted Veil
Marx, Groucho
  Copacabana
Massey, Ilona
  Balalaika
  Jet Over the Atlantic
Mature, Victor
  The Shanghai Gesture
Mayo, Virginia
  Jet Over the Atlantic
  Pearl of the South
    Pacific
McBain, Diane
  The Caretakers
  Parrish
McCambridge, Mercedes
  99 Women
McCrea, Joel
  The Silver Cord
McDowall, Roddy
  The Loved One

McEnery, Peter
  Entertaining Mr.
    Sloane
  Victim
McShane, Ian
  Tam Lin
Medina, Patricia
  The Beast of Hollow
    Mountain
  The Killing of Sister
    George
Merkel, Una
  Destry Rides Again
  The Merry Widow
Merton, John
  Slaves in Bondage
Michaels, Marion
  Liane, Jungle Goddess
Midler, Bette
  Big Business
  Ruthless People
  The Thorn
Miles, Sarah
  The Servant
Miles, Sylvia
  Parrish
Mineo, Sal
  Dino
Miranda, Carmen
  Copacabana
  Greenwich Village
  If I'm Lucky
  That Night in Rio
  Week-end in Havana
Mitchell, Gordon
  The Giant of
    Metropolis
Mitchum, James
  The Tramplers
Montez, Maria
  Arabian Nights
  Gypsy Wildcat
  Mystery of Marie
    Roget
  Sudan
  That Night in Rio
  White Savage
Moorehead, Agnes
  What's the Matter
    with Helen?

Moreau, Jeanne
  Mademoiselle
Morgan, Ralph
  Little Men
Morley, Robert
  The Loved One
Morris, Kirk
  Colossus and the
    Headhunters
  The Terror of the
    Steppes
Morse, Robert
  The Loved One
Munson, Ona
  The Shanghai Gesture
Murray, Bill
  Ed Wood
Nader, George
  Carnival Story
  The Female Animal
Nazimova, Alla
  Blood and Sand
Nelson, Ricky
  Love and Kisses
Nero, Franco
  The Tramplers
Novak, Kim
  Just a Gigolo
Nureyev, Rudolf
  Valentino
O'Brian, Hugh
  Love Has Many Faces
O'Brien, Edmond
  The Girl Can't Help It
O'Brien-Moore, Erin
  Little Men
Ogata, Ken
  Mishima: A Life in
    Four Chapters
Oliver, Susan
  The Caretakers
Ouspenskaya, Maria
  Mystery of Marie
    Roget
  The Shanghai Gesture
Oxenberg, Catherine
  The Lair of the White
    Worm
Paige, Janis
  The Caretakers

Palance, Jack
  Bagdad Cafe
  Sudden Fear
Palmer, Betsy
  Queen Bee
Pangborn, Franklin
  Design for Living
Papas, Irene
  Theodora, Slave
    Empress
Park, Reg
  Hercules in the
    Haunted World
Patterson, Elizabeth
  Go West, Young Man
Paule, Alan
  Macho Dancer
Payne, George
  Kiss Today Goodbye
Payne, John
  Week-end in Havana
Phillips, Michelle
  Valentino
Phoenix, River
  My Own Private
    Idaho
Pitts, ZaSu
  So's Your Aunt
    Emma!
Pleasence, Donald
  Land of the Minotaur
Pounder, CCH
  Bagdad Cafe
Powell, Jane
  Athena
  The Female Animal
Power, Tyrone
  Blood and Sand
  Thin Ice
Powers, Stefanie
  Die! Die! My Darling!
  Love Has Many Faces
Price, Dennis
  Venus in Furs
  Victim
Purdom, Edmund
  Athena
Quinn, Anthony
  Blood and Sand
  Hercules and the
    Amazon Women

Hercules and the Lost
    Kingdom
Quinn, Pat
  Zachariah
Raft, George
  Jet Over the Atlantic
Rathbone, Basil
  The Garden of Allah
  The Spider Woman
Reagan, Ronald
  Dark Victory
Reason, Rhodes
  Voodoo Island
  Yellowstone Kelly
Reeves, Keanu
  My Own Private
    Idaho
Reeves, Steve
  Athena
  The Last Days of
    Pompeii
  Morgan the Pirate
  The White Warrior
Reid, Beryl
  Entertaining Mr.
    Sloane
  The Killing of Sister
    George
Rettig, Tommy
  The Cobweb
Reynolds, Debbie
  Athena
  What's the Matter
    with Helen?
Ritter, Thelma
  The Mating Season
Robertson, Cliff
  Love Has Many Faces
Rohm, Maria
  99 Women
  Venus in Furs
Roland, Gilbert
  The Furies
Roman, Ruth
  Look in Any Window
  Love Has Many Faces
Romero, Cesar
  Week-end in Havana
Roth, Lillian
  Ladies They Talk
    About

Royce, Morgan
  Song of the Loon
Rubinstein, John
  Zachariah
Ruffo, Leonora
  Hercules in the
    Haunted World
Russell, Elizabeth
  So's Your Aunt Emma!
Russell, Gail
  Song of India
Russell, Jane
  Montana Belle
Russell, Rosalind
  Auntie Mame
  Gypsy
Sabu
  Arabian Nights
  The Jungle Book
  Jungle Hell
  Song of India
  White Savage
Sägebrecht, Marianne
  Bagdad Cafe
St. John, Jill
  The Oscar
Sanders, George
  Ecco
  Jupiter's Darling
Schell, Maria
  Just a Gigolo
  99 Women
Schildkraut, Joseph
  Cleopatra
  The Garden of Allah
Schygulla, Hanna
  The Bitter Tears of
    Petra Von Kant
Scott, Gordon
  The Conquest of
    Mycenae
  Goliath and the
    Vampires
  Hero of Babylon
  The Lion of St. Mark
  The Tramplers
Scott, Imogen Millais
  Salome's Last Dance
Scott, Randolph
  Go West, Young Man
  She

Seager, Lew
  Kiss Today Goodbye
Sears, Heather
  *The Story of Esther
  Costello*
Seyrig, Delphine
  *Daughters of
  Darkness*
Sheffield, Johnny
  *Bomba and the Jungle
  Girl*
Silvers, Phil
  Cover Girl
  If I'm Lucky
Smith, C. Aubrey
  Balalaika
  Cleopatra
  The Garden of Allah
Sondergaard, Gale
  The Climax
  Gypsy Wildcat
  *Hollywood Horror
  House*
  Isle of Forgotten Sins
  The Spider Woman
  *The Spider Woman
  Strikes Back*
Sorbo, Kevin
  *Hercules and the
  Amazon Women*
  *Hercules and the Lost
  Kingdom*
Stachura, Joseph
  Jerker
Stack, Robert
  The Caretakers
Stanwyck, Barbara
  Crime of Passion
  The Furies
  *Ladies They Talk
  About*
  The Night Walker
  The Purchase Price
  Stella Dallas
  To Please a Lady
  *Walk on the Wild
  Side*
Steel, Alan
  *Hercules and the
  Masked Rider*

Steiger, Rod
  The Loved One
Sterling, Jan
  The Female Animal
  Female on the Beach
  The Mating Season
Stevens, Connie
  Parrish
Stewart, James
  Destry Rides Again
Stole, Mink
  Serial Mom
Stone, Milburn
  The Mad Ghoul
Stryker, Jeff
  Powertool
Sullivan, Barry
  Queen Bee
Sutherland, Donald
  Die! Die! My Darling!
Swinton, Tilda
  Caravaggio
  Edward II
Talbot, Lyle
  Go West, Young Man
  *Ladies They Talk
  About*
  The Purchase Price
Talbott, Gloria
  Girls Town
  The Leech Woman
Tcherina, Ludmilla
  Sins of Rome
Terry, Nigel
  Caravaggio
  Edward II
Terry, Phillip
  Balalaika
  The Leech Woman
Thulin, Ingrid
  Salon Kitty
Tiernan, Andrew
  Edward II
Tierney, Gene
  The Mating Season
  The Shanghai Gesture
Toler, Sidney
  Isle of Forgotten Sins
  That Certain Woman
  White Savage

Tomlin, Lily
  Big Business
Tone, Franchot
  Dancing Lady
Treacher, Arthur
  Thin Ice
Tune, Tommy
  The Boy Friend
Turner, Kathleen
  Serial Mom
Turner, Lana
  Imitation of Life
  Love Has Many Faces
  Madame X
Twiggy
  The Boy Friend
Tyrrell, Susan
  Andy Warhol's Bad
Vadis, Dan
  *The Triumph of
  Hercules*
Valli, Alida
  Killer Nun
Van Doren, Mamie
  Girls Town
Vaughn, Robert
  The Caretakers
Vickers, Yvette
  *What's the Matter
  with Helen?*
Waddington, Steven
  Edward II
Wagner, Tom
  Jerker
  Love Bites
Waite, Michael
  Fun Down There
Walker, Clint
  Yellowstone Kelly
Walker, Helen
  Problem Girls
Webb, Clifton
  Woman's World
West, Mae
  Belle of the Nineties
  Go West, Young Man
  Goin' to Town
  Klondike Annie
Widmark, Richard
  The Cobweb

221

Wilcoxon, Henry
  Cleopatra
Wilding, Michael
  Torch Song
William, Warren
  Cleopatra
  Go West, Young
    Man
Williams, Esther
  Jupiter's Darling
Wilson, Stuart
  No Escape

Winters, Jonathan
  The Loved One
Winters, Shelley
  South Sea Sinner
  What's the Matter
    with Helen?
Wood, Natalie
  Gypsy
Wrangler, Jack
  Kansas City Trucking
    Co.

Wray, Fay
  The Cobweb
  Crime of Passion
  Queen Bee
York, Susannah
  The Killing of Sister
    George
Yurka, Blanche
  The Furies
Zucco, George
  The Mad Ghoul
  Sudan

BOOKS FROM LEYLAND PUBLICATIONS / G.S PRESS

ABOUT THE AUTHOR

Paul Roen (born 1948), whom *Inches* magazine has dubbed "the Maria Montez of gay intellectuals," lives in the woods near Two Harbors, Minnesota. He graduated summa cum laude from the University of Minnesota (Duluth). For the past twenty-six years, he has been employed by the Duluth Public Library.